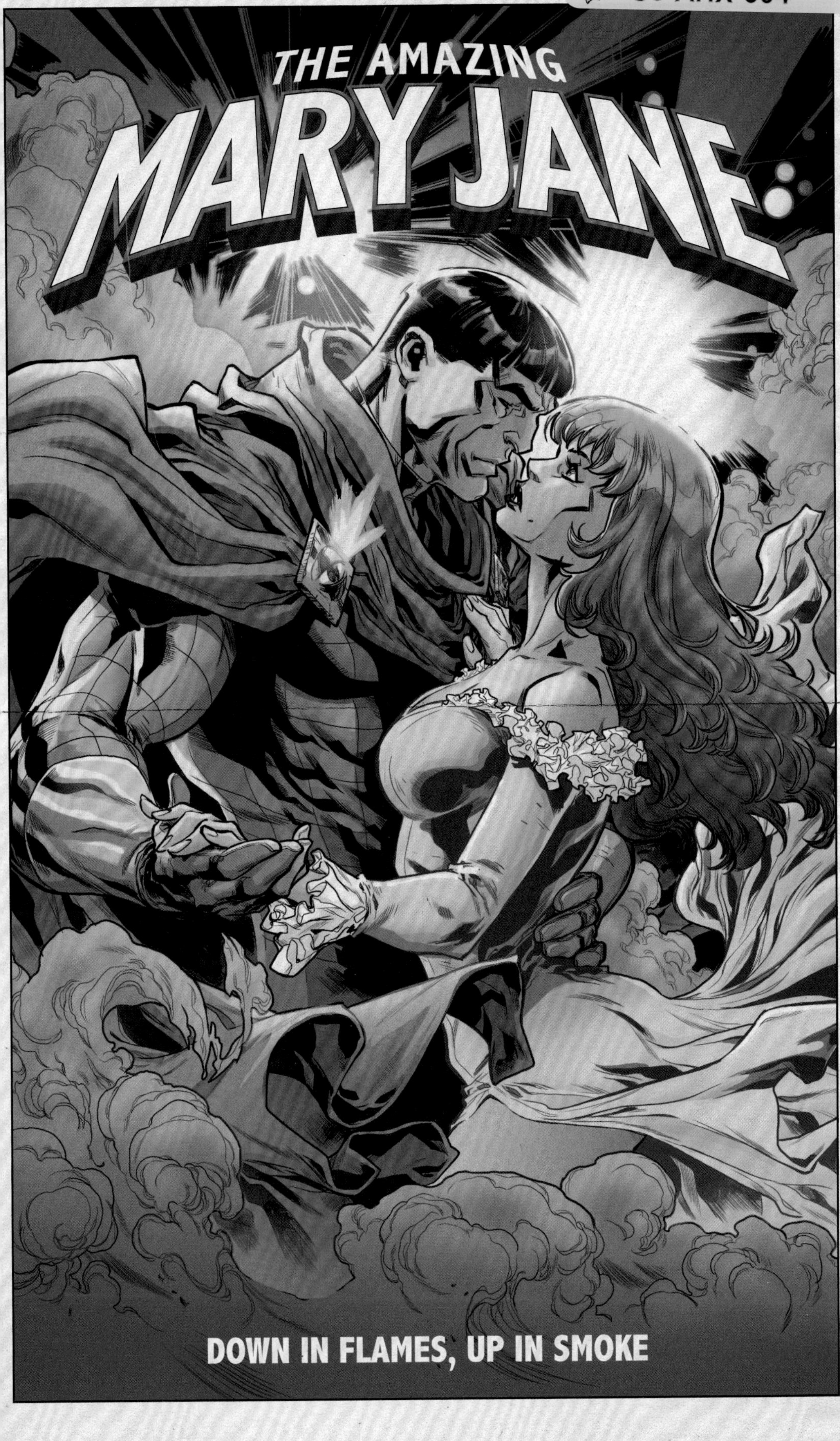
THE AMAZING
MARY JANE
DOWN IN FLAMES, UP IN SMOKE

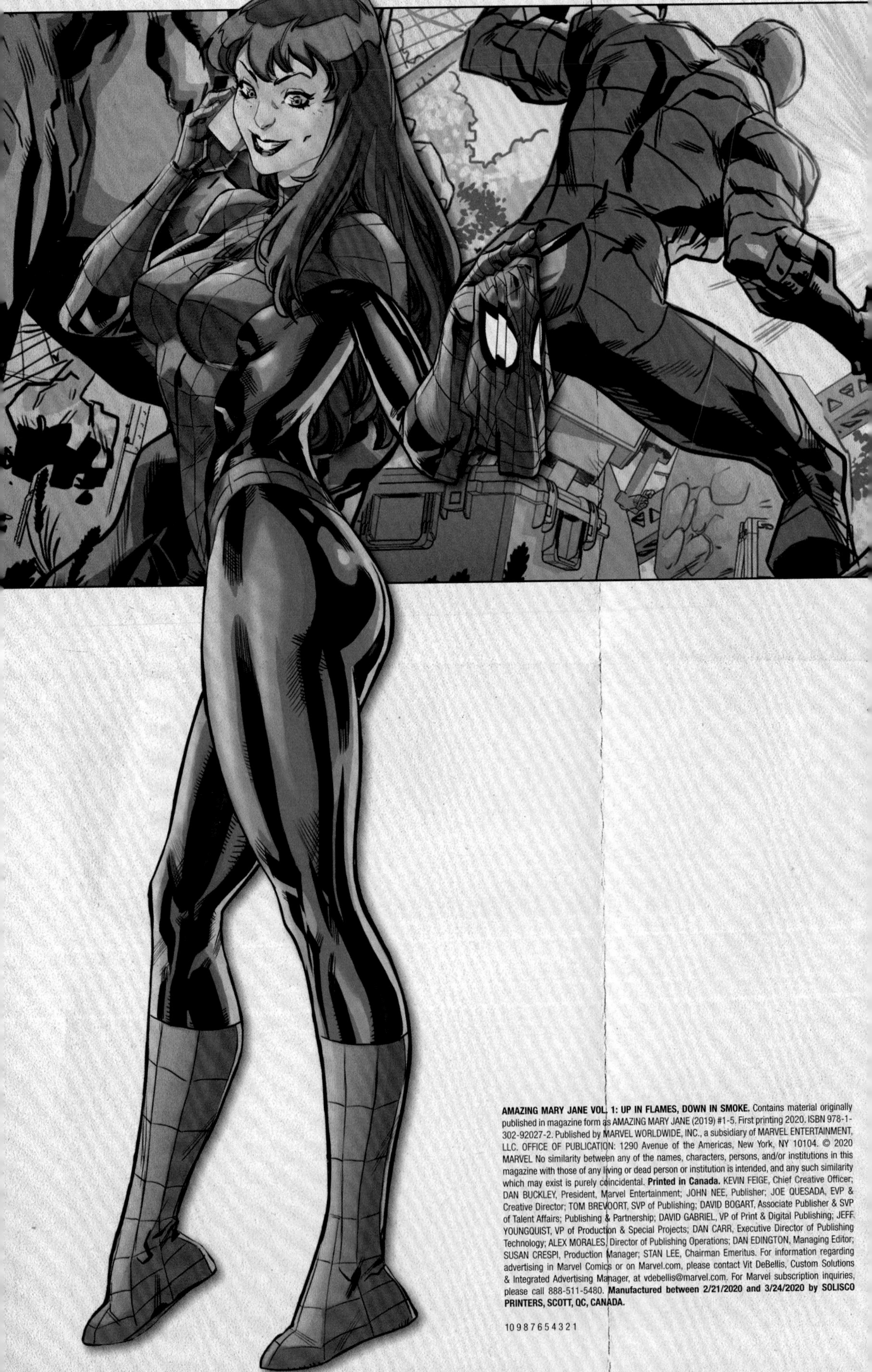

AMAZING MARY JANE VOL. 1: UP IN FLAMES, DOWN IN SMOKE. Contains material originally published in magazine form as AMAZING MARY JANE (2019) #1-5. First printing 2020. ISBN 978-1-302-92027-2. Published by MARVEL WORLDWIDE, INC., a subsidiary of MARVEL ENTERTAINMENT, LLC. OFFICE OF PUBLICATION: 1290 Avenue of the Americas, New York, NY 10104. **Printed in Canada.** KEVIN FEIGE, Chief Creative Officer; DAN BUCKLEY, President, Marvel Entertainment; JOHN NEE, Publisher; JOE QUESADA, EVP & Creative Director; TOM BREVOORT, SVP of Publishing; DAVID BOGART, Associate Publisher & SVP of Talent Affairs; Publishing & Partnership; DAVID GABRIEL, VP of Print & Digital Publishing; JEFF YOUNGQUIST, VP of Production & Special Projects; DAN CARR, Executive Director of Publishing Technology; ALEX MORALES, Director of Publishing Operations; DAN EDINGTON, Managing Editor; SUSAN CRESPI, Production Manager; STAN LEE, Chairman Emeritus. For information regarding advertising in Marvel Comics or on Marvel.com, please contact Vit DeBellis, Custom Solutions & Integrated Advertising Manager, at vdebellis@marvel.com. For Marvel subscription inquiries, please call 888-511-5480. **Manufactured between 2/21/2020 and 3/24/2020 by SOLISCO PRINTERS, SCOTT, QC, CANADA.**

10 9 8 7 6 5 4 3 2 1

THE AMAZING
MARY JANE

DOWN IN FLAMES, UP IN SMOKE

WRITTEN BY
LEAH WILLIAMS

ART BY
CARLOS GÓMEZ
WITH **LUCAS WERNECK** (#3)

COLORED BY
CARLOS LOPEZ

LETTERERED BY
VC'S JOE CARAMAGNA

COVERS BY
HUMBERTO RAMOS & **EDGARD DELGADO**

EDITOR
KATHLEEN WISNESKI

EXECUTIVE EDITOR
NICK LOWE

COLLECTION EDITOR JENNIFER GRÜNWALD
ASSISTANT MANAGING EDITOR MAIA LOY
ASSISTANT MANAGING EDITOR LISA MONTALBANO
EDITOR, SPECIAL PROJECTS MARK D. BEAZLEY

VP PRODUCTION & SPECIAL PROJECTS JEFF YOUNGQUIST
BOOK DESIGNER ADAM DEL RE
SVP PRINT, SALES & MARKETING DAVID GABRIEL
EDITOR IN CHIEF C.B. CEBULSKI

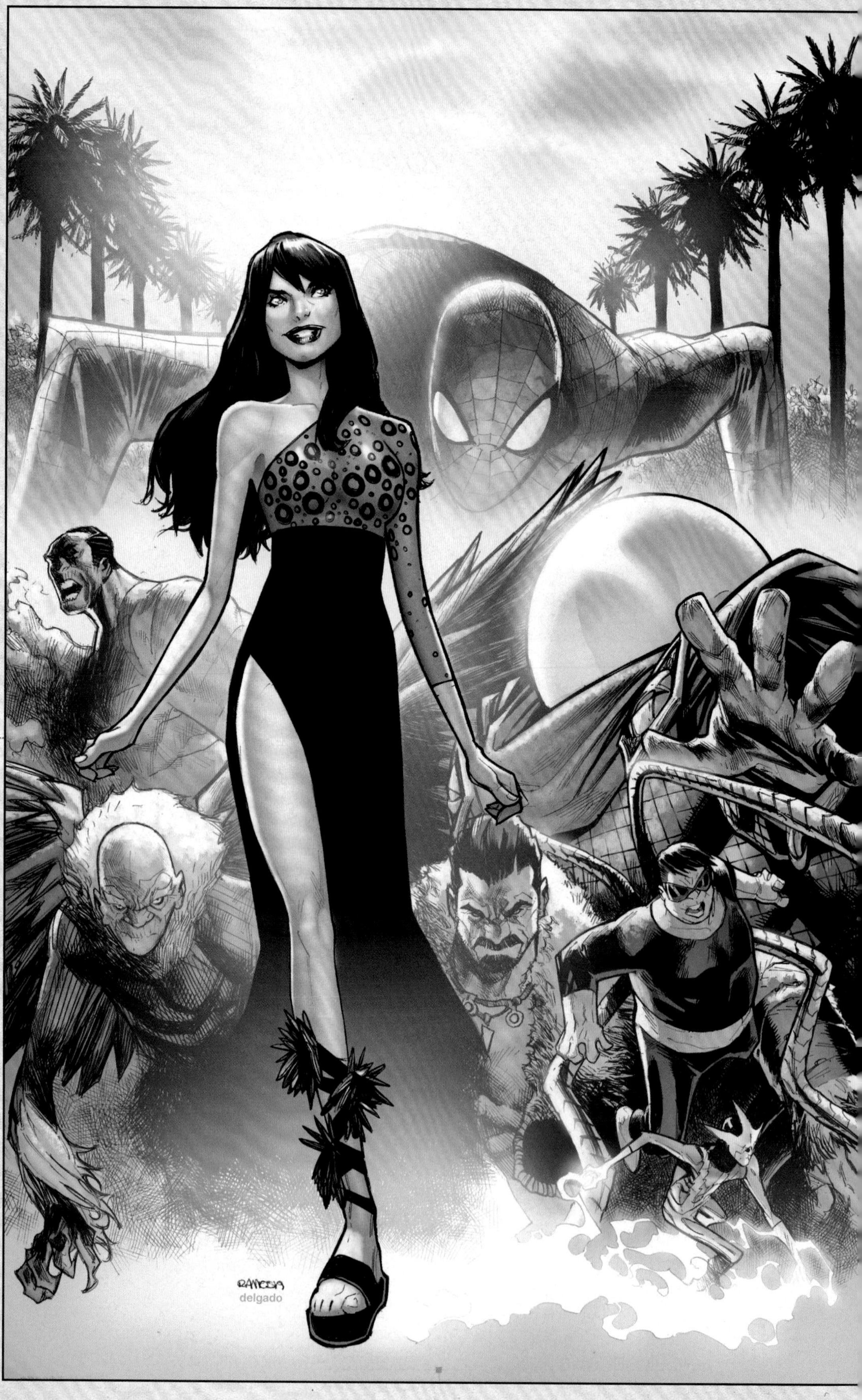
RAMOS 19
delgado

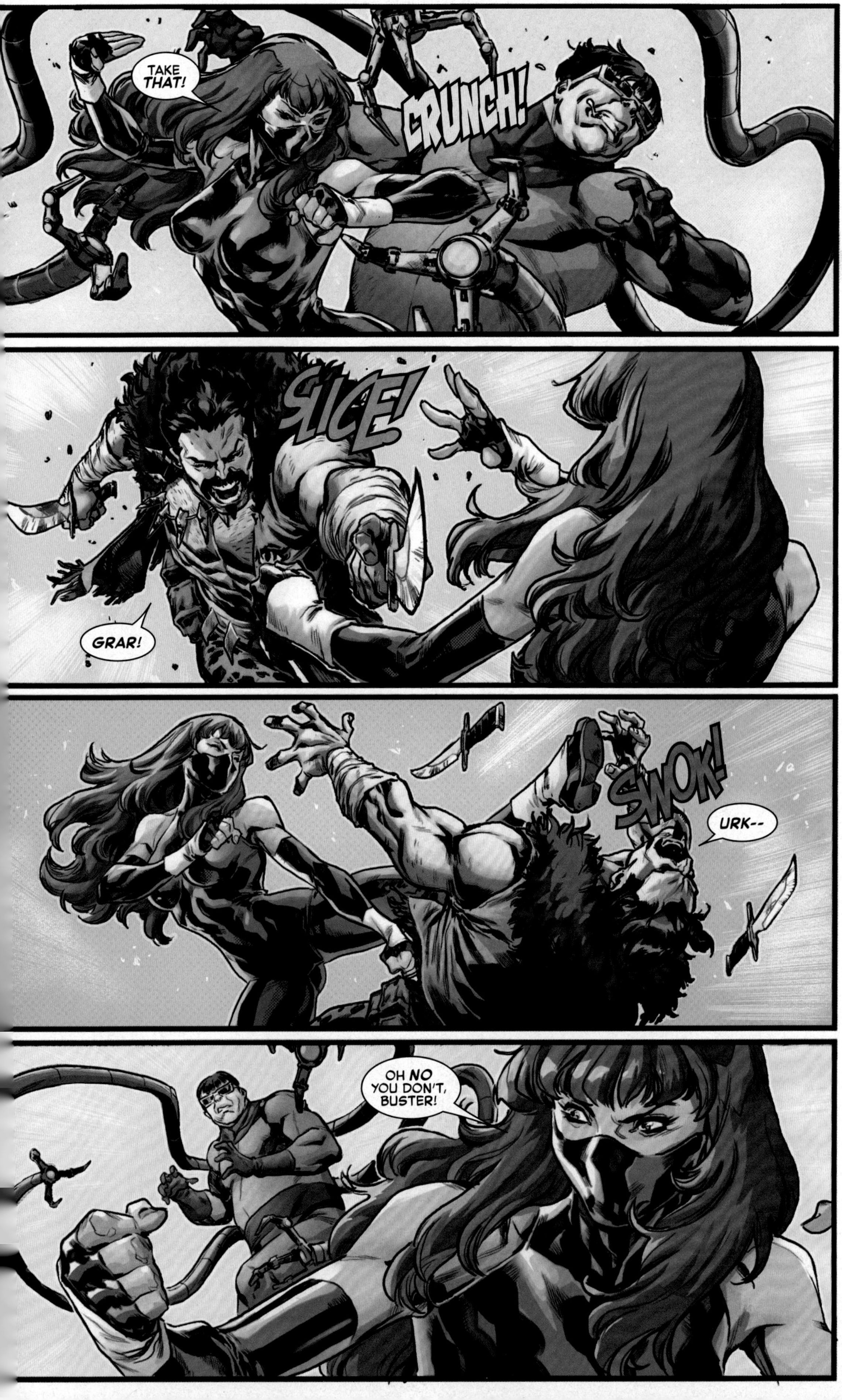
TAKE THAT!
CRUNCH!
SLICE!
GRAR!
SWOK!
URK--
OH NO YOU DON'T, BUSTER!

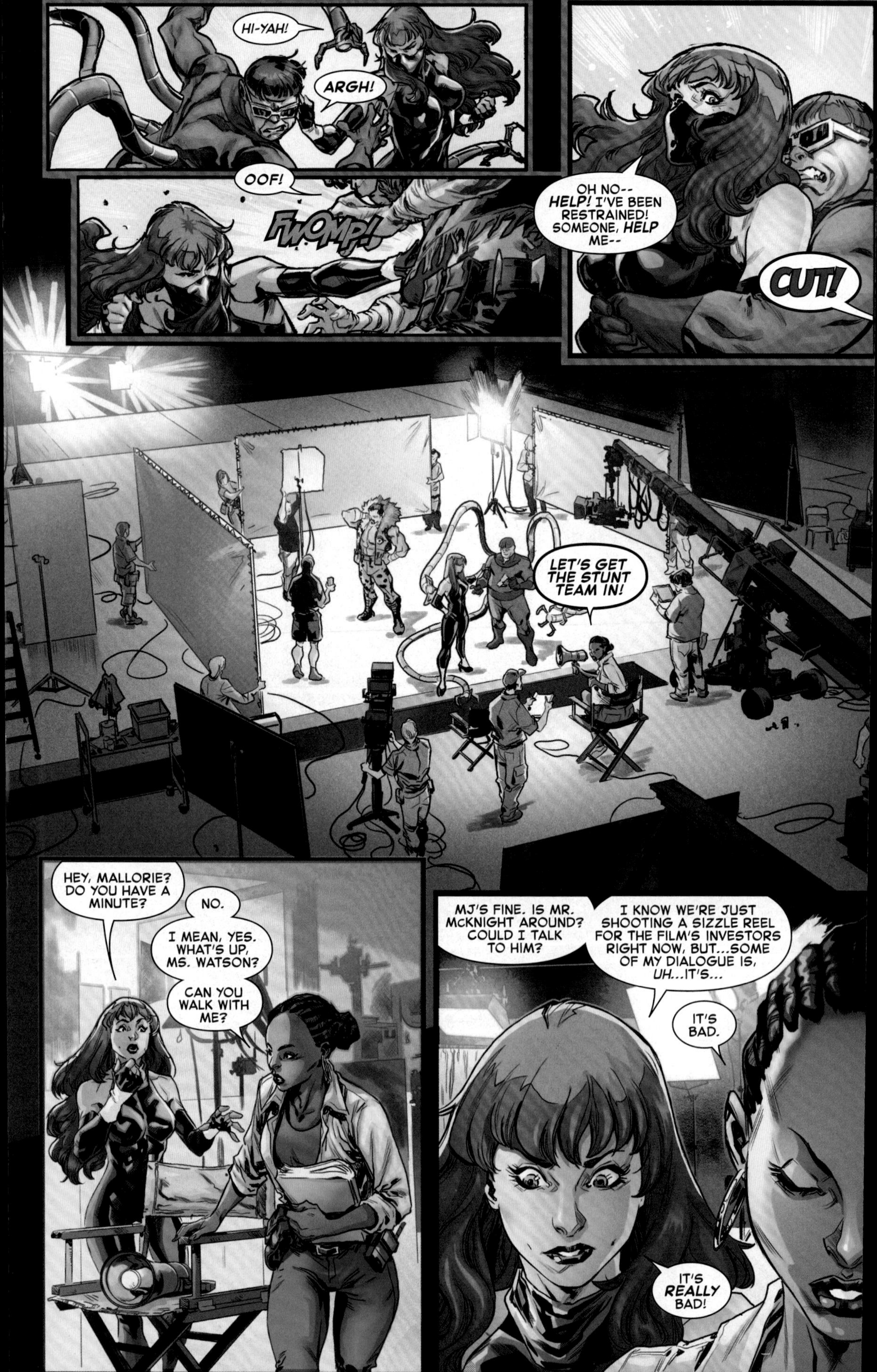
HI-YAH!
ARGH!
OOF!
FWOMP!
OH NO-- HELP! I'VE BEEN RESTRAINED! SOMEONE, HELP ME--
CUT!
LET'S GET THE STUNT TEAM IN!
HEY, MALLORIE? DO YOU HAVE A MINUTE?
NO.
I MEAN, YES. WHAT'S UP, MS. WATSON?
CAN YOU WALK WITH ME?
MJ'S FINE. IS MR. McKNIGHT AROUND? COULD I TALK TO HIM?
I KNOW WE'RE JUST SHOOTING A SIZZLE REEL FOR THE FILM'S INVESTORS RIGHT NOW, BUT...SOME OF MY DIALOGUE IS, UH...IT'S...
IT'S BAD.
IT'S REALLY BAD!

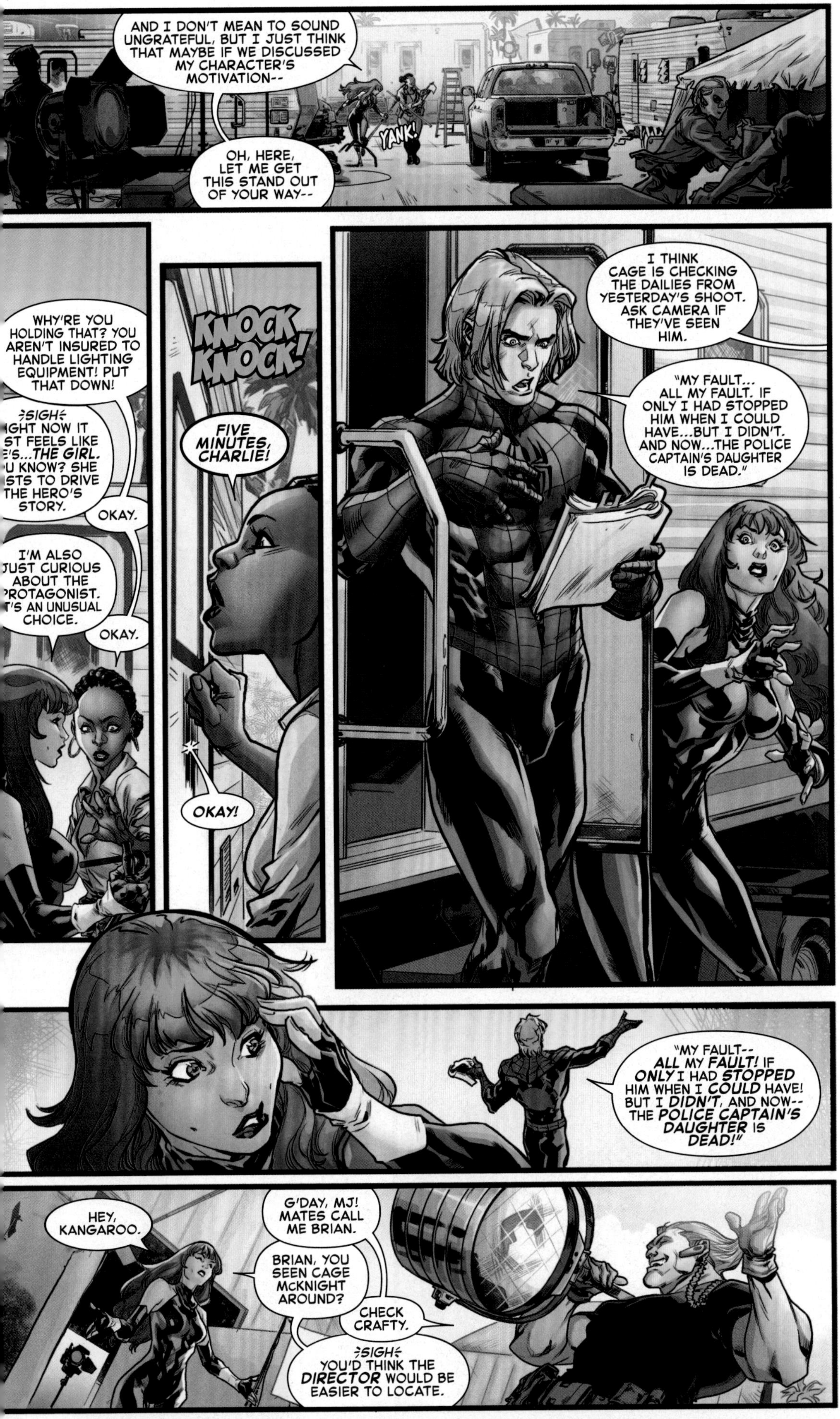
AND I DON'T MEAN TO SOUND UNGRATEFUL, BUT I JUST THINK THAT MAYBE IF WE DISCUSSED MY CHARACTER'S MOTIVATION--
OH, HERE, LET ME GET THIS STAND OUT OF YOUR WAY--
YANK!
WHY'RE YOU HOLDING THAT? YOU AREN'T INSURED TO HANDLE LIGHTING EQUIPMENT! PUT THAT DOWN!
SIGH
OKAY.
I'M ALSO
OKAY.
KNOCK KNOCK!
FIVE MINUTES, CHARLIE!
OKAY!
I THINK CAGE IS CHECKING THE DAILIES FROM YESTERDAY'S SHOOT. ASK CAMERA IF THEY'VE SEEN HIM.
"MY FAULT... ALL MY FAULT. IF ONLY I HAD STOPPED HIM WHEN I COULD HAVE...BUT I DIDN'T. AND NOW...THE POLICE CAPTAIN'S DAUGHTER IS DEAD."
"MY FAULT-- ALL MY FAULT! IF ONLY I HAD STOPPED HIM WHEN I COULD HAVE! BUT I DIDN'T, AND NOW-- THE POLICE CAPTAIN'S DAUGHTER IS DEAD!"
HEY, KANGAROO.
G'DAY, MJ! MATES CALL ME BRIAN.
BRIAN, YOU SEEN CAGE McKNIGHT AROUND?
CHECK CRAFTY.
SIGH YOU'D THINK THE DIRECTOR WOULD BE EASIER TO LOCATE.

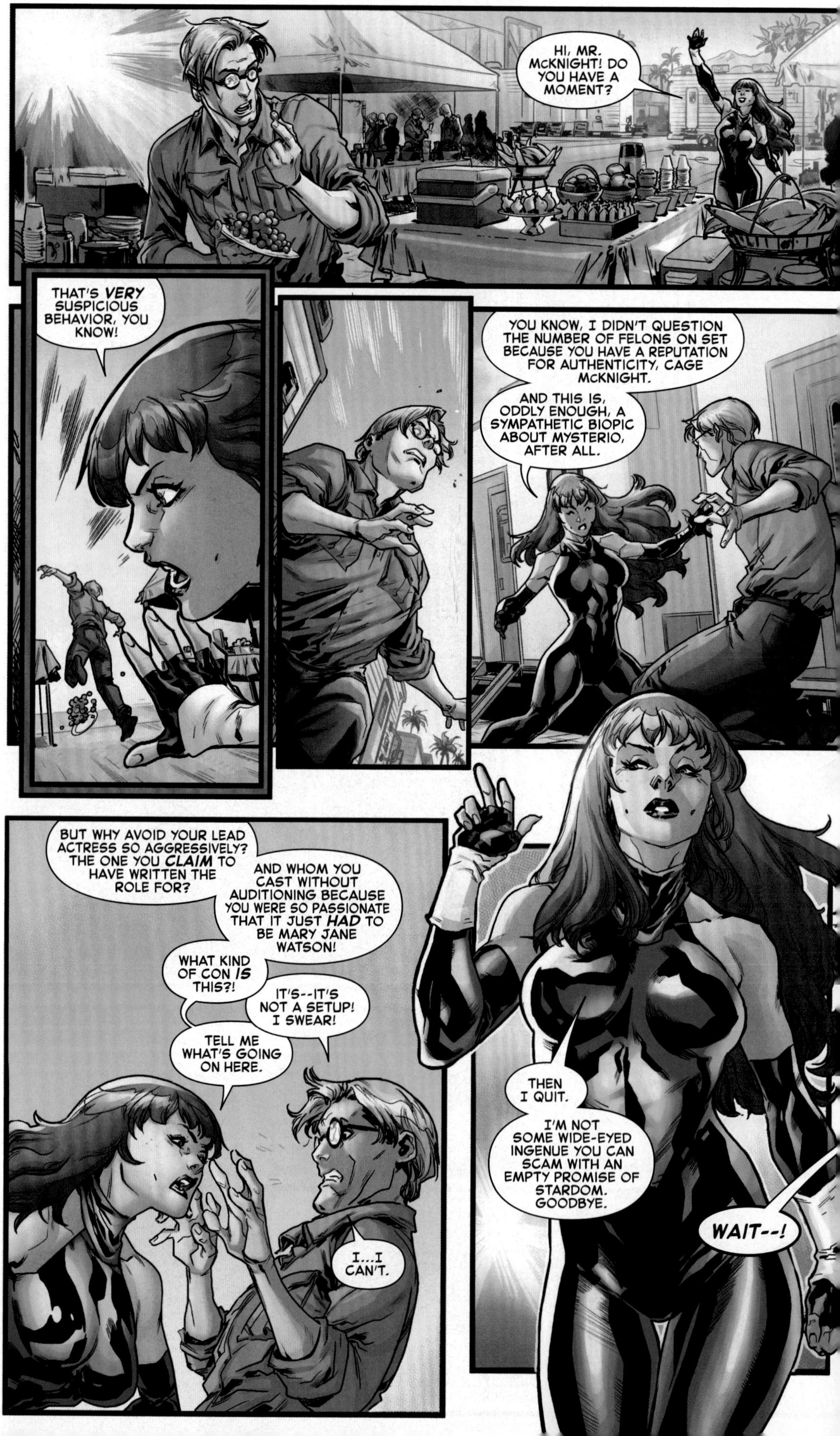
HI, MR. McKNIGHT! DO YOU HAVE A MOMENT?
THAT'S VERY SUSPICIOUS BEHAVIOR, YOU KNOW!
YOU KNOW, I DIDN'T QUESTION THE NUMBER OF FELONS ON SET BECAUSE YOU HAVE A REPUTATION FOR AUTHENTICITY, CAGE McKNIGHT.
AND THIS IS, ODDLY ENOUGH, A SYMPATHETIC BIOPIC ABOUT MYSTERIO, AFTER ALL.
BUT WHY AVOID YOUR LEAD ACTRESS SO AGGRESSIVELY? THE ONE YOU CLAIM TO HAVE WRITTEN THE ROLE FOR?
AND WHOM YOU CAST WITHOUT AUDITIONING BECAUSE YOU WERE SO PASSIONATE THAT IT JUST HAD TO BE MARY JANE WATSON!
WHAT KIND OF CON IS THIS?!
IT'S--IT'S NOT A SETUP! I SWEAR!
TELL ME WHAT'S GOING ON HERE.
I...I CAN'T.
THEN I QUIT.
I'M NOT SOME WIDE-EYED INGENUE YOU CAN SCAM WITH AN EMPTY PROMISE OF STARDOM. GOODBYE.
WAIT--!

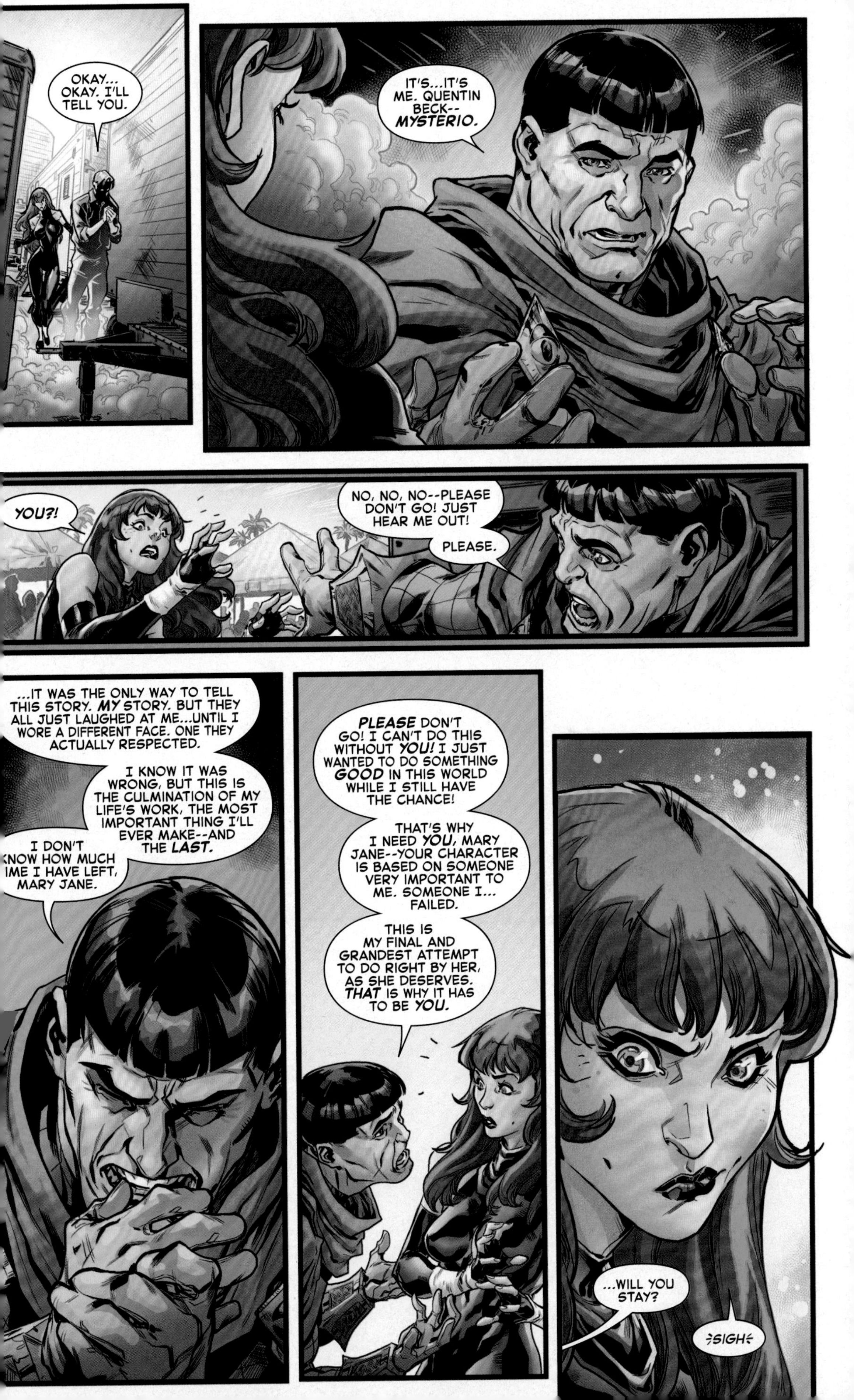
OKAY... OKAY. I'LL TELL YOU.
IT'S...IT'S ME. QUENTIN BECK-- MYSTERIO.
YOU?!
NO, NO, NO--PLEASE DON'T GO! JUST HEAR ME OUT!
PLEASE.
...IT WAS THE ONLY WAY TO TELL THIS STORY. MY STORY. BUT THEY ALL JUST LAUGHED AT ME...UNTIL I WORE A DIFFERENT FACE. ONE THEY ACTUALLY RESPECTED.
I KNOW IT WAS WRONG, BUT THIS IS THE CULMINATION OF MY LIFE'S WORK, THE MOST IMPORTANT THING I'LL EVER MAKE--AND THE LAST.
I DON'T KNOW HOW MUCH TIME I HAVE LEFT, MARY JANE.
PLEASE DON'T GO! I CAN'T DO THIS WITHOUT YOU! I JUST WANTED TO DO SOMETHING GOOD IN THIS WORLD WHILE I STILL HAVE THE CHANCE!
THAT'S WHY I NEED YOU, MARY JANE--YOUR CHARACTER IS BASED ON SOMEONE VERY IMPORTANT TO ME. SOMEONE I... FAILED.
THIS IS MY FINAL AND GRANDEST ATTEMPT TO DO RIGHT BY HER, AS SHE DESERVES. THAT IS WHY IT HAS TO BE YOU.
...WILL YOU STAY?
SIGH

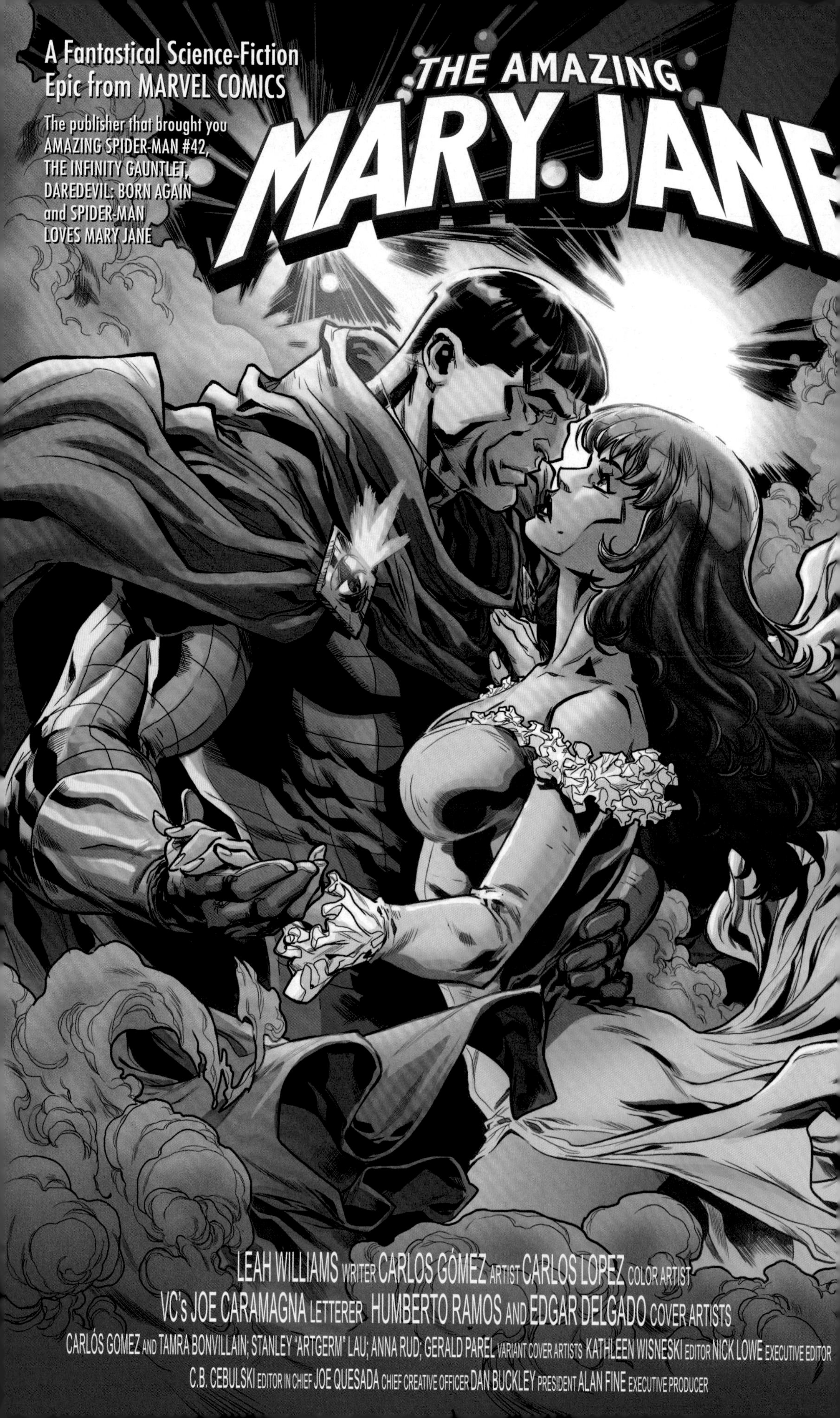
A Fantastical Science-Fiction Epic from MARVEL COMICS
The publisher that brought you AMAZING SPIDER-MAN #42, THE INFINITY GAUNTLET, DAREDEVIL: BORN AGAIN and SPIDER-MAN LOVES MARY JANE
THE AMAZING
MARY JANE
LEAH WILLIAMS WRITER CARLOS GÓMEZ ARTIST CARLOS LOPEZ COLOR ARTIST
VC's JOE CARAMAGNA LETTERER HUMBERTO RAMOS AND EDGAR DELGADO COVER ARTISTS
CARLÓS GOMEZ AND TAMRA BONVILLAIN; STANLEY "ARTGERM" LAU; ANNA RUD; GERALD PAREL VARIANT COVER ARTISTS KATHLEEN WISNESKI EDITOR NICK LOWE EXECUTIVE EDITOR
C.B. CEBULSKI EDITOR IN CHIEF JOE QUESADA CHIEF CREATIVE OFFICER DAN BUCKLEY PRESIDENT ALAN FINE EXECUTIVE PRODUCER

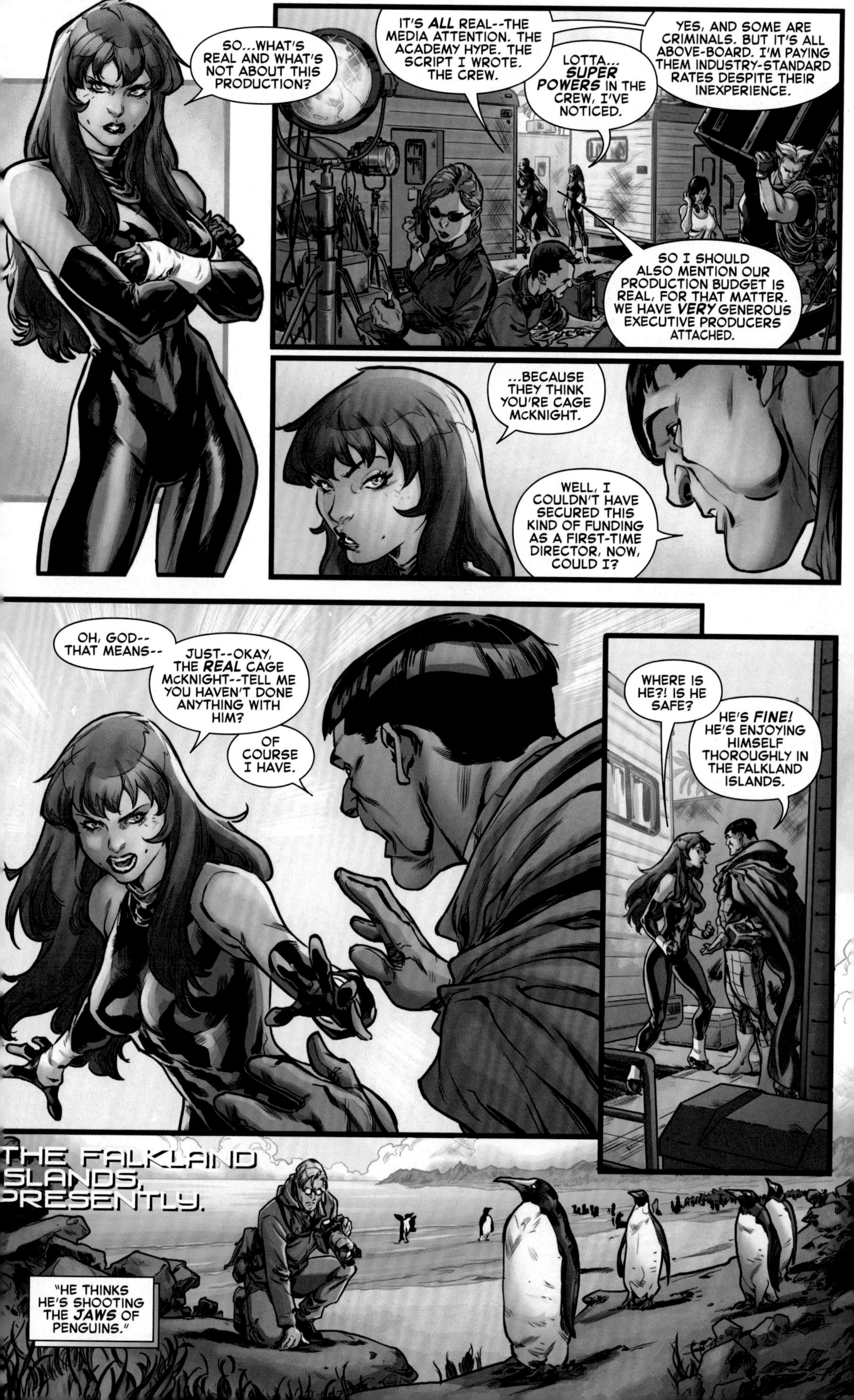

SO...WHAT'S REAL AND WHAT'S NOT ABOUT THIS PRODUCTION?
IT'S ALL REAL--THE MEDIA ATTENTION. THE ACADEMY HYPE. THE SCRIPT I WROTE. THE CREW.
LOTTA... SUPER POWERS IN THE CREW, I'VE NOTICED.
YES, AND SOME ARE CRIMINALS. BUT IT'S ALL ABOVE-BOARD. I'M PAYING THEM INDUSTRY-STANDARD RATES DESPITE THEIR INEXPERIENCE.
SO I SHOULD ALSO MENTION OUR PRODUCTION BUDGET IS REAL, FOR THAT MATTER. WE HAVE VERY GENEROUS EXECUTIVE PRODUCERS ATTACHED.
...BECAUSE THEY THINK YOU'RE CAGE McKNIGHT.
WELL, I COULDN'T HAVE SECURED THIS KIND OF FUNDING AS A FIRST-TIME DIRECTOR, NOW, COULD I?
OH, GOD--THAT MEANS--
JUST--OKAY, THE REAL CAGE McKNIGHT--TELL ME YOU HAVEN'T DONE ANYTHING WITH HIM?
OF COURSE I HAVE.
WHERE IS HE?! IS HE SAFE?
HE'S FINE! HE'S ENJOYING HIMSELF THOROUGHLY IN THE FALKLAND ISLANDS.
THE FALKLAND ISLANDS, PRESENTLY.
"HE THINKS HE'S SHOOTING THE JAWS OF PENGUINS."

LOOK. SEE? I EVEN HAVE A BABY MONITOR APP JUST TO MAKE SURE HE'S OKAY.

HE'S A *VERY* IMMERSIVE AUTEUR, WHICH I RESPECT. ONLY USES PRACTICAL EFFECTS AND HIGHLY AUTHENTIC PERFORMANCES.

CASTING THE RIGHT PENGUIN WILL KEEP HIM BUSY AND HAPPY FOR AT LEAST A YEAR.

MORE THAN ENOUGH TIME TO COMPLETE MY MAGNUM OPUS.

...OUR MAGNUM OPUS?

I CAN FEEL A WRINKLE FORMING. RIGHT HERE.

SO, LET ME MAKE SURE I'VE UNDERSTOOD--

YOU'RE MAKING A BIOPIC THAT EMPATHIZES WITH YOU AS A VILLAIN, DOESN'T APOLOGIZE FOR IT, YOU'VE SECURED FUNDING THROUGH *FRAUD,* AND YOU'VE STAFFED THIS PRODUCTION WITH FORMER FELONS AND CURRENT VILLAINS AS WELL.

...YES.

I WANTED TO GIVE THEM A CHAN[CE] TO CREAT[E] SOMETHIN[G] MEANINGF[UL]

THIS IS. *INSANE.*

...I'M IN.

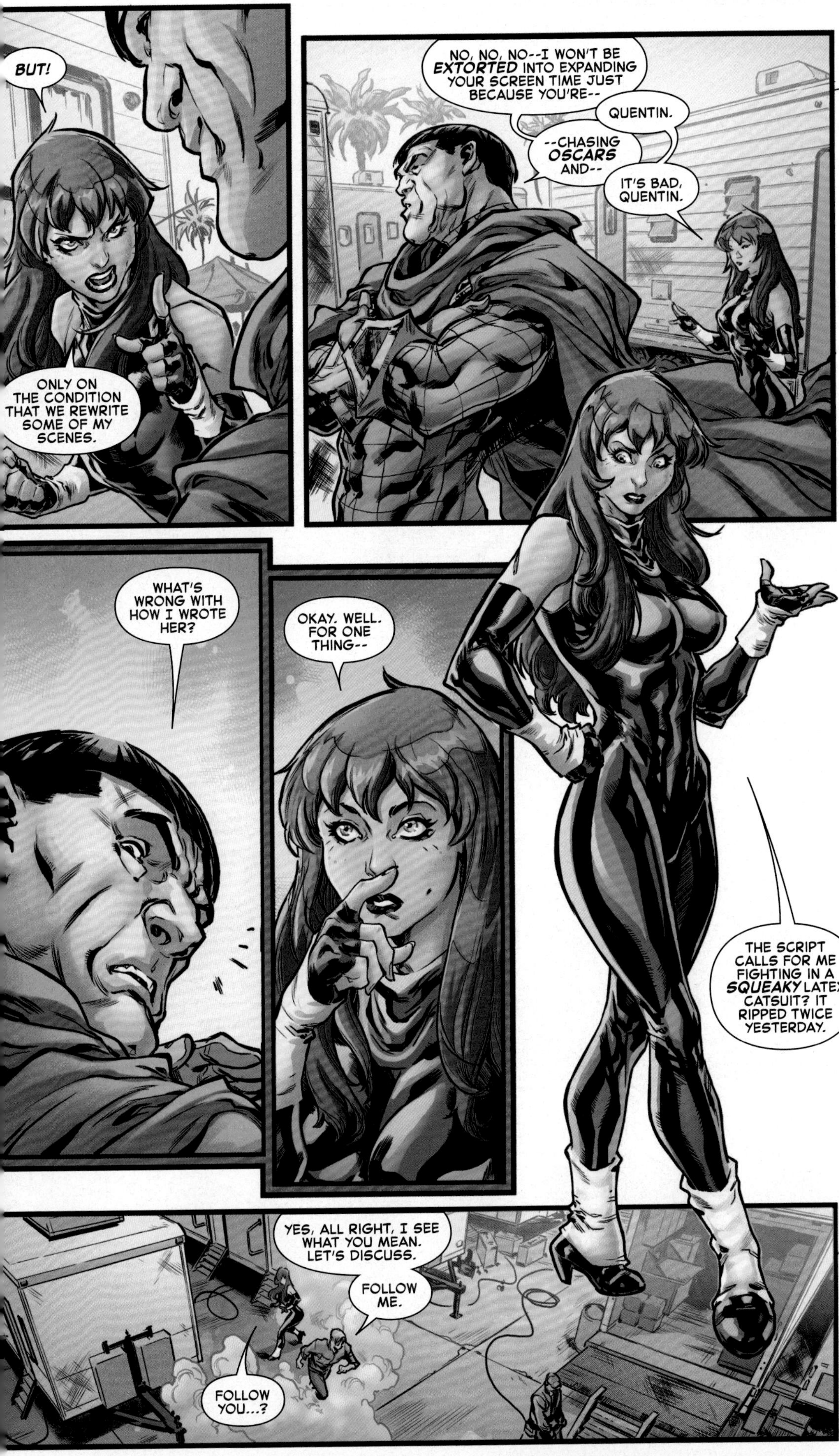
BUT!
ONLY ON THE CONDITION THAT WE REWRITE SOME OF MY SCENES.
NO, NO, NO--I WON'T BE EXTORTED INTO EXPANDING YOUR SCREEN TIME JUST BECAUSE YOU'RE--
QUENTIN.
--CHASING OSCARS AND--
IT'S BAD, QUENTIN.
WHAT'S WRONG WITH HOW I WROTE HER?
OKAY. WELL. FOR ONE THING--
THE SCRIPT CALLS FOR ME FIGHTING IN A SQUEAKY LATEX CATSUIT? IT RIPPED TWICE YESTERDAY.
YES, ALL RIGHT, I SEE WHAT YOU MEAN. LET'S DISCUSS.
FOLLOW ME.
FOLLOW YOU...?

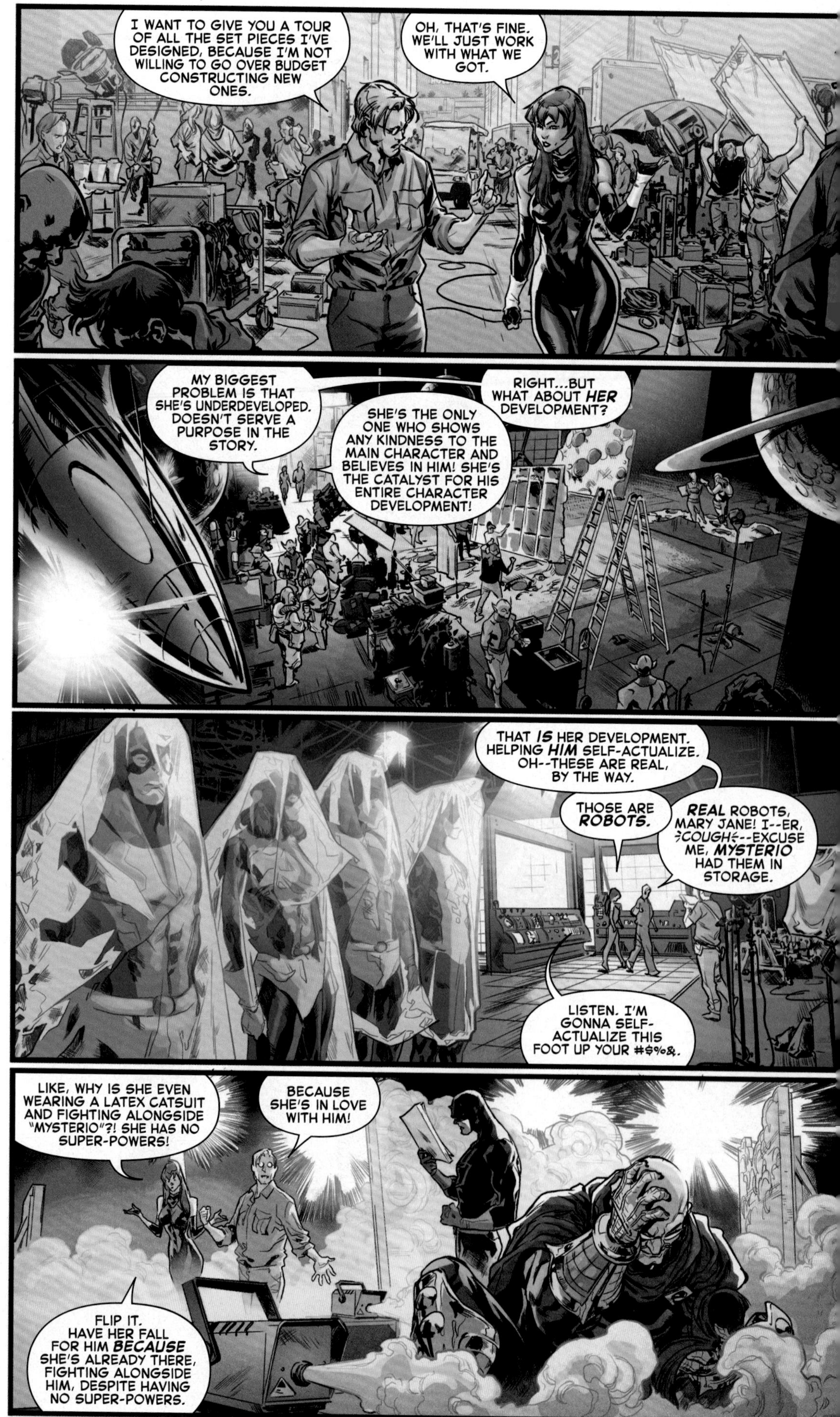

I WANT TO GIVE YOU A TOUR OF ALL THE SET PIECES I'VE DESIGNED, BECAUSE I'M NOT WILLING TO GO OVER BUDGET CONSTRUCTING NEW ONES.
OH, THAT'S FINE. WE'LL JUST WORK WITH WHAT WE GOT.
MY BIGGEST PROBLEM IS THAT SHE'S UNDERDEVELOPED. DOESN'T SERVE A PURPOSE IN THE STORY.
RIGHT...BUT WHAT ABOUT HER DEVELOPMENT?
SHE'S THE ONLY ONE WHO SHOWS ANY KINDNESS TO THE MAIN CHARACTER AND BELIEVES IN HIM! SHE'S THE CATALYST FOR HIS ENTIRE CHARACTER DEVELOPMENT!
THAT IS HER DEVELOPMENT. HELPING HIM SELF-ACTUALIZE. OH--THESE ARE REAL, BY THE WAY.
THOSE ARE ROBOTS.
REAL ROBOTS, MARY JANE! I--ER, COUGH--EXCUSE ME, MYSTERIO HAD THEM IN STORAGE.
LISTEN. I'M GONNA SELF-ACTUALIZE THIS FOOT UP YOUR #$%&.
LIKE, WHY IS SHE EVEN WEARING A LATEX CATSUIT AND FIGHTING ALONGSIDE "MYSTERIO"?! SHE HAS NO SUPER-POWERS!
BECAUSE SHE'S IN LOVE WITH HIM!
FLIP IT. HAVE HER FALL FOR HIM BECAUSE SHE'S ALREADY THERE, FIGHTING ALONGSIDE HIM, DESPITE HAVING NO SUPER-POWERS.

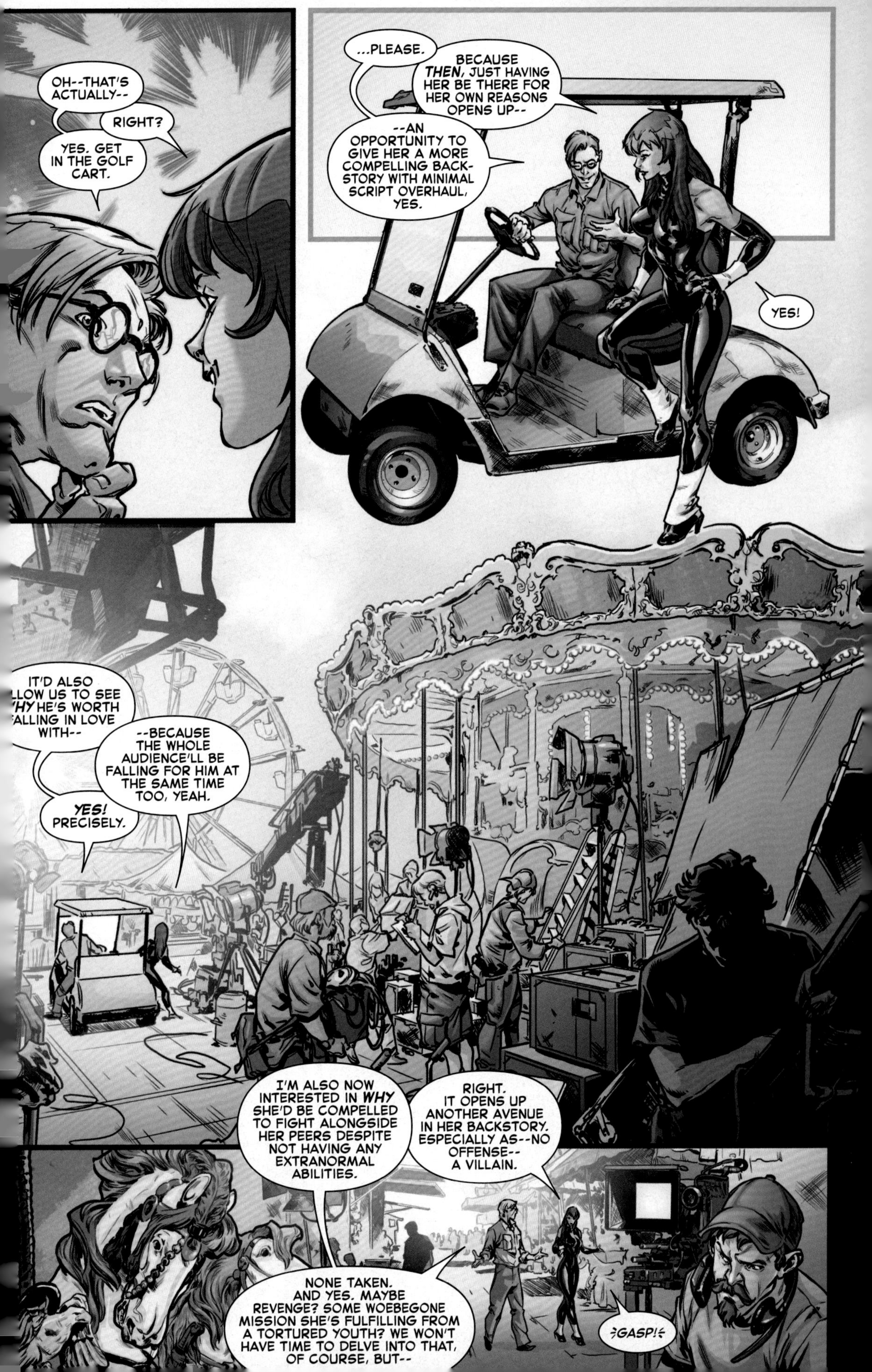

OH--THAT'S ACTUALLY--
RIGHT?
YES. GET IN THE GOLF CART.
...PLEASE.
BECAUSE THEN, JUST HAVING HER BE THERE FOR HER OWN REASONS OPENS UP--
--AN OPPORTUNITY TO GIVE HER A MORE COMPELLING BACK-STORY WITH MINIMAL SCRIPT OVERHAUL, YES.
YES!
IT'D ALSO LLOW US TO SEE WHY HE'S WORTH ALLING IN LOVE WITH--
--BECAUSE THE WHOLE AUDIENCE'LL BE FALLING FOR HIM AT THE SAME TIME TOO, YEAH.
YES! PRECISELY.
I'M ALSO NOW INTERESTED IN WHY SHE'D BE COMPELLED TO FIGHT ALONGSIDE HER PEERS DESPITE NOT HAVING ANY EXTRANORMAL ABILITIES.
RIGHT. IT OPENS UP ANOTHER AVENUE IN HER BACKSTORY. ESPECIALLY AS--NO OFFENSE--A VILLAIN.
NONE TAKEN. AND YES. MAYBE REVENGE? SOME WOEBEGONE MISSION SHE'S FULFILLING FROM A TORTURED YOUTH? WE WON'T HAVE TIME TO DELVE INTO THAT, OF COURSE, BUT--
GASP!

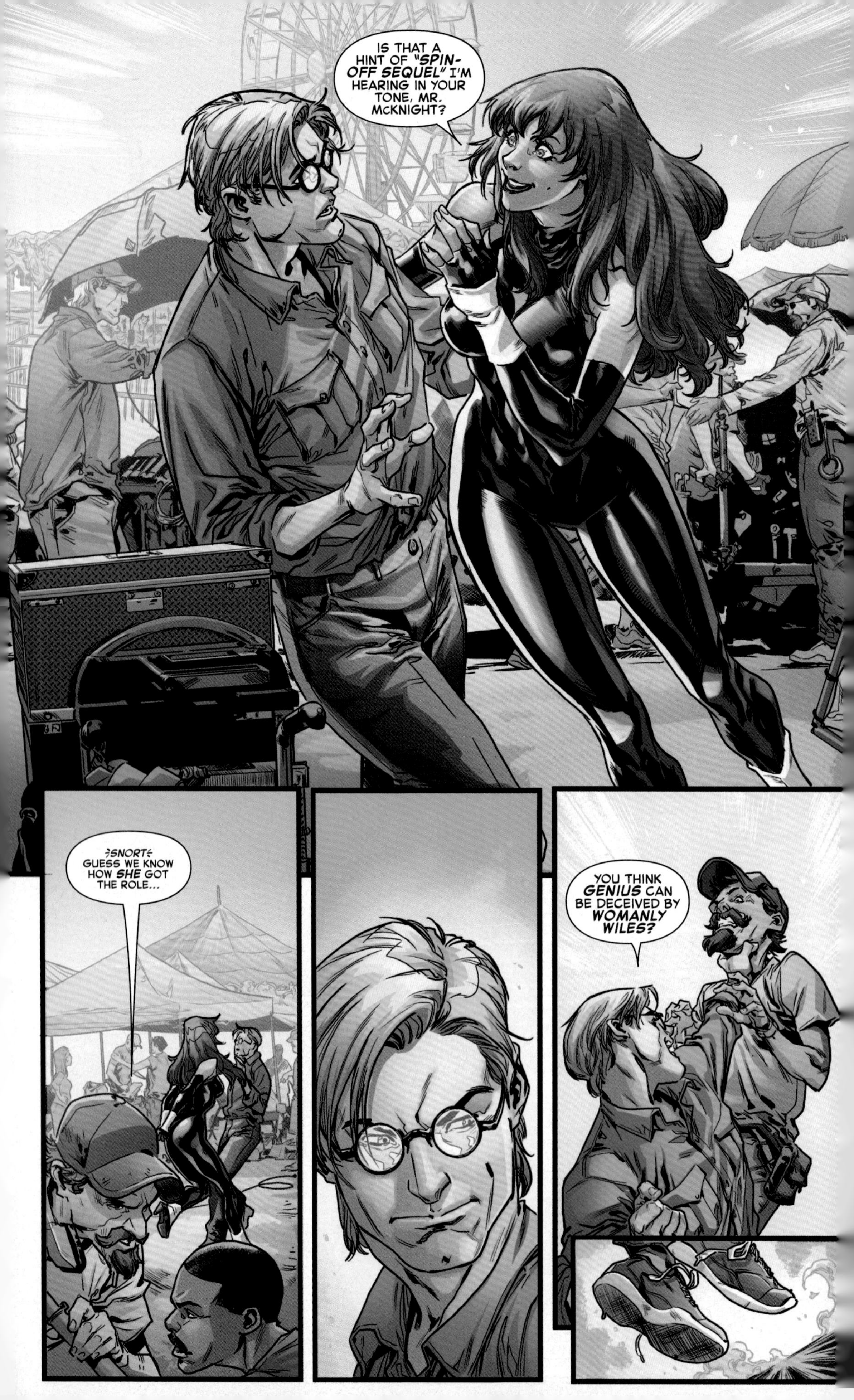
IS THAT A HINT OF "SPIN-OFF SEQUEL" I'M HEARING IN YOUR TONE, MR. McKNIGHT?
SNORT GUESS WE KNOW HOW SHE GOT THE ROLE...
YOU THINK GENIUS CAN BE DECEIVED BY WOMANLY WILES?

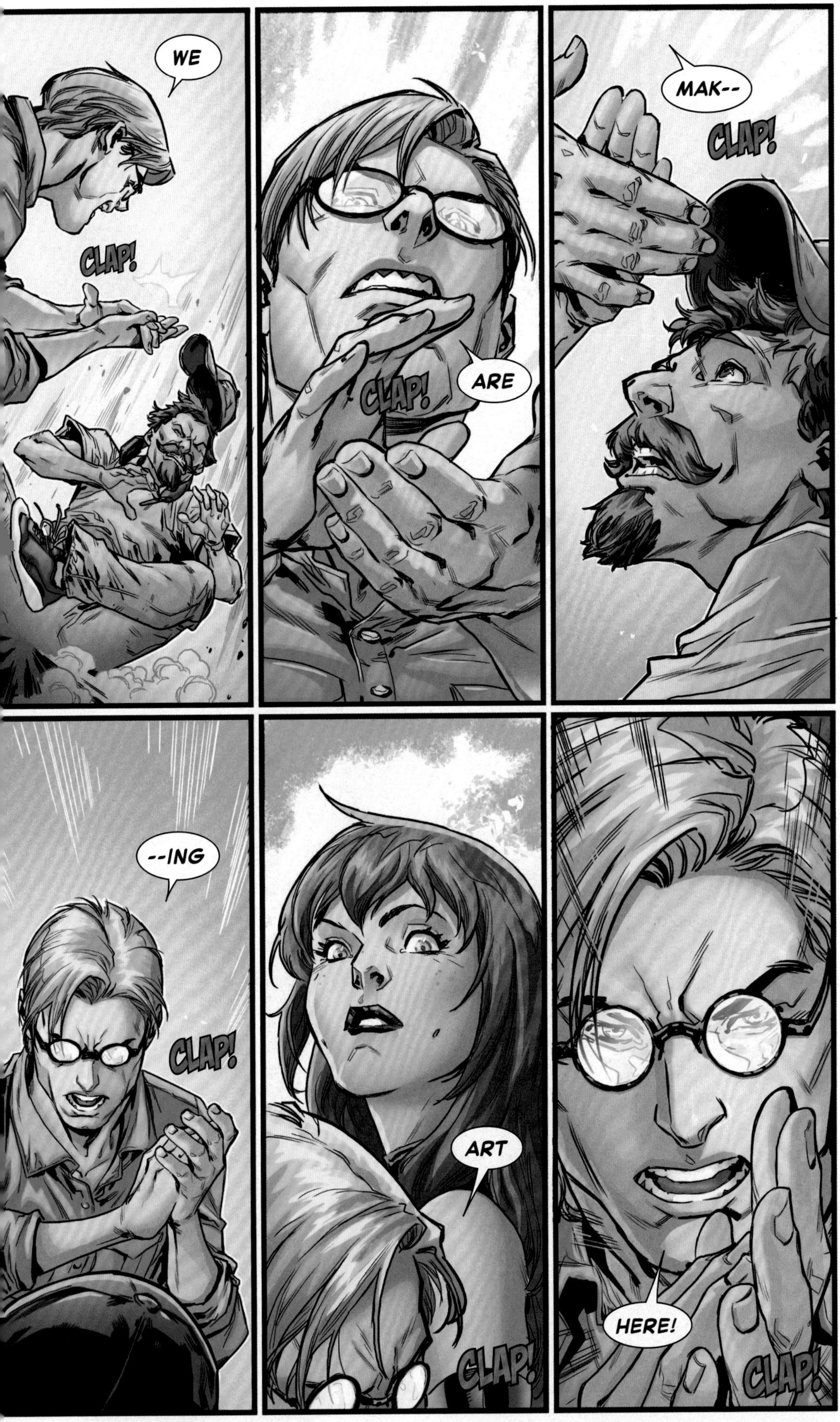
WE
CLAP!
CLAP!
ARE
MAK--
CLAP!
--ING
CLAP!
ART
CLAP!
HERE!
CLAP!

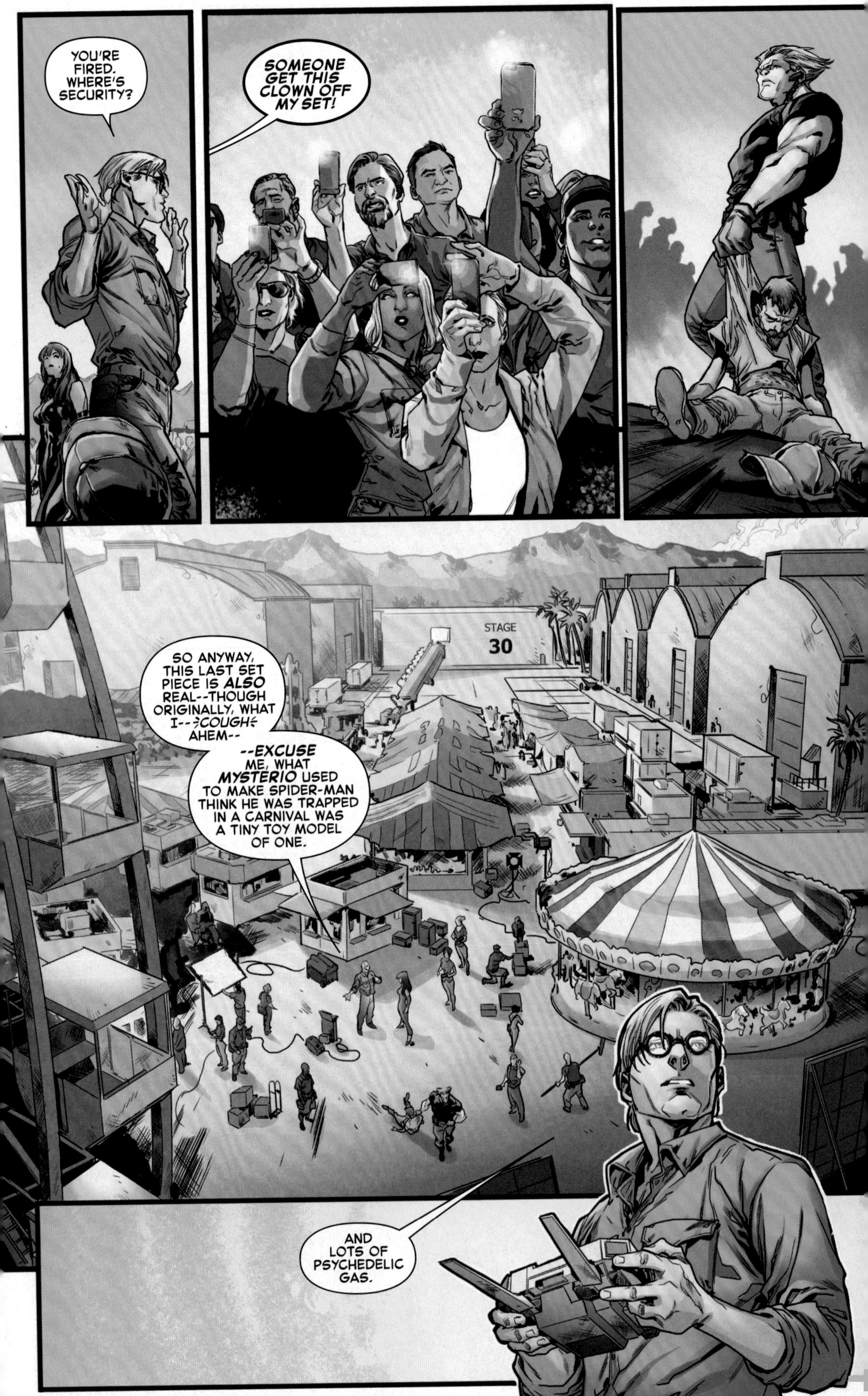
YOU'RE FIRED. WHERE'S SECURITY?
SOMEONE GET THIS CLOWN OFF MY SET!
STAGE 30
SO ANYWAY, THIS LAST SET PIECE IS ALSO REAL--THOUGH ORIGINALLY, WHAT I-- *COUGH* AHEM--
--EXCUSE ME, WHAT MYSTERIO USED TO MAKE SPIDER-MAN THINK HE WAS TRAPPED IN A CARNIVAL WAS A TINY TOY MODEL OF ONE.
AND LOTS OF PSYCHEDELIC GAS.

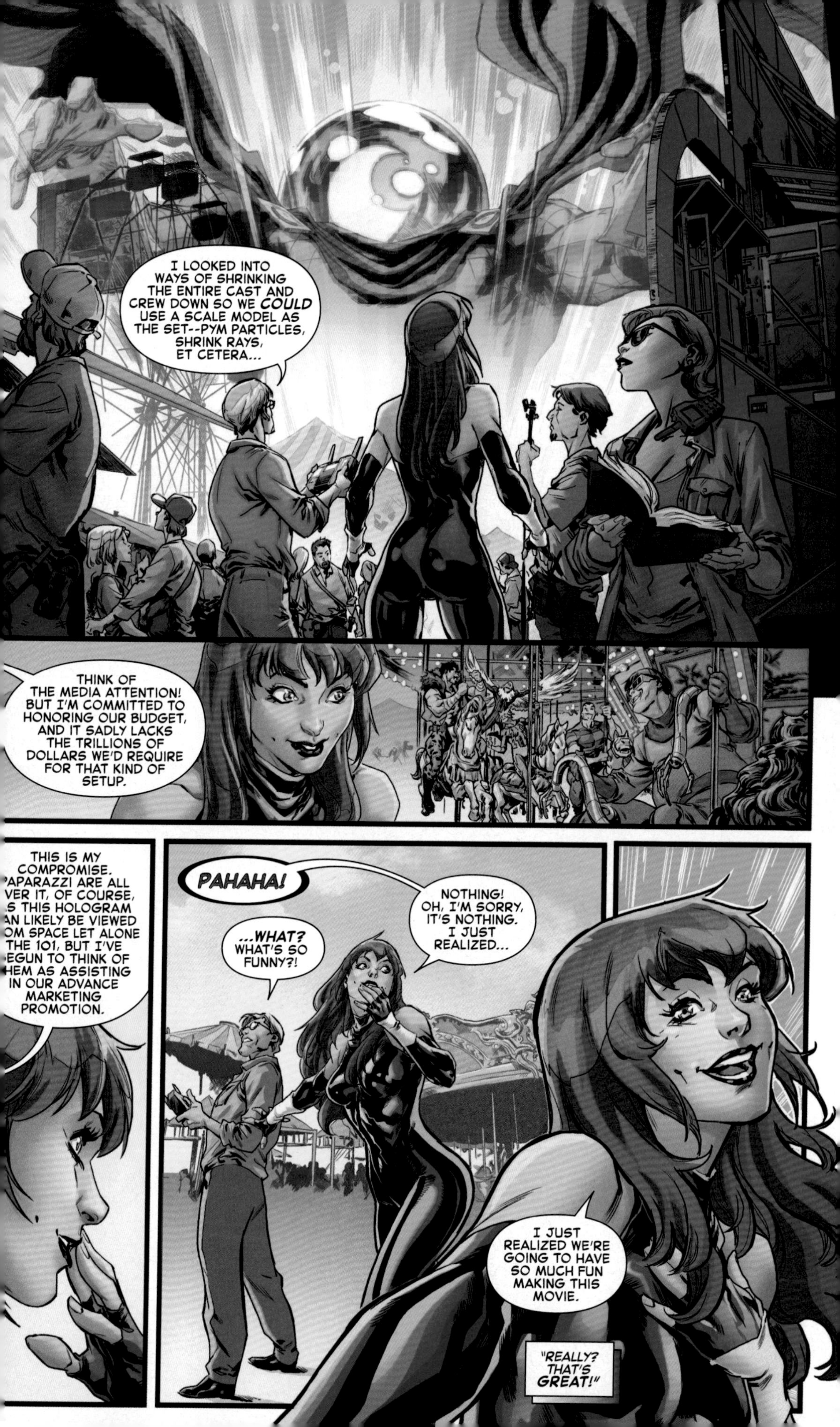

I LOOKED INTO WAYS OF SHRINKING THE ENTIRE CAST AND CREW DOWN SO WE COULD USE A SCALE MODEL AS THE SET--PYM PARTICLES, SHRINK RAYS, ET CETERA...
THINK OF THE MEDIA ATTENTION! BUT I'M COMMITTED TO HONORING OUR BUDGET, AND IT SADLY LACKS THE TRILLIONS OF DOLLARS WE'D REQUIRE FOR THAT KIND OF SETUP.
THIS IS MY COMPROMISE. PAPARAZZI ARE ALL VER IT, OF COURSE, S THIS HOLOGRAM AN LIKELY BE VIEWED OM SPACE LET ALONE THE 101, BUT I'VE EGUN TO THINK OF HEM AS ASSISTING IN OUR ADVANCE MARKETING PROMOTION.
PAHAHA!
...WHAT? WHAT'S SO FUNNY?!
NOTHING! OH, I'M SORRY, IT'S NOTHING. I JUST REALIZED...
I JUST REALIZED WE'RE GOING TO HAVE SO MUCH FUN MAKING THIS MOVIE.
"REALLY? THAT'S GREAT!"

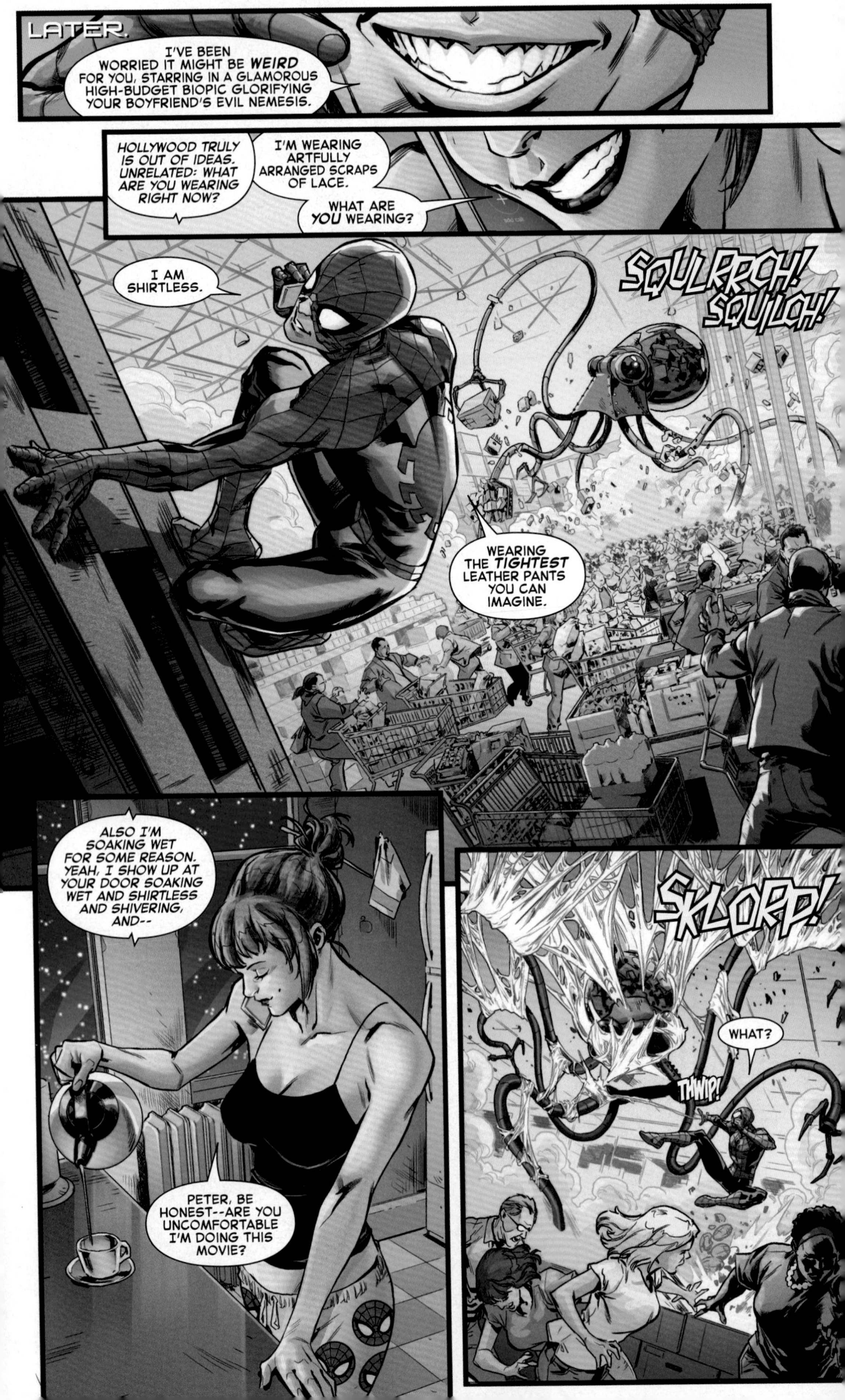
LATER.
I'VE BEEN WORRIED IT MIGHT BE WEIRD FOR YOU, STARRING IN A GLAMOROUS HIGH-BUDGET BIOPIC GLORIFYING YOUR BOYFRIEND'S EVIL NEMESIS.
HOLLYWOOD TRULY IS OUT OF IDEAS. UNRELATED: WHAT ARE YOU WEARING RIGHT NOW?
I'M WEARING ARTFULLY ARRANGED SCRAPS OF LACE.
WHAT ARE YOU WEARING?
I AM SHIRTLESS.
SQULRRCH! SQUILCH!
WEARING THE TIGHTEST LEATHER PANTS YOU CAN IMAGINE.
ALSO I'M SOAKING WET FOR SOME REASON. YEAH, I SHOW UP AT YOUR DOOR SOAKING WET AND SHIRTLESS AND SHIVERING, AND--
PETER, BE HONEST--ARE YOU UNCOMFORTABLE I'M DOING THIS MOVIE?
SKLORP!
WHAT?
THWIP!

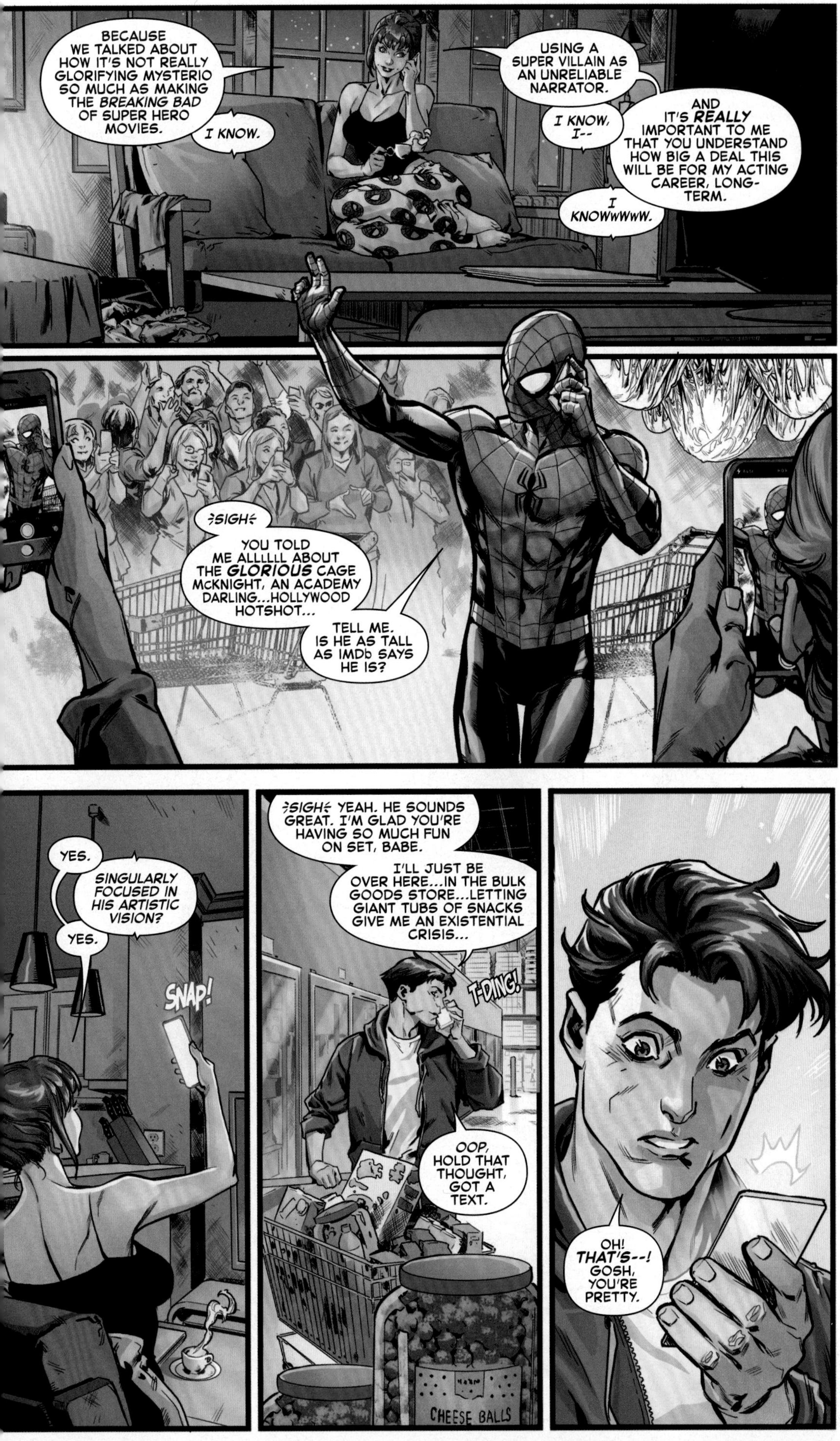
BECAUSE WE TALKED ABOUT HOW IT'S NOT REALLY GLORIFYING MYSTERIO SO MUCH AS MAKING THE *BREAKING BAD* OF SUPER HERO MOVIES.
I KNOW.
USING A SUPER VILLAIN AS AN UNRELIABLE NARRATOR.
I KNOW, I--
AND IT'S ***REALLY*** IMPORTANT TO ME THAT YOU UNDERSTAND HOW BIG A DEAL THIS WILL BE FOR MY ACTING CAREER, LONG-TERM.
I KNOWwWWW.
SIGH
YOU TOLD ME ALLLLLL ABOUT THE ***GLORIOUS*** CAGE McKNIGHT, AN ACADEMY DARLING...HOLLYWOOD HOTSHOT...
TELL ME. IS HE AS TALL AS IMDb SAYS HE IS?
YES.
SINGULARLY FOCUSED IN HIS ARTISTIC VISION?
YES.
SNAP!
SIGH YEAH. HE SOUNDS GREAT. I'M GLAD YOU'RE HAVING SO MUCH FUN ON SET, BABE.
I'LL JUST BE OVER HERE...IN THE BULK GOODS STORE...LETTING GIANT TUBS OF SNACKS GIVE ME AN EXISTENTIAL CRISIS...
T-DING!
OOP, HOLD THAT THOUGHT, GOT A TEXT.
CHEESE BALLS
OH! ***THAT'S--!*** GOSH, YOU'RE PRETTY.

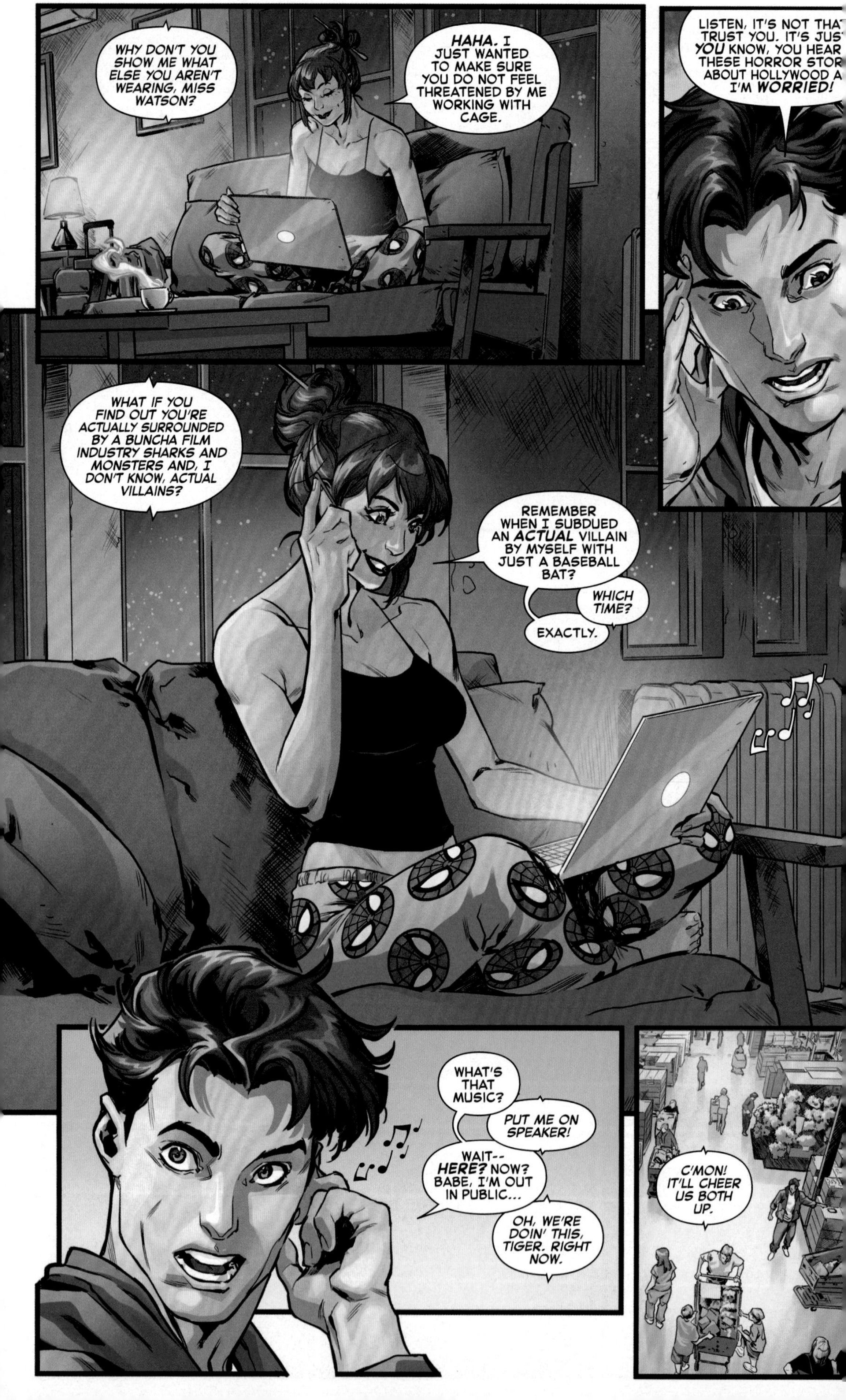

WHY DON'T YOU SHOW ME WHAT ELSE YOU AREN'T WEARING, MISS WATSON?
HAHA. I JUST WANTED TO MAKE SURE YOU DO NOT FEEL THREATENED BY ME WORKING WITH CAGE.
LISTEN, IT'S NOT THAT TRUST YOU. IT'S JUST YOU KNOW, YOU HEAR THESE HORROR STOR ABOUT HOLLYWOOD A I'M WORRIED!
WHAT IF YOU FIND OUT YOU'RE ACTUALLY SURROUNDED BY A BUNCHA FILM INDUSTRY SHARKS AND MONSTERS AND, I DON'T KNOW, ACTUAL VILLAINS?
REMEMBER WHEN I SUBDUED AN ACTUAL VILLAIN BY MYSELF WITH JUST A BASEBALL BAT?
WHICH TIME?
EXACTLY.
WHAT'S THAT MUSIC?
PUT ME ON SPEAKER!
WAIT-- HERE? NOW? BABE, I'M OUT IN PUBLIC...
OH, WE'RE DOIN' THIS, TIGER. RIGHT NOW.
C'MON! IT'LL CHEER US BOTH UP.

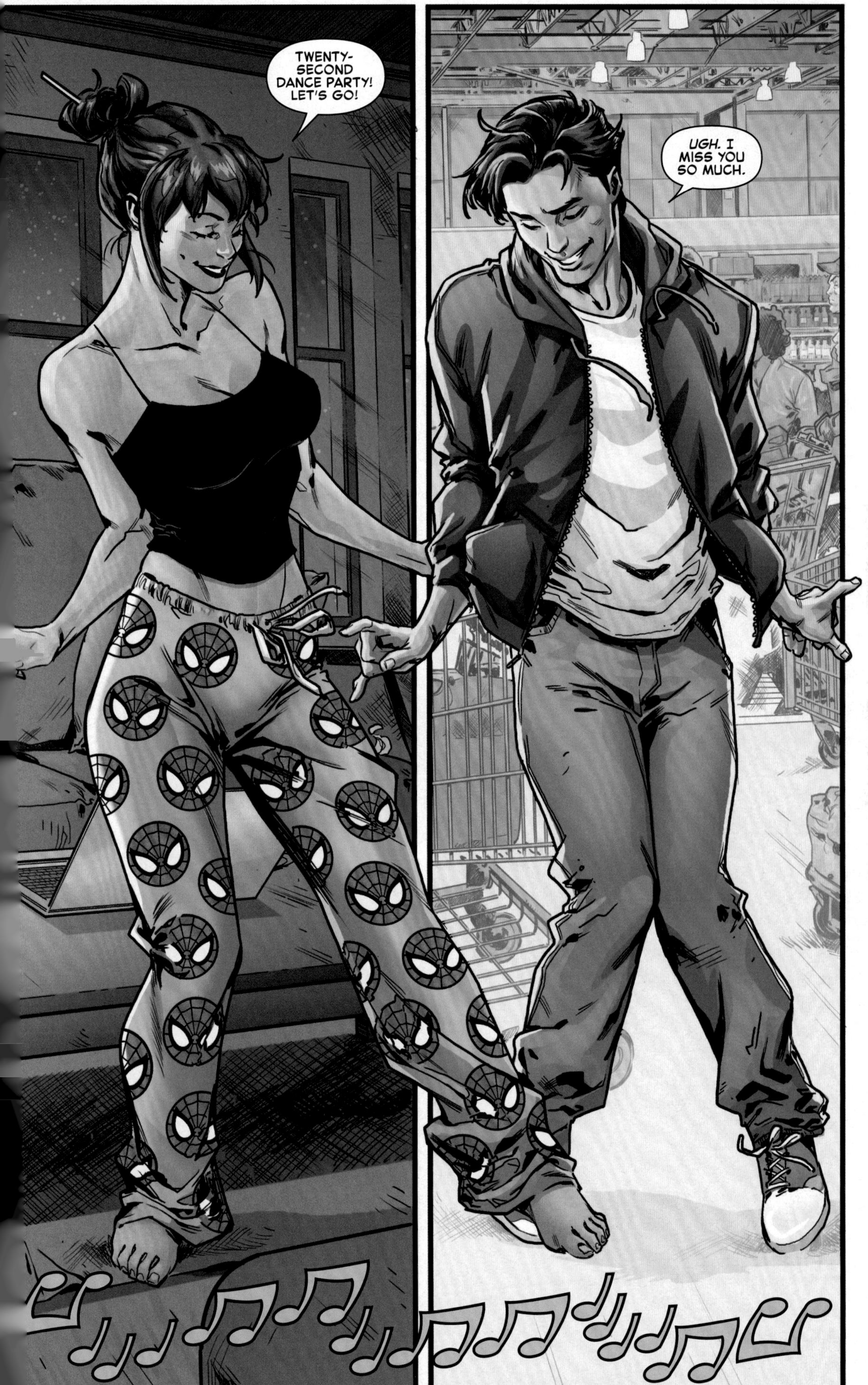
TWENTY-SECOND DANCE PARTY! LET'S GO!
UGH. I MISS YOU SO MUCH.

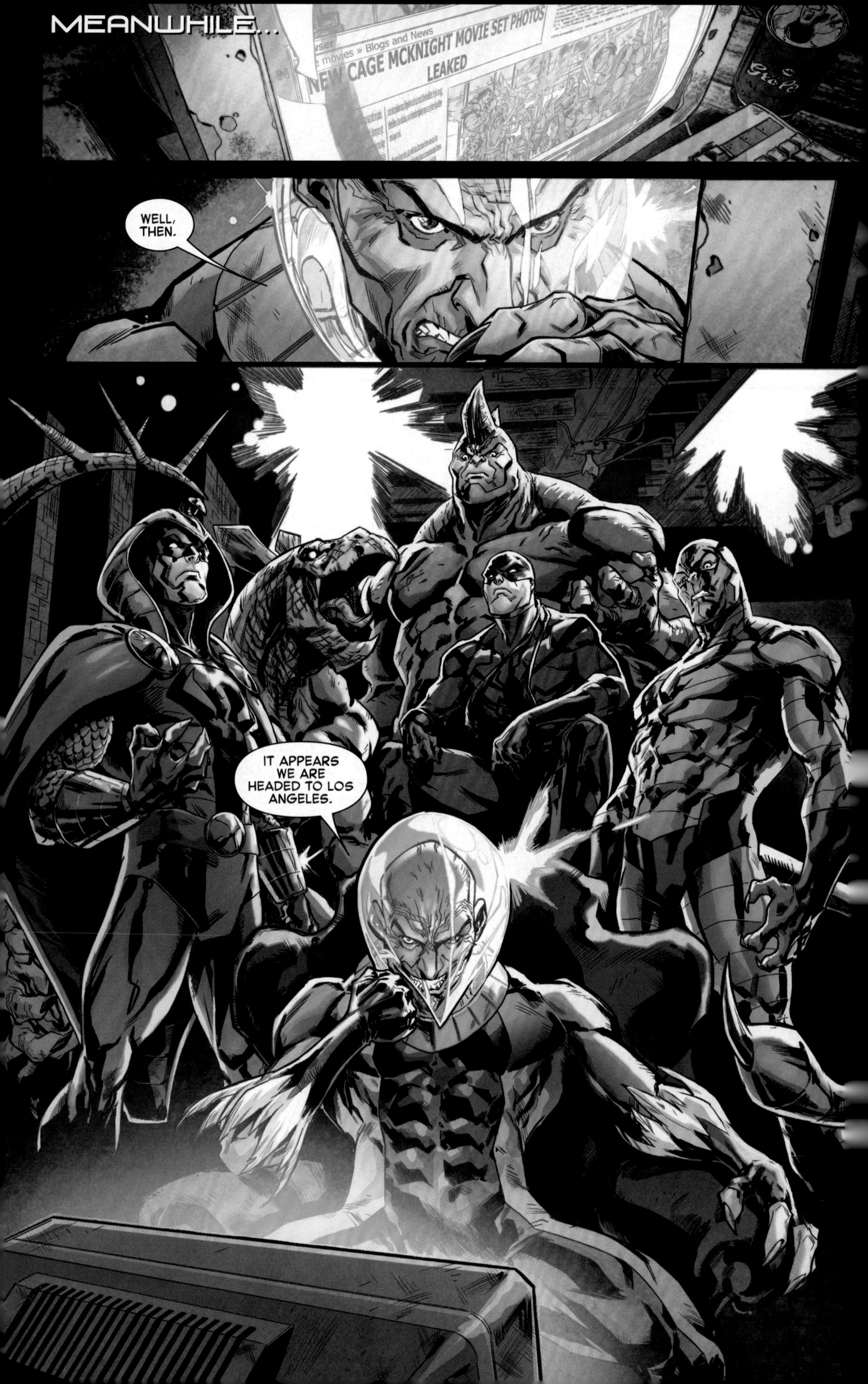
MEANWHILE...
Blogs and News
NEW CAGE MCKNIGHT MOVIE SET PHOTOS LEAKED
WELL, THEN.
IT APPEARS WE ARE HEADED TO LOS ANGELES.

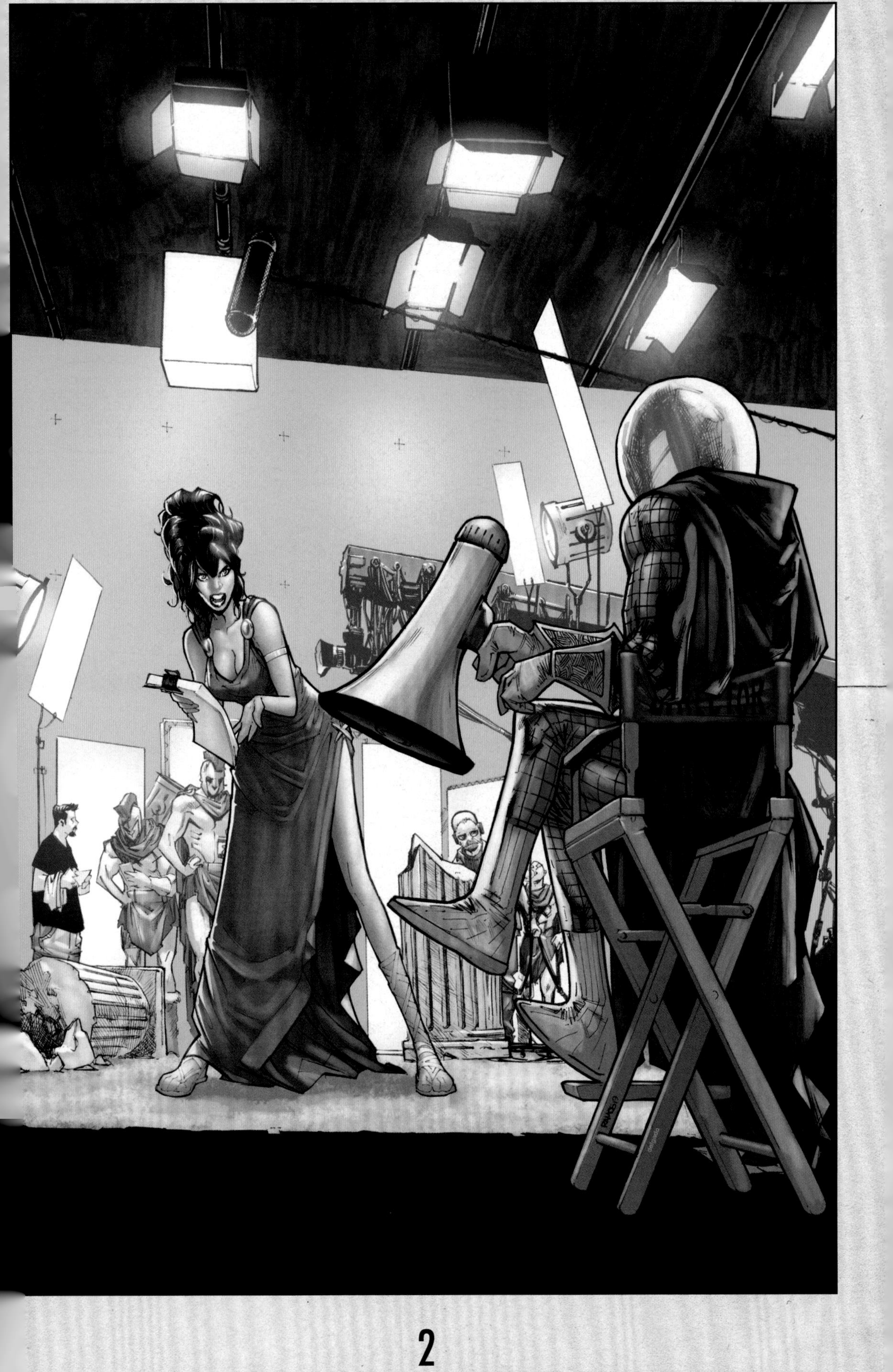

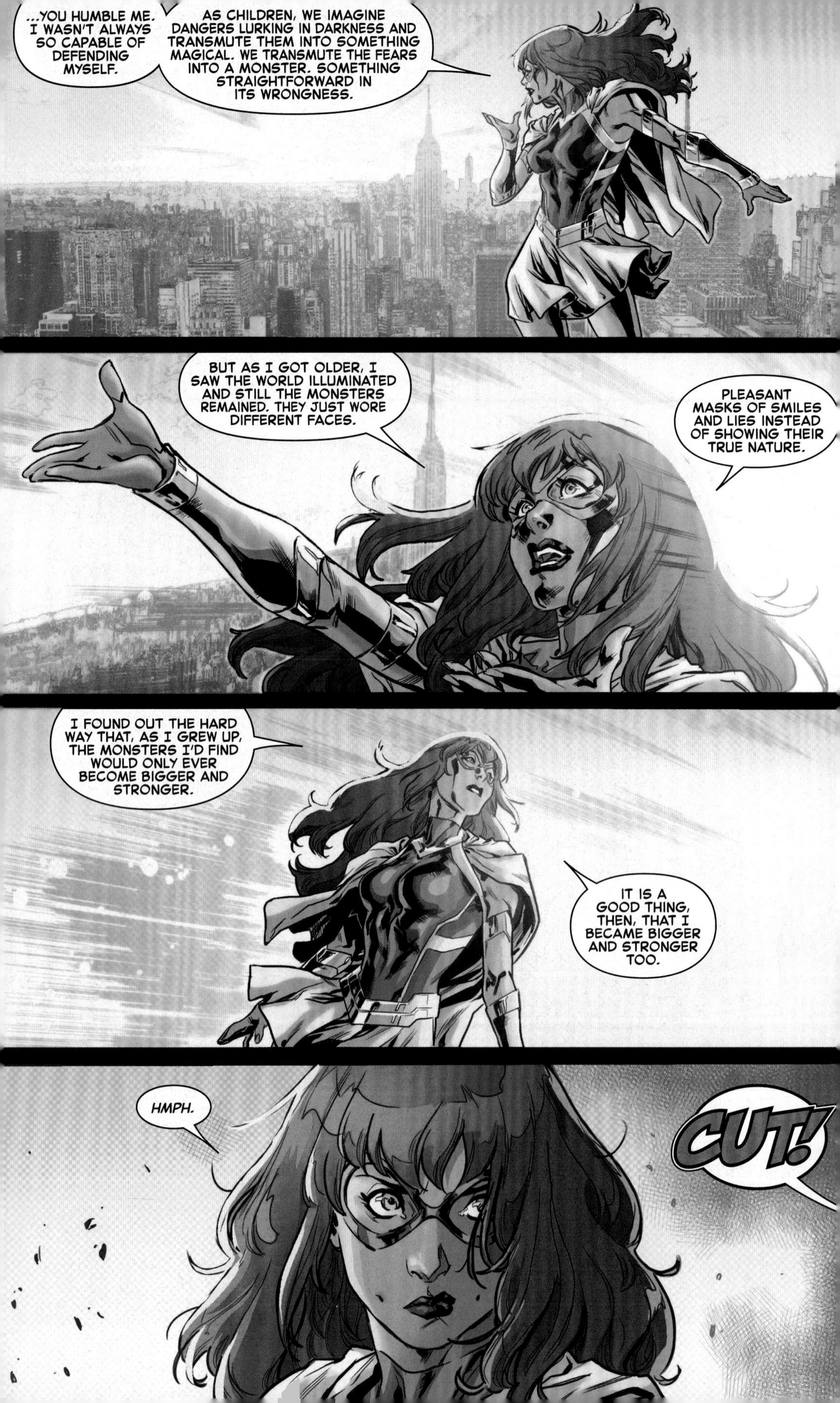
...YOU HUMBLE ME. I WASN'T ALWAYS SO CAPABLE OF DEFENDING MYSELF.
AS CHILDREN, WE IMAGINE DANGERS LURKING IN DARKNESS AND TRANSMUTE THEM INTO SOMETHING MAGICAL. WE TRANSMUTE THE FEARS INTO A MONSTER. SOMETHING STRAIGHTFORWARD IN ITS WRONGNESS.
BUT AS I GOT OLDER, I SAW THE WORLD ILLUMINATED AND STILL THE MONSTERS REMAINED. THEY JUST WORE DIFFERENT FACES.
PLEASANT MASKS OF SMILES AND LIES INSTEAD OF SHOWING THEIR TRUE NATURE.
I FOUND OUT THE HARD WAY THAT, AS I GREW UP, THE MONSTERS I'D FIND WOULD ONLY EVER BECOME BIGGER AND STRONGER.
IT IS A GOOD THING, THEN, THAT I BECAME BIGGER AND STRONGER TOO.
HMPH.
CUT!

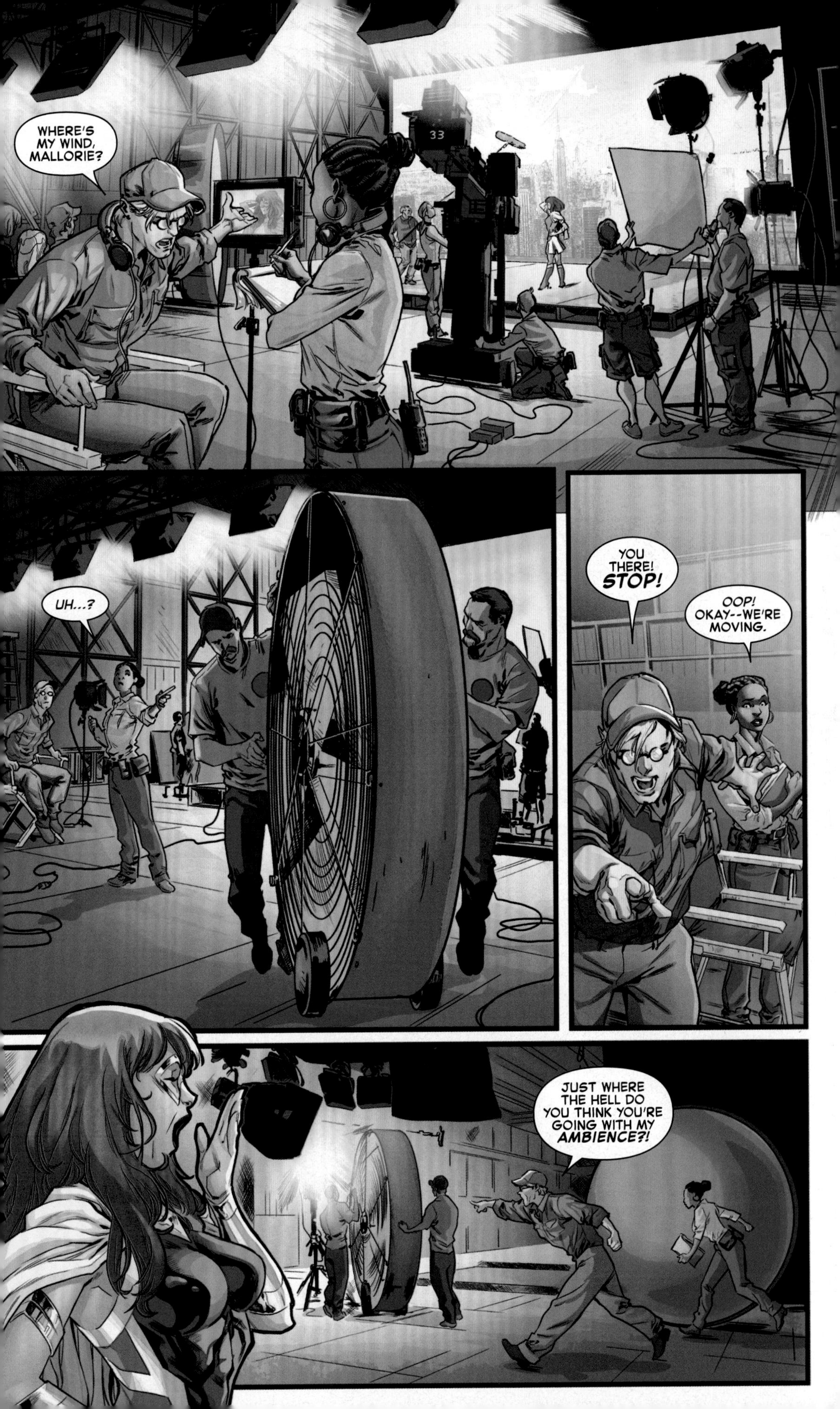
WHERE'S MY WIND, MALLORIE?
UH...?
YOU THERE! STOP!
OOP! OKAY--WE'RE MOVING.
JUST WHERE THE HELL DO YOU THINK YOU'RE GOING WITH MY AMBIENCE?!

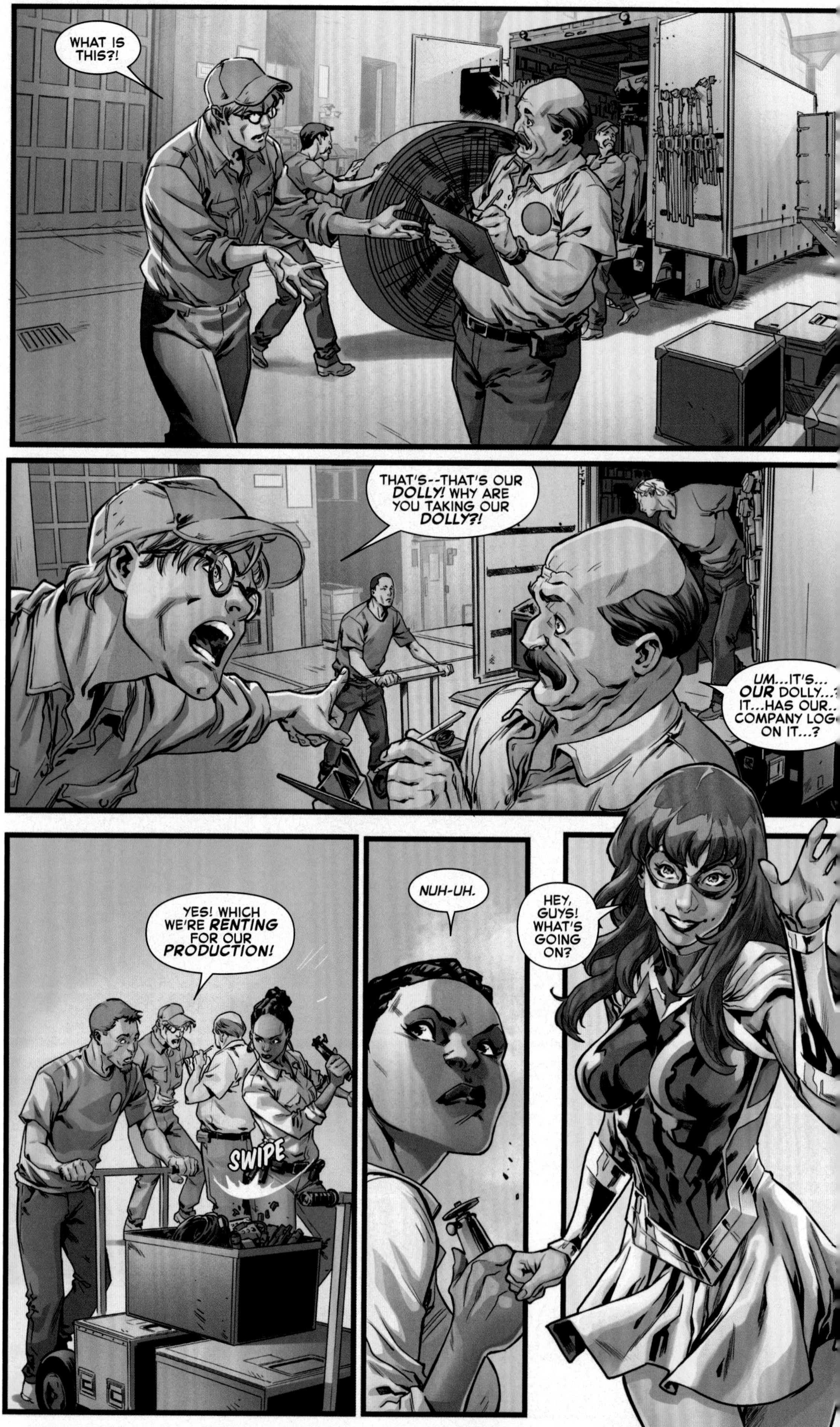
WHAT IS THIS?!
THAT'S--THAT'S OUR DOLLY! WHY ARE YOU TAKING OUR DOLLY?!
UM...IT'S... OUR DOLLY...? IT...HAS OUR... COMPANY LOG ON IT...?
YES! WHICH WE'RE RENTING FOR OUR PRODUCTION!
SWIPE
NUH-UH.
HEY, GUYS! WHAT'S GOING ON?

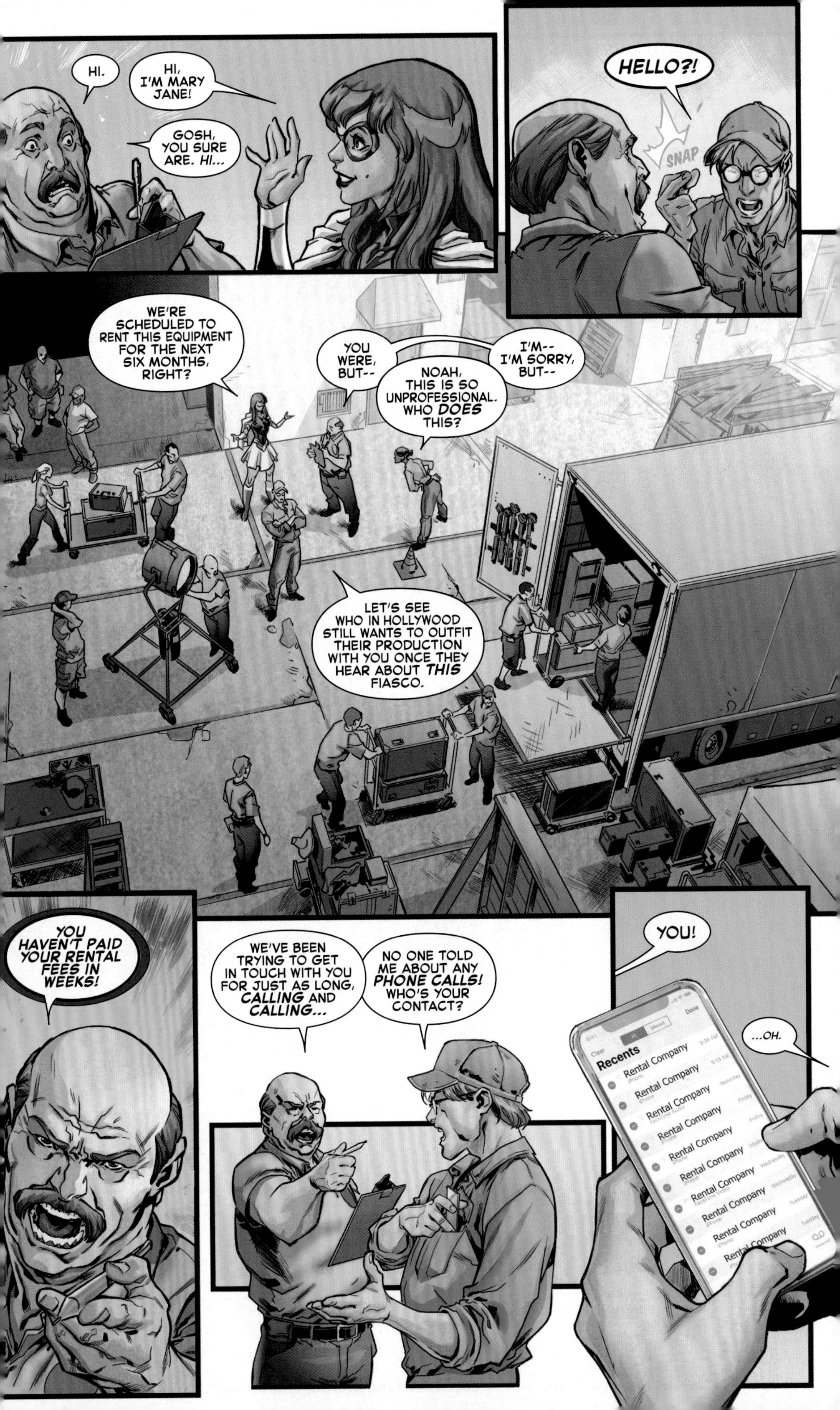
HI.
HI, I'M MARY JANE!
GOSH, YOU SURE ARE. HI...
HELLO?!
SNAP
WE'RE SCHEDULED TO RENT THIS EQUIPMENT FOR THE NEXT SIX MONTHS, RIGHT?
YOU WERE, BUT--
I'M-- I'M SORRY, BUT--
NOAH, THIS IS SO UNPROFESSIONAL. WHO DOES THIS?
LET'S SEE WHO IN HOLLYWOOD STILL WANTS TO OUTFIT THEIR PRODUCTION WITH YOU ONCE THEY HEAR ABOUT THIS FIASCO.
YOU HAVEN'T PAID YOUR RENTAL FEES IN WEEKS!
WE'VE BEEN TRYING TO GET IN TOUCH WITH YOU FOR JUST AS LONG, CALLING AND CALLING...
NO ONE TOLD ME ABOUT ANY PHONE CALLS! WHO'S YOUR CONTACT?
YOU!
...OH.
Recents
Rental Company
Rental Company
Rental Company
Rental Company
Rental Company
Rental Company
Rental Company
Rental Company
Rental Company
Rental Company

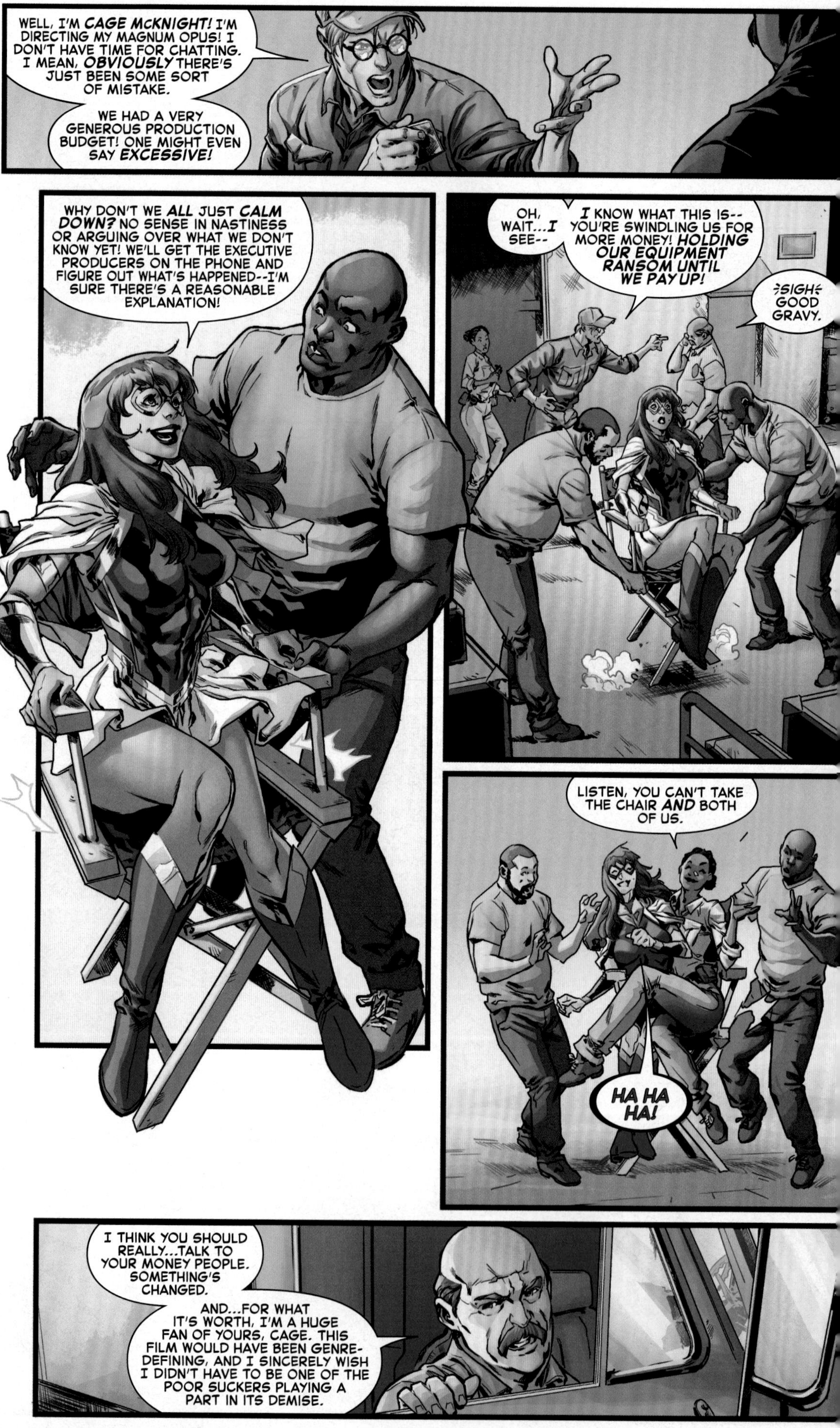

WELL, I'M CAGE McKNIGHT! I'M DIRECTING MY MAGNUM OPUS! I DON'T HAVE TIME FOR CHATTING. I MEAN, OBVIOUSLY THERE'S JUST BEEN SOME SORT OF MISTAKE.
WE HAD A VERY GENEROUS PRODUCTION BUDGET! ONE MIGHT EVEN SAY EXCESSIVE!
WHY DON'T WE ALL JUST CALM DOWN? NO SENSE IN NASTINESS OR ARGUING OVER WHAT WE DON'T KNOW YET! WE'LL GET THE EXECUTIVE PRODUCERS ON THE PHONE AND FIGURE OUT WHAT'S HAPPENED--I'M SURE THERE'S A REASONABLE EXPLANATION!
OH, WAIT...I SEE--
I KNOW WHAT THIS IS--YOU'RE SWINDLING US FOR MORE MONEY! HOLDING OUR EQUIPMENT RANSOM UNTIL WE PAY UP!
SIGH GOOD GRAVY.
LISTEN, YOU CAN'T TAKE THE CHAIR AND BOTH OF US.
HA HA HA!
I THINK YOU SHOULD REALLY...TALK TO YOUR MONEY PEOPLE. SOMETHING'S CHANGED.
AND...FOR WHAT IT'S WORTH, I'M A HUGE FAN OF YOURS, CAGE. THIS FILM WOULD HAVE BEEN GENRE-DEFINING, AND I SINCERELY WISH I DIDN'T HAVE TO BE ONE OF THE POOR SUCKERS PLAYING A PART IN ITS DEMISE.

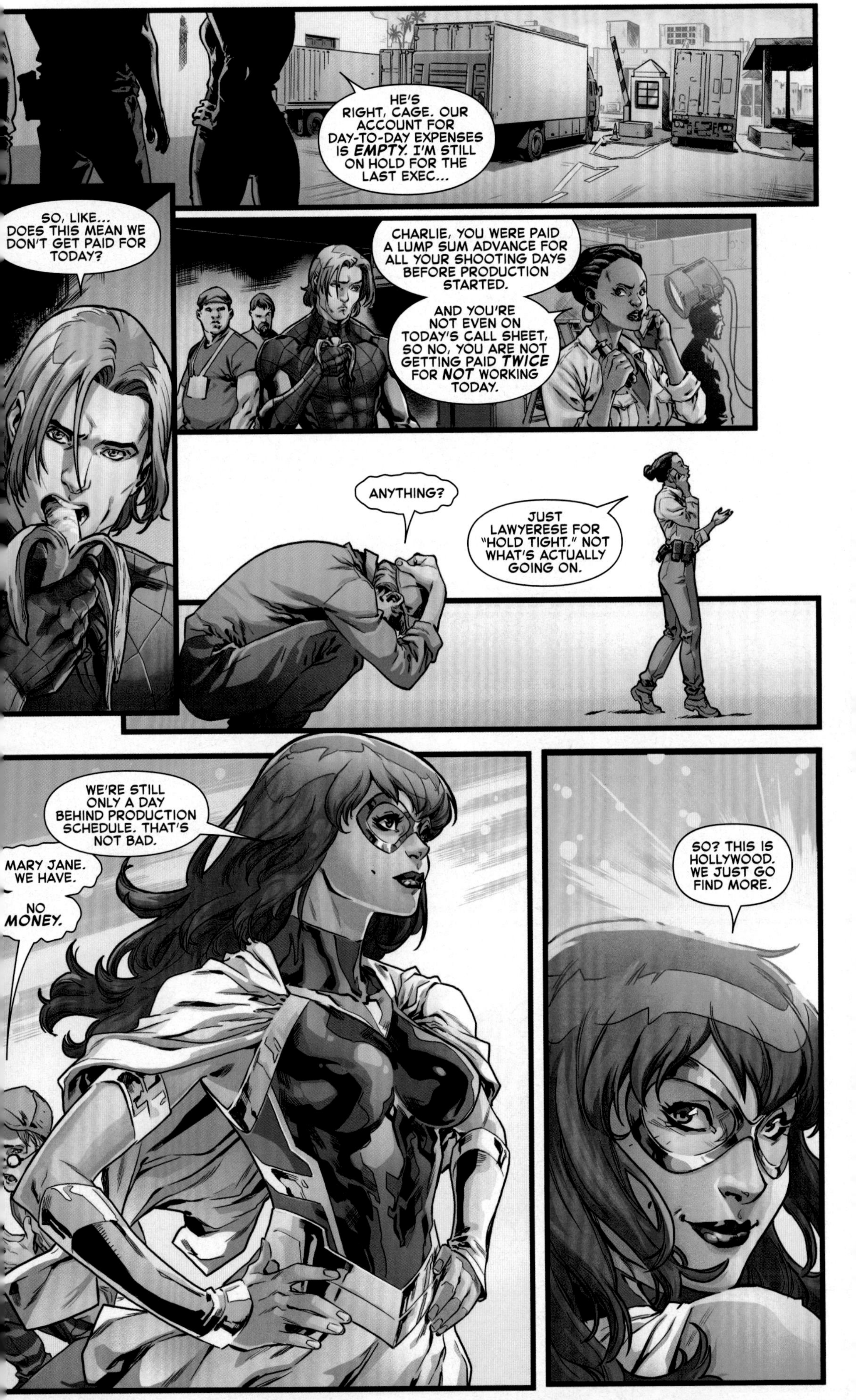
HE'S RIGHT, CAGE. OUR ACCOUNT FOR DAY-TO-DAY EXPENSES IS EMPTY. I'M STILL ON HOLD FOR THE LAST EXEC...
SO, LIKE... DOES THIS MEAN WE DON'T GET PAID FOR TODAY?
CHARLIE, YOU WERE PAID A LUMP SUM ADVANCE FOR ALL YOUR SHOOTING DAYS BEFORE PRODUCTION STARTED.
AND YOU'RE NOT EVEN ON TODAY'S CALL SHEET, SO NO, YOU ARE NOT GETTING PAID TWICE FOR NOT WORKING TODAY.
ANYTHING?
JUST LAWYERESE FOR "HOLD TIGHT." NOT WHAT'S ACTUALLY GOING ON.
WE'RE STILL ONLY A DAY BEHIND PRODUCTION SCHEDULE. THAT'S NOT BAD.
MARY JANE. WE HAVE.
NO MONEY.
SO? THIS IS HOLLYWOOD. WE JUST GO FIND MORE.

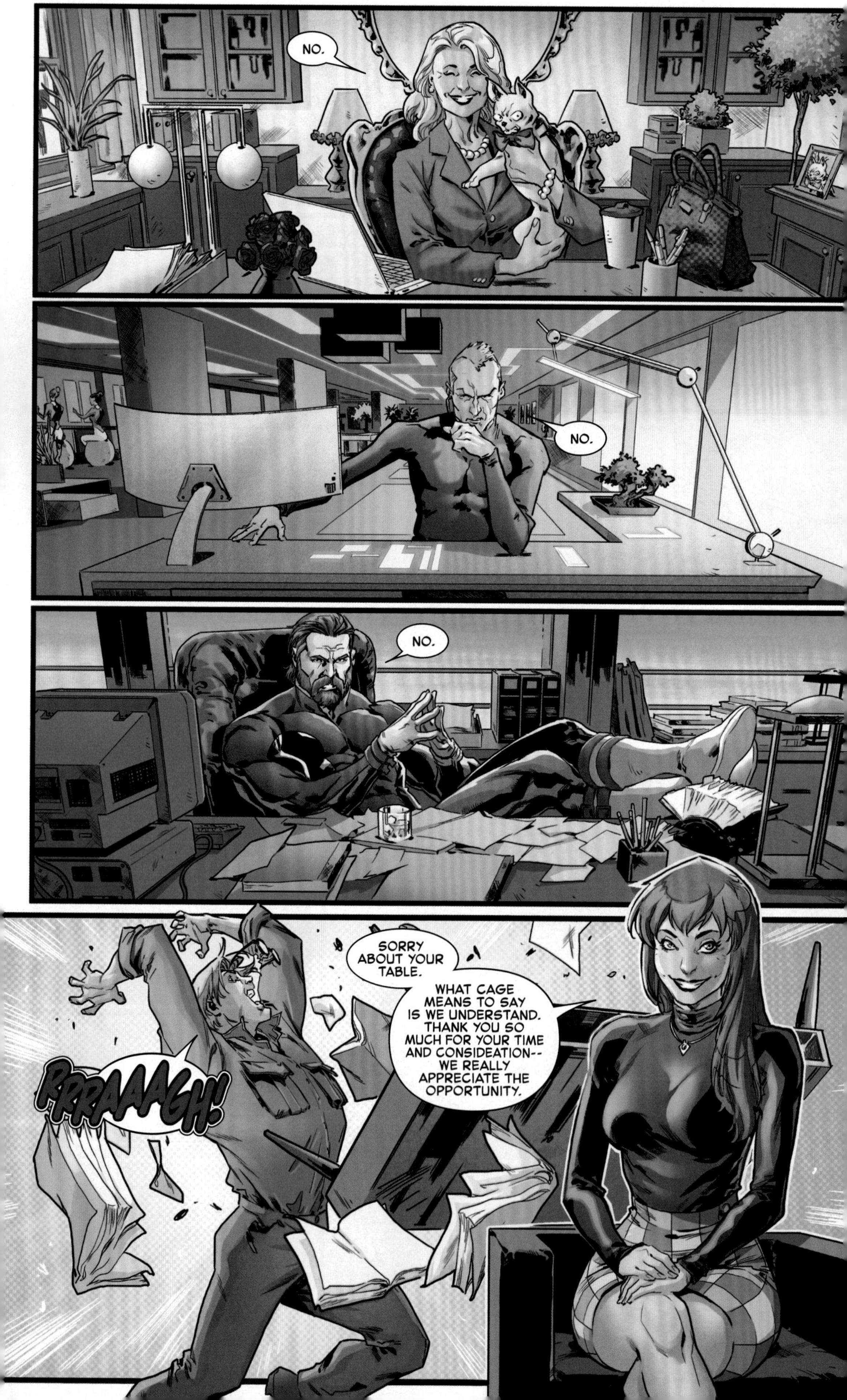
NO.
NO.
NO.
SORRY ABOUT YOUR TABLE.
WHAT CAGE MEANS TO SAY IS WE UNDERSTAND. THANK YOU SO MUCH FOR YOUR TIME AND CONSIDEATION-- WE REALLY APPRECIATE THE OPPORTUNITY.
RRRAAAAGH!

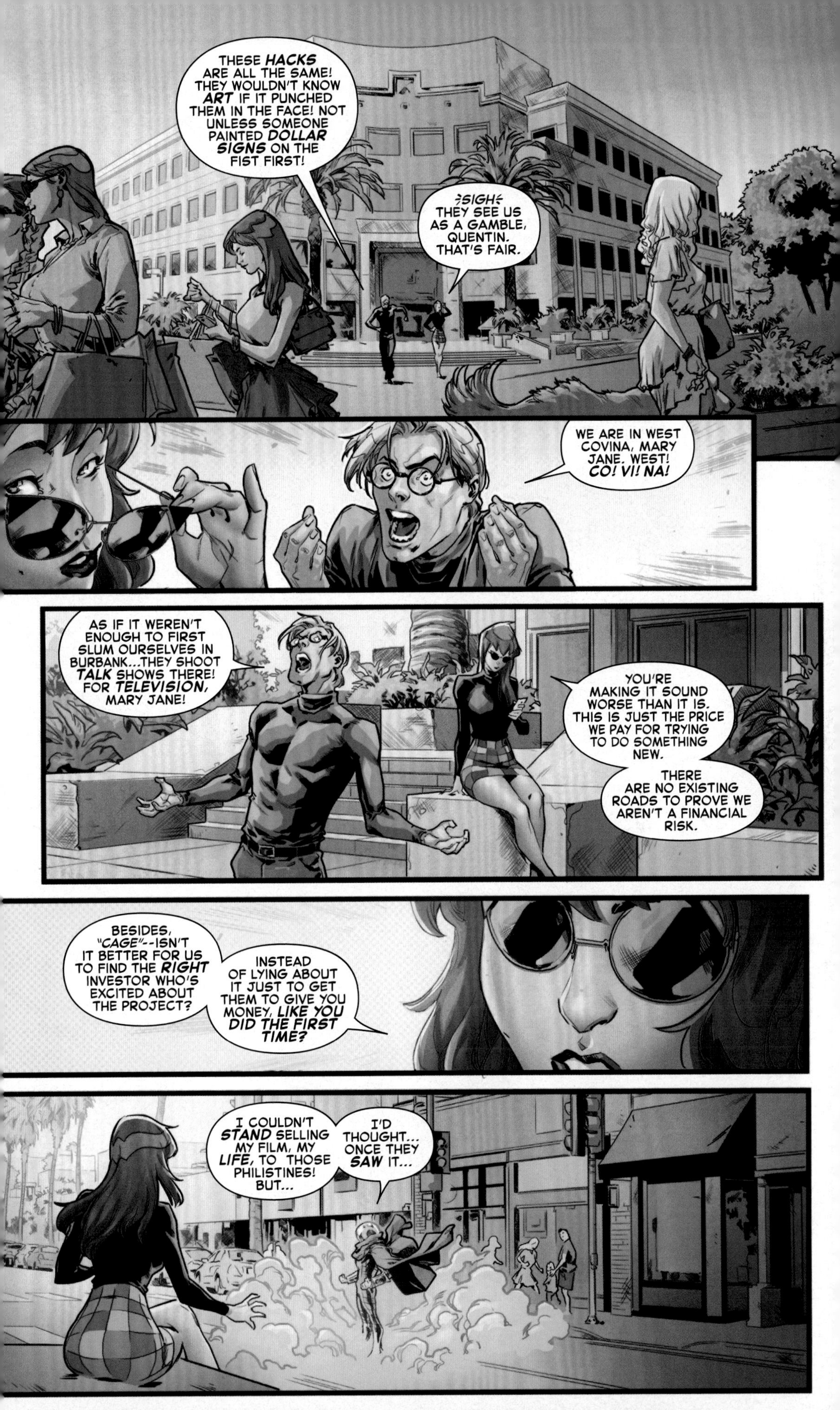
THESE HACKS ARE ALL THE SAME! THEY WOULDN'T KNOW ART IF IT PUNCHED THEM IN THE FACE! NOT UNLESS SOMEONE PAINTED DOLLAR SIGNS ON THE FIST FIRST!
SIGH THEY SEE US AS A GAMBLE, QUENTIN. THAT'S FAIR.
WE ARE IN WEST COVINA, MARY JANE. WEST! CO! VI! NA!
AS IF IT WEREN'T ENOUGH TO FIRST SLUM OURSELVES IN BURBANK...THEY SHOOT TALK SHOWS THERE! FOR TELEVISION, MARY JANE!
YOU'RE MAKING IT SOUND WORSE THAN IT IS. THIS IS JUST THE PRICE WE PAY FOR TRYING TO DO SOMETHING NEW.
THERE ARE NO EXISTING ROADS TO PROVE WE AREN'T A FINANCIAL RISK.
BESIDES, "CAGE"--ISN'T IT BETTER FOR US TO FIND THE RIGHT INVESTOR WHO'S EXCITED ABOUT THE PROJECT?
INSTEAD OF LYING ABOUT IT JUST TO GET THEM TO GIVE YOU MONEY, LIKE YOU DID THE FIRST TIME?
I COULDN'T STAND SELLING MY FILM, MY LIFE, TO THOSE PHILISTINES! BUT...
I'D THOUGHT... ONCE THEY SAW IT...

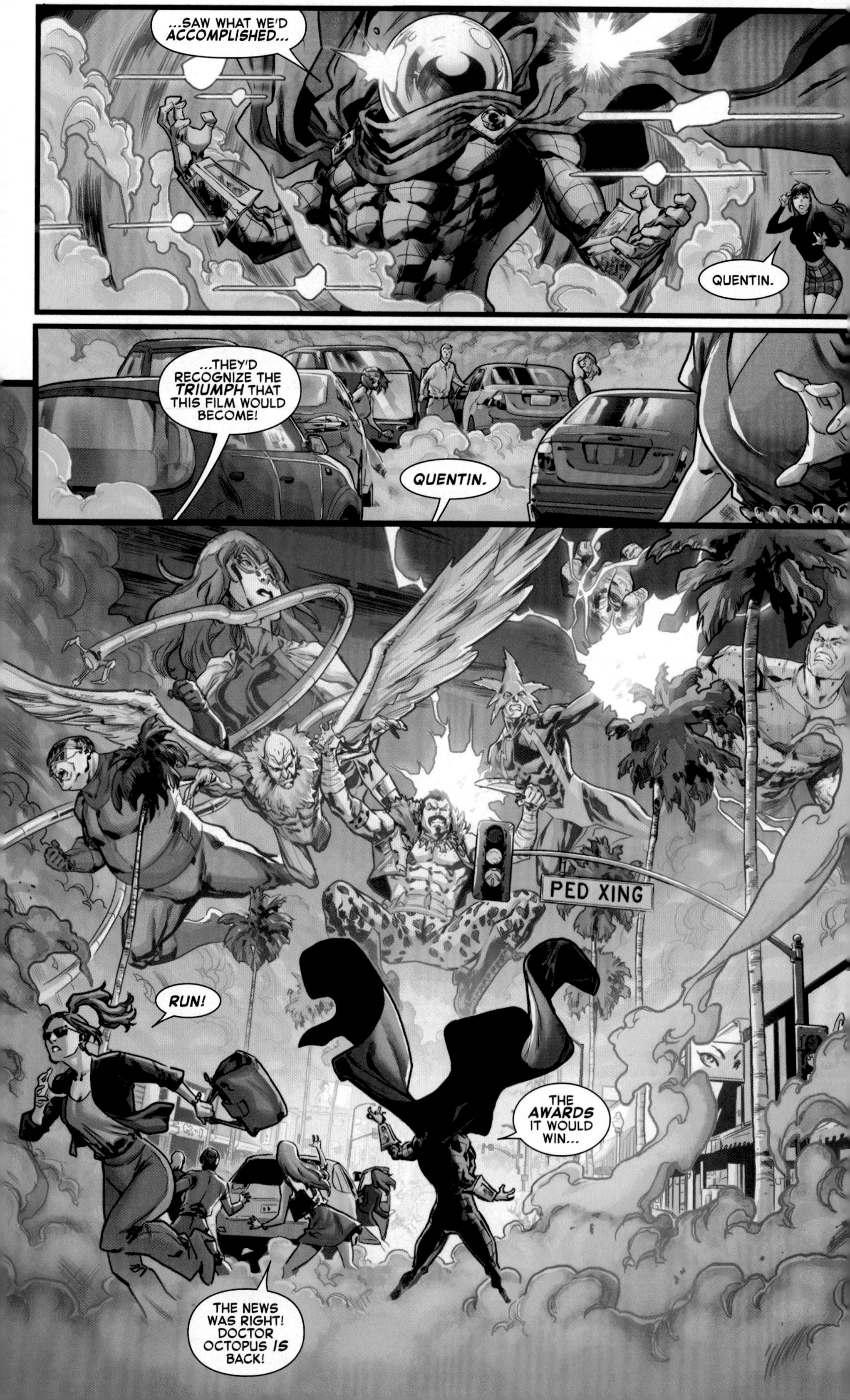
...SAW WHAT WE'D ACCOMPLISHED...
QUENTIN.
...THEY'D RECOGNIZE THE TRIUMPH THAT THIS FILM WOULD BECOME!
QUENTIN.
RUN!
PED XING
THE AWARDS IT WOULD WIN...
THE NEWS WAS RIGHT! DOCTOR OCTOPUS IS BACK!

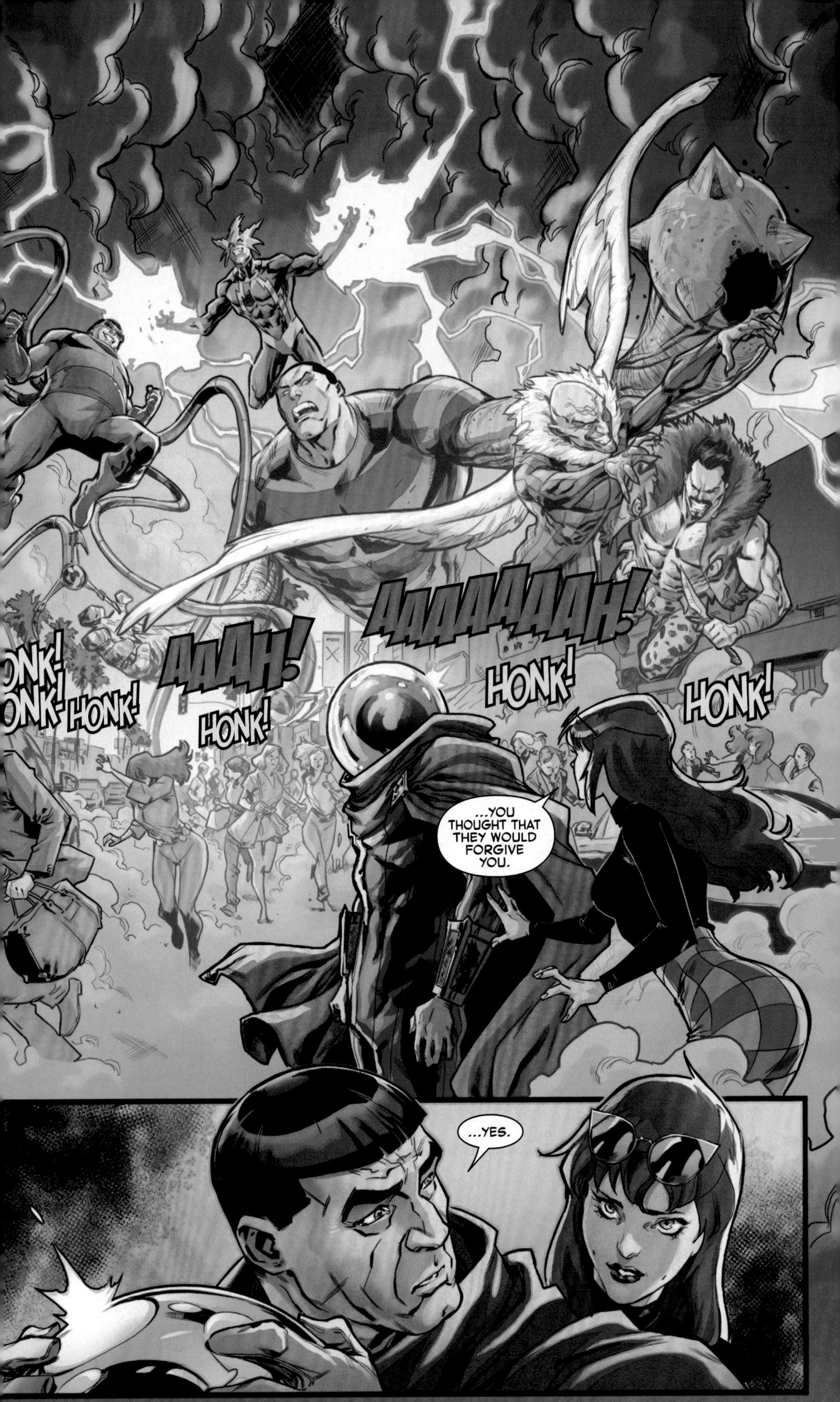
AAAAAAAAH!
AAAH!
HONK!
HONK!
HONK!
HONK!
HONK!
HONK!
HONK!
...YOU THOUGHT THAT THEY WOULD FORGIVE YOU.
...YES.

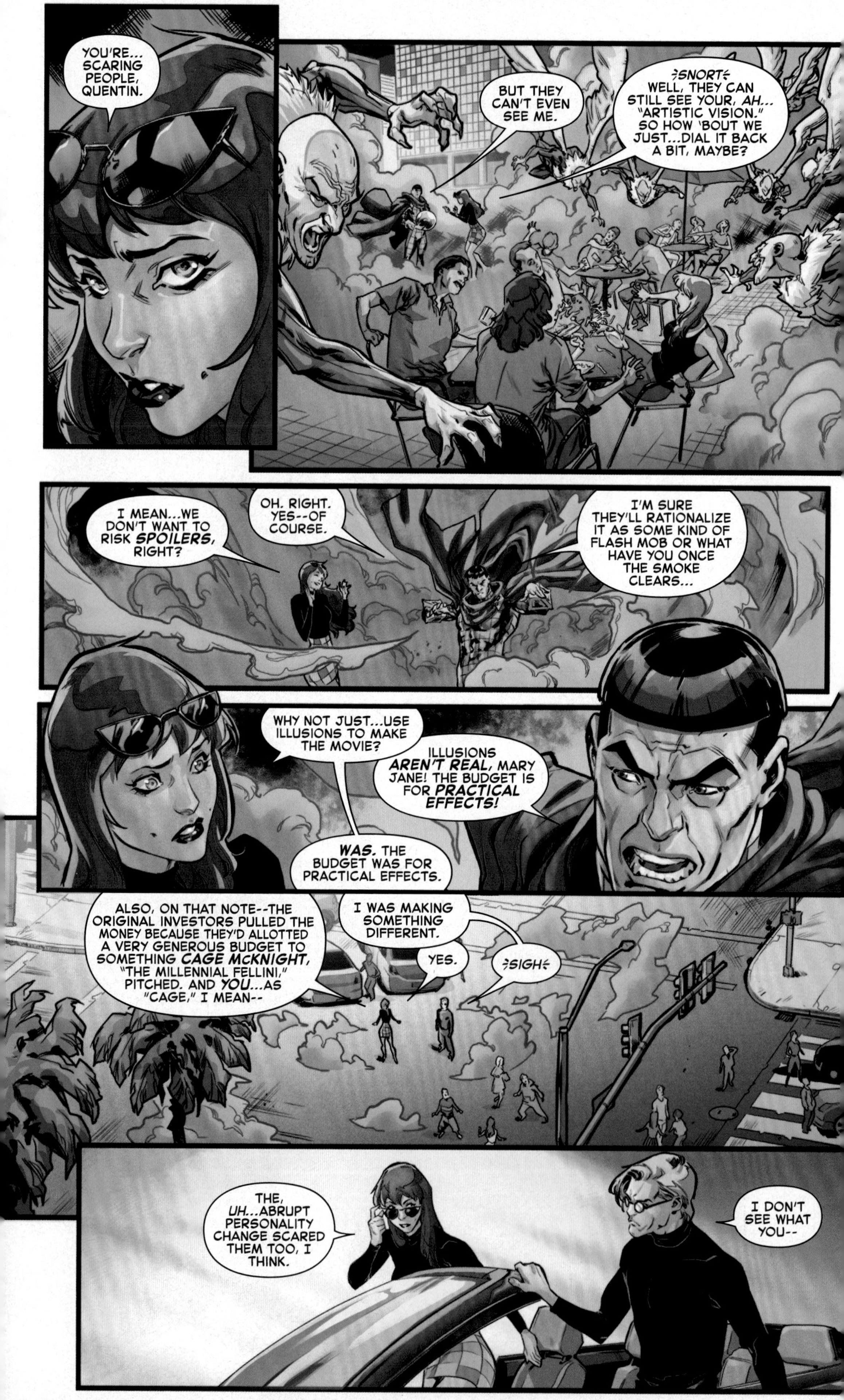
YOU'RE... SCARING PEOPLE, QUENTIN.
BUT THEY CAN'T EVEN SEE ME.
≶SNORT≶ WELL, THEY CAN STILL SEE YOUR, AH... "ARTISTIC VISION." SO HOW 'BOUT WE JUST...DIAL IT BACK A BIT, MAYBE?
I MEAN...WE DON'T WANT TO RISK SPOILERS, RIGHT?
OH. RIGHT. YES--OF COURSE.
I'M SURE THEY'LL RATIONALIZE IT AS SOME KIND OF FLASH MOB OR WHAT HAVE YOU ONCE THE SMOKE CLEARS...
WHY NOT JUST...USE ILLUSIONS TO MAKE THE MOVIE?
ILLUSIONS AREN'T REAL, MARY JANE! THE BUDGET IS FOR PRACTICAL EFFECTS!
WAS. THE BUDGET WAS FOR PRACTICAL EFFECTS.
ALSO, ON THAT NOTE--THE ORIGINAL INVESTORS PULLED THE MONEY BECAUSE THEY'D ALLOTTED A VERY GENEROUS BUDGET TO SOMETHING CAGE McKNIGHT, "THE MILLENNIAL FELLINI," PITCHED. AND YOU...AS "CAGE," I MEAN--
I WAS MAKING SOMETHING DIFFERENT.
YES.
≶SIGH≶
THE, UH...ABRUPT PERSONALITY CHANGE SCARED THEM TOO, I THINK.
I DON'T SEE WHAT YOU--

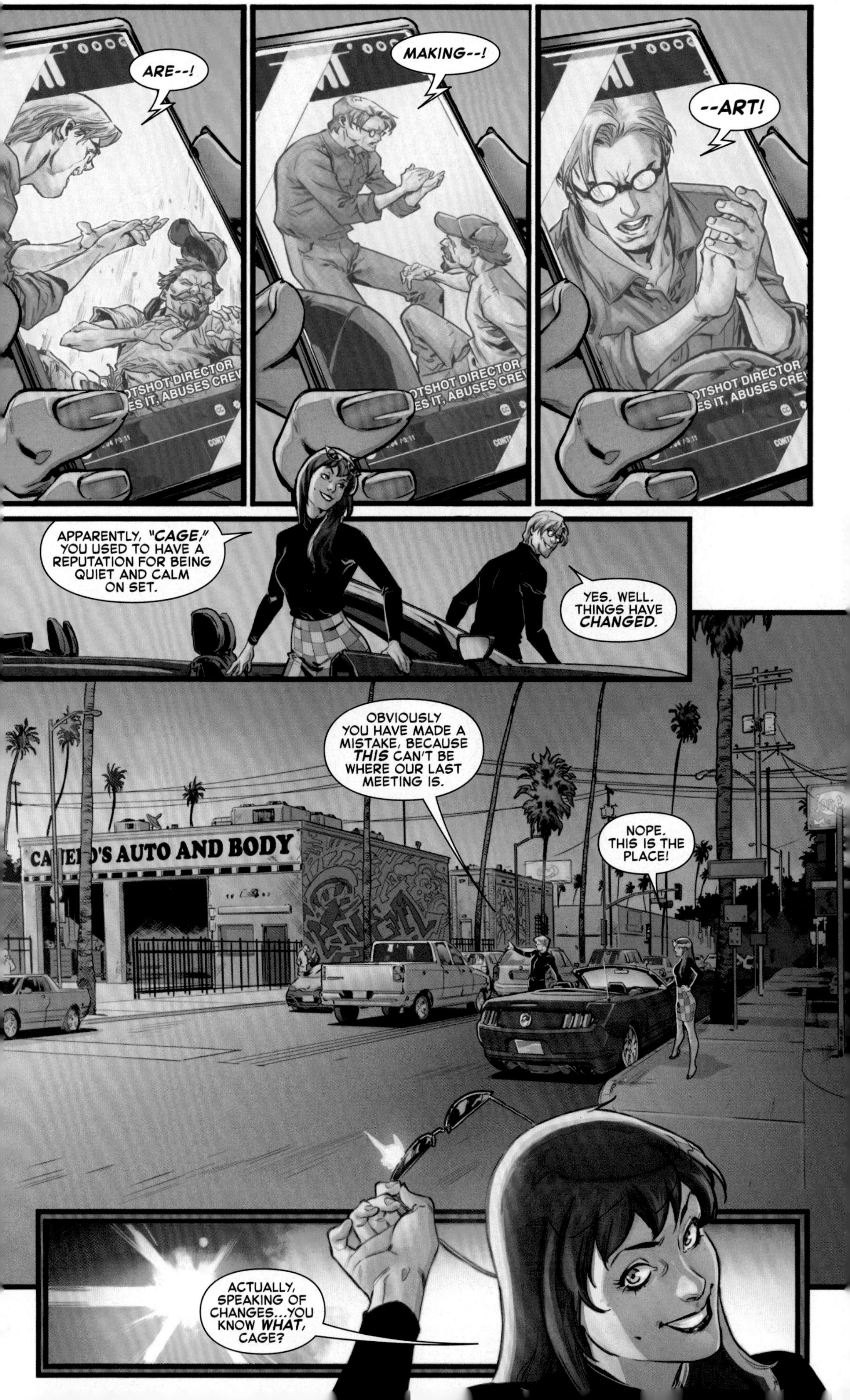
ARE--!
OTSHOT DIRECTOR
ES IT, ABUSES CREV
MAKING--!
--ART!
APPARENTLY, "CAGE," YOU USED TO HAVE A REPUTATION FOR BEING QUIET AND CALM ON SET.
YES. WELL. THINGS HAVE CHANGED.
OBVIOUSLY YOU HAVE MADE A MISTAKE, BECAUSE THIS CAN'T BE WHERE OUR LAST MEETING IS.
NOPE. THIS IS THE PLACE!
'S AUTO AND BODY
ACTUALLY, SPEAKING OF CHANGES...YOU KNOW WHAT, CAGE?

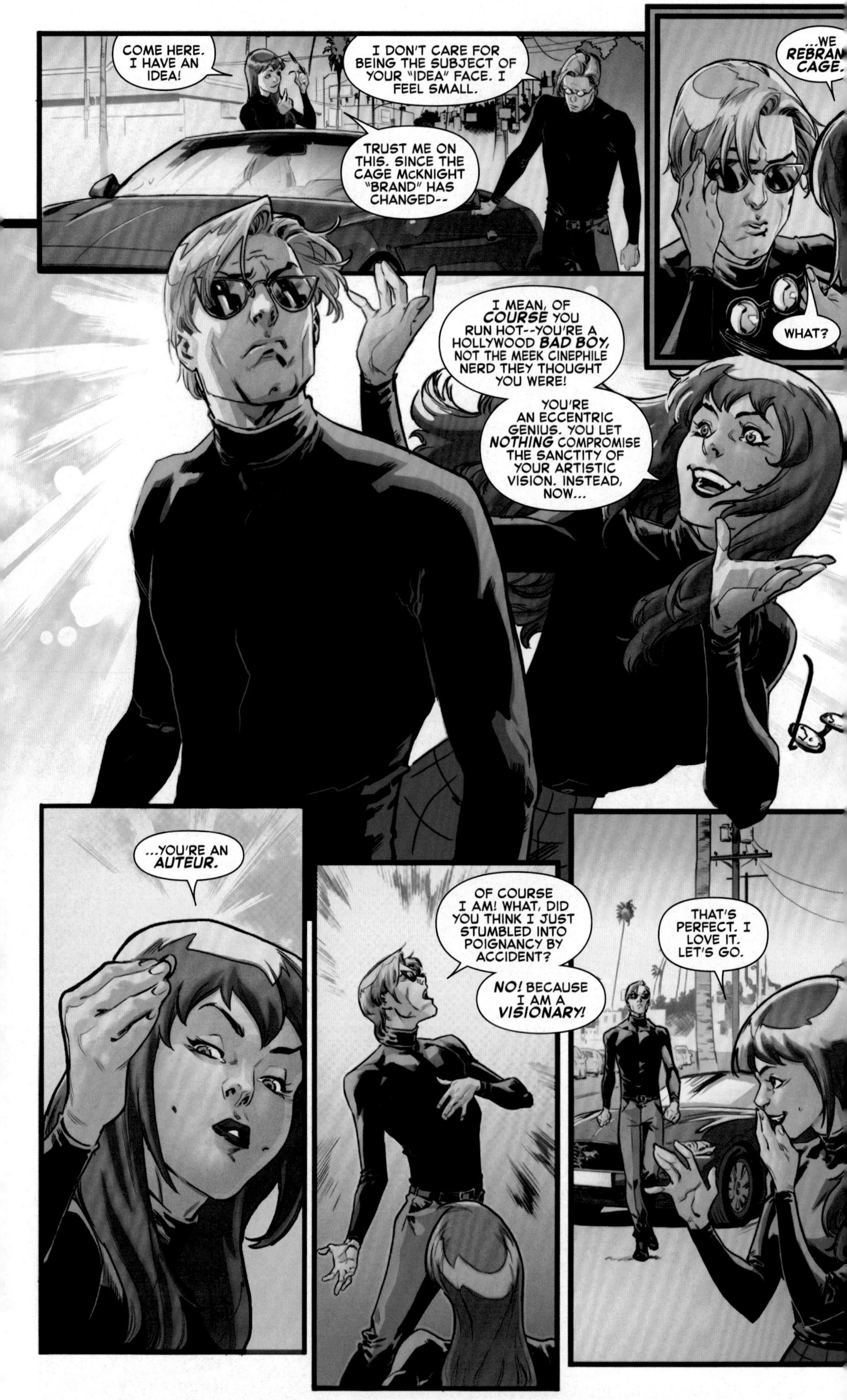

COME HERE. I HAVE AN IDEA!
I DON'T CARE FOR BEING THE SUBJECT OF YOUR "IDEA" FACE. I FEEL SMALL.
TRUST ME ON THIS. SINCE THE CAGE McKNIGHT "BRAND" HAS CHANGED--
...WE REBRAN CAGE.
WHAT?
I MEAN, OF COURSE YOU RUN HOT--YOU'RE A HOLLYWOOD BAD BOY, NOT THE MEEK CINEPHILE NERD THEY THOUGHT YOU WERE!
YOU'RE AN ECCENTRIC GENIUS. YOU LET NOTHING COMPROMISE THE SANCTITY OF YOUR ARTISTIC VISION. INSTEAD, NOW...
...YOU'RE AN AUTEUR.
OF COURSE I AM! WHAT, DID YOU THINK I JUST STUMBLED INTO POIGNANCY BY ACCIDENT?
NO! BECAUSE I AM A VISIONARY!
THAT'S PERFECT. I LOVE IT. LET'S GO.

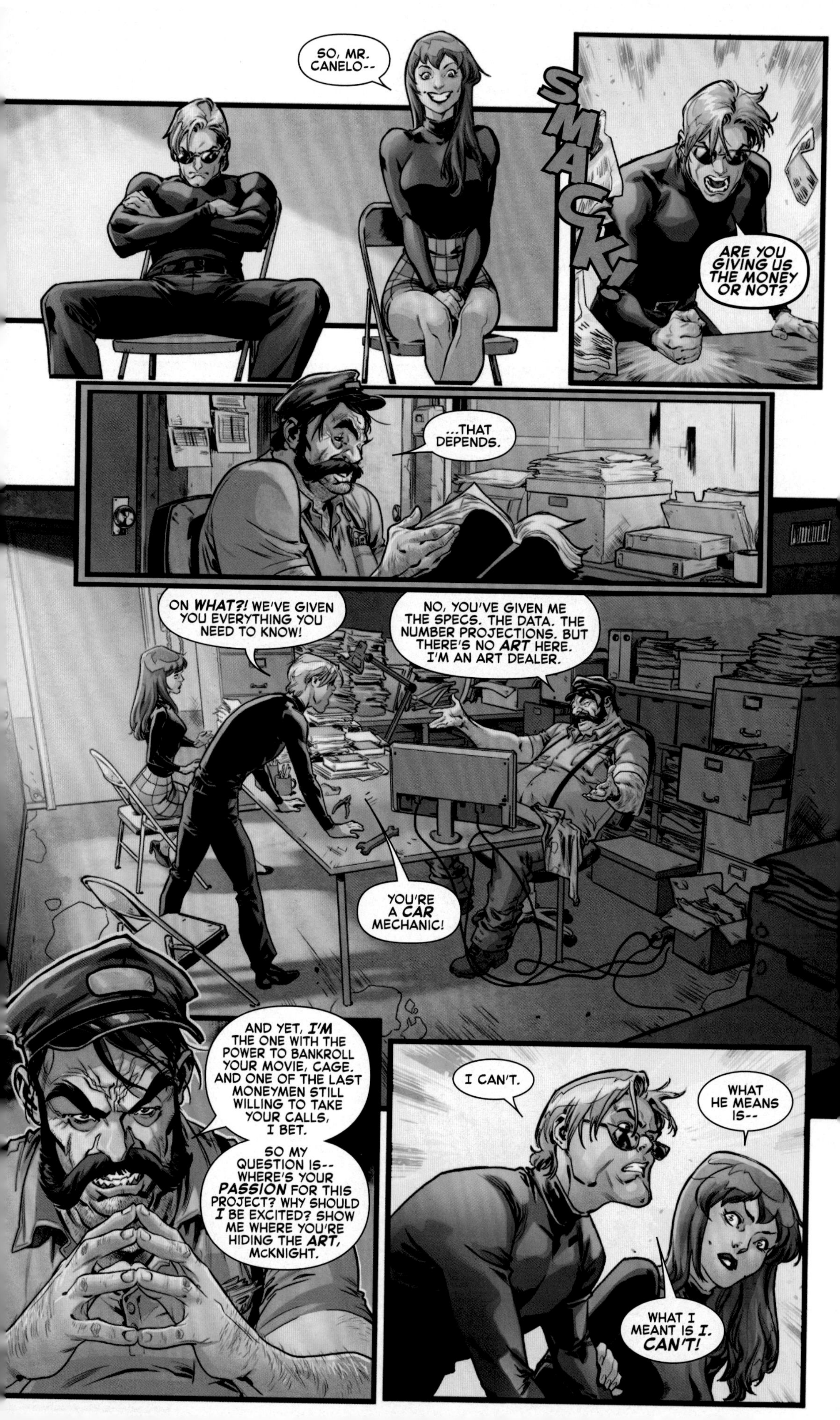
SO, MR. CANELO--
SMACK!
ARE YOU GIVING US THE MONEY OR NOT?
...THAT DEPENDS.
ON WHAT?! WE'VE GIVEN YOU EVERYTHING YOU NEED TO KNOW!
NO, YOU'VE GIVEN ME THE SPECS. THE DATA. THE NUMBER PROJECTIONS. BUT THERE'S NO ART HERE. I'M AN ART DEALER.
YOU'RE A CAR MECHANIC!
AND YET, I'M THE ONE WITH THE POWER TO BANKROLL YOUR MOVIE, CAGE. AND ONE OF THE LAST MONEYMEN STILL WILLING TO TAKE YOUR CALLS, I BET.
SO MY QUESTION IS-- WHERE'S YOUR PASSION FOR THIS PROJECT? WHY SHOULD I BE EXCITED? SHOW ME WHERE YOU'RE HIDING THE ART, McKNIGHT.
I CAN'T.
WHAT HE MEANS IS--
WHAT I MEANT IS I. CAN'T!

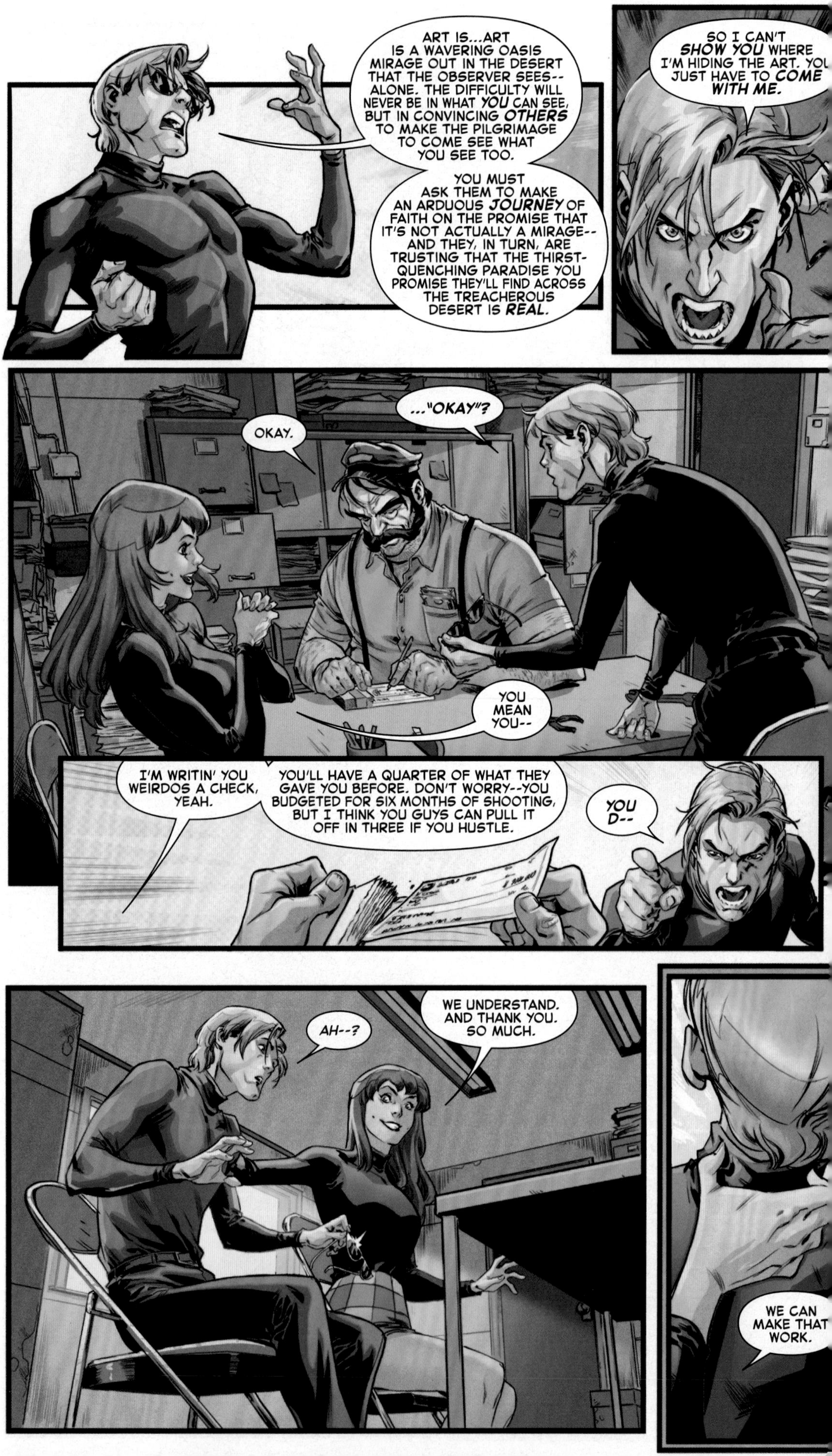

ART IS...ART IS A WAVERING OASIS MIRAGE OUT IN THE DESERT THAT THE OBSERVER SEES--ALONE. THE DIFFICULTY WILL NEVER BE IN WHAT *YOU* CAN SEE, BUT IN CONVINCING *OTHERS* TO MAKE THE PILGRIMAGE TO COME SEE WHAT YOU SEE TOO.
YOU MUST ASK THEM TO MAKE AN ARDUOUS *JOURNEY* OF FAITH ON THE PROMISE THAT IT'S NOT ACTUALLY A MIRAGE--AND THEY, IN TURN, ARE TRUSTING THAT THE THIRST-QUENCHING PARADISE YOU PROMISE THEY'LL FIND ACROSS THE TREACHEROUS DESERT IS *REAL*.
SO I CAN'T *SHOW YOU* WHERE I'M HIDING THE ART. YOU JUST HAVE TO *COME WITH ME.*
OKAY.
..."OKAY"?
YOU MEAN YOU--
I'M WRITIN' YOU WEIRDOS A CHECK, YEAH.
YOU'LL HAVE A QUARTER OF WHAT THEY GAVE YOU BEFORE. DON'T WORRY--YOU BUDGETED FOR SIX MONTHS OF SHOOTING, BUT I THINK YOU GUYS CAN PULL IT OFF IN THREE IF YOU HUSTLE.
YOU D--
AH--?
WE UNDERSTAND. AND THANK YOU. SO MUCH.
WE CAN MAKE THAT WORK.

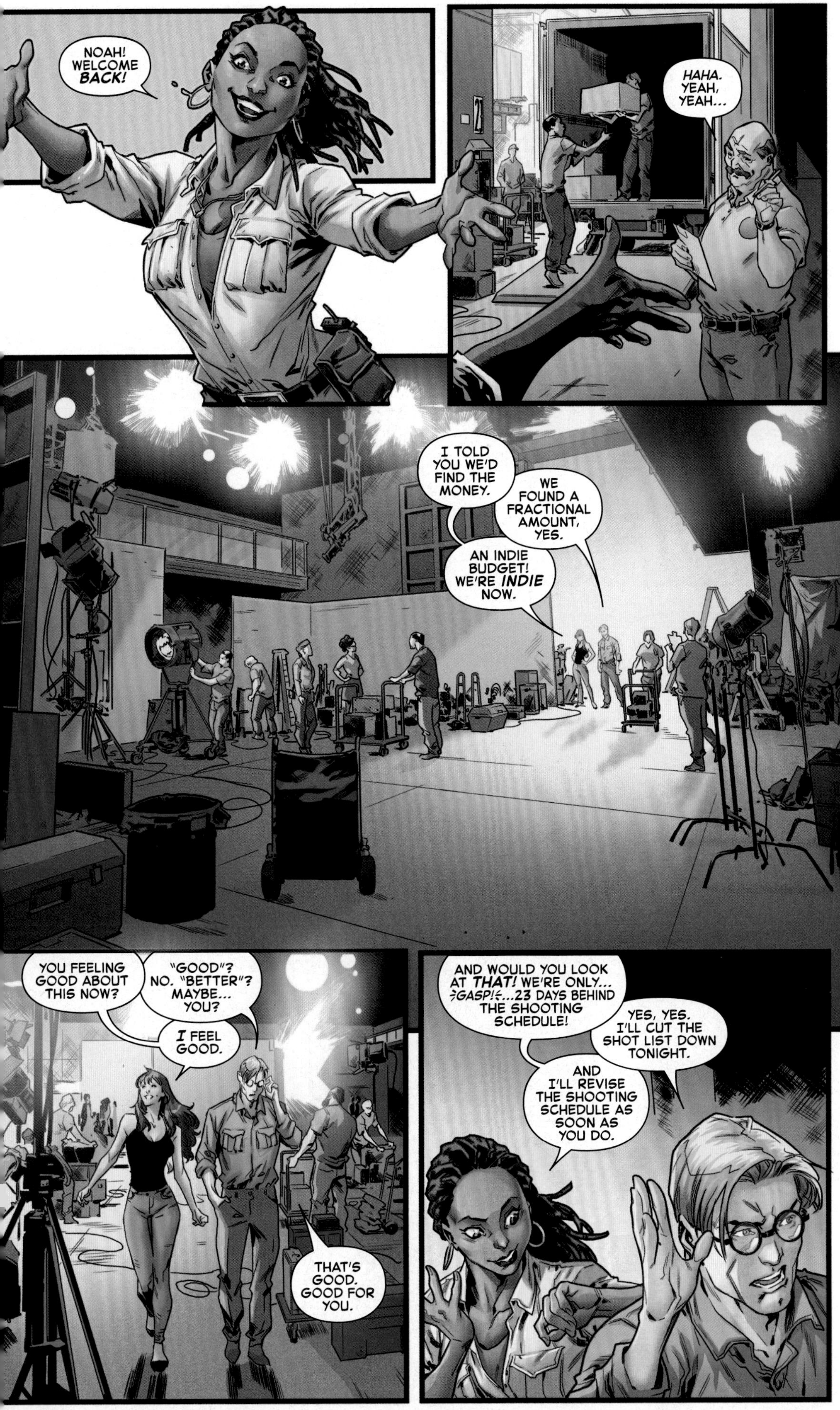

NOAH! WELCOME *BACK!*
HAHA. YEAH, YEAH...
I TOLD YOU WE'D FIND THE MONEY.
WE FOUND A FRACTIONAL AMOUNT, YES.
AN INDIE BUDGET! WE'RE *INDIE* NOW.
YOU FEELING GOOD ABOUT THIS NOW?
"GOOD"? NO. "BETTER"? MAYBE... YOU?
I FEEL GOOD.
THAT'S GOOD. GOOD FOR YOU.
AND WOULD YOU LOOK AT *THAT!* WE'RE ONLY... *GASP!*...23 DAYS BEHIND THE SHOOTING SCHEDULE!
YES, YES. I'LL CUT THE SHOT LIST DOWN TONIGHT.
AND I'LL REVISE THE SHOOTING SCHEDULE AS SOON AS YOU DO.

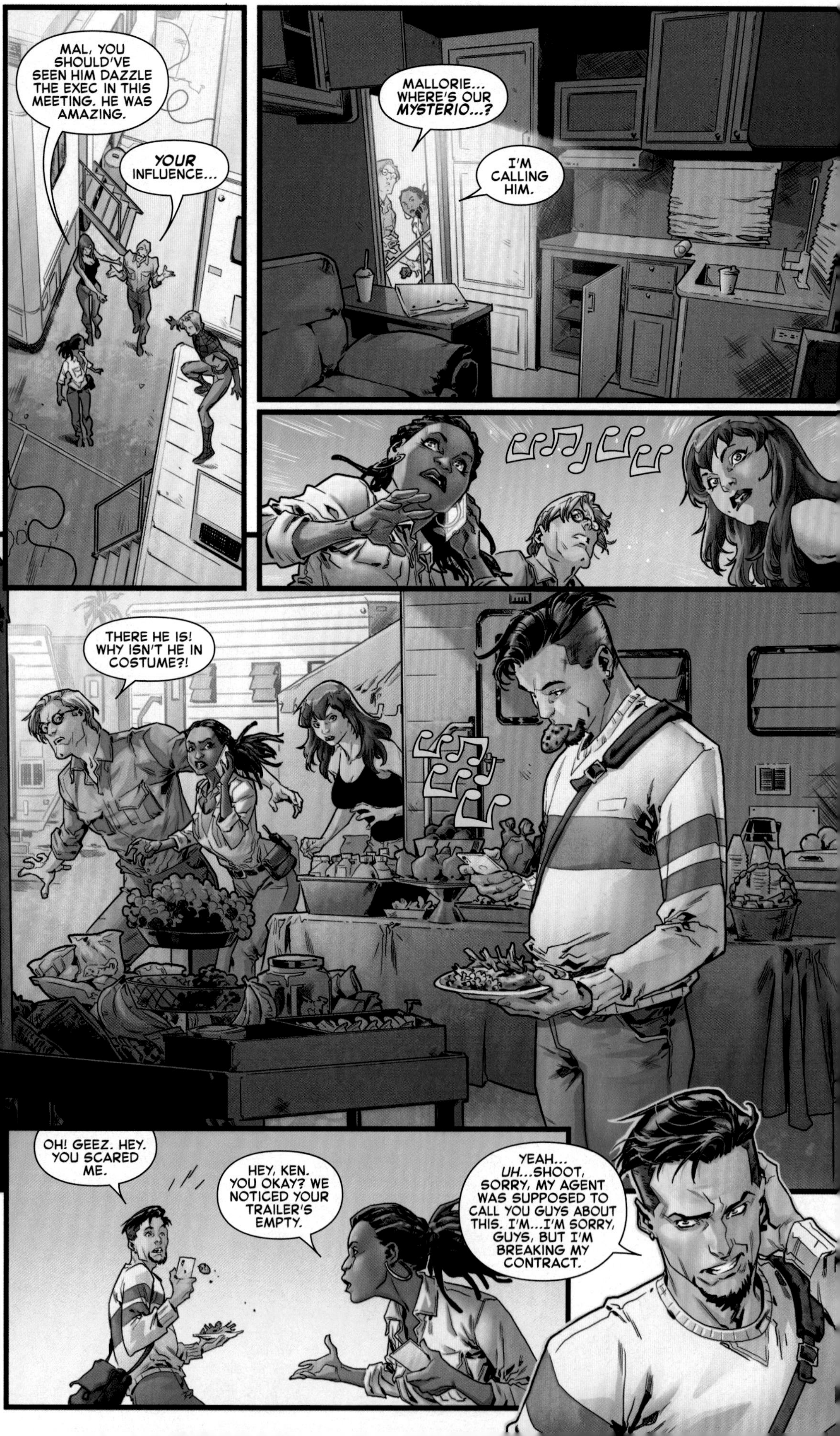
MAL, YOU SHOULD'VE SEEN HIM DAZZLE THE EXEC IN THIS MEETING. HE WAS AMAZING.
YOUR INFLUENCE...
MALLORIE... WHERE'S OUR MYSTERIO...?
I'M CALLING HIM.
THERE HE IS! WHY ISN'T HE IN COSTUME?!
OH! GEEZ. HEY. YOU SCARED ME.
HEY, KEN. YOU OKAY? WE NOTICED YOUR TRAILER'S EMPTY.
YEAH... UH...SHOOT, SORRY, MY AGENT WAS SUPPOSED TO CALL YOU GUYS ABOUT THIS. I'M...I'M SORRY, GUYS, BUT I'M BREAKING MY CONTRACT.

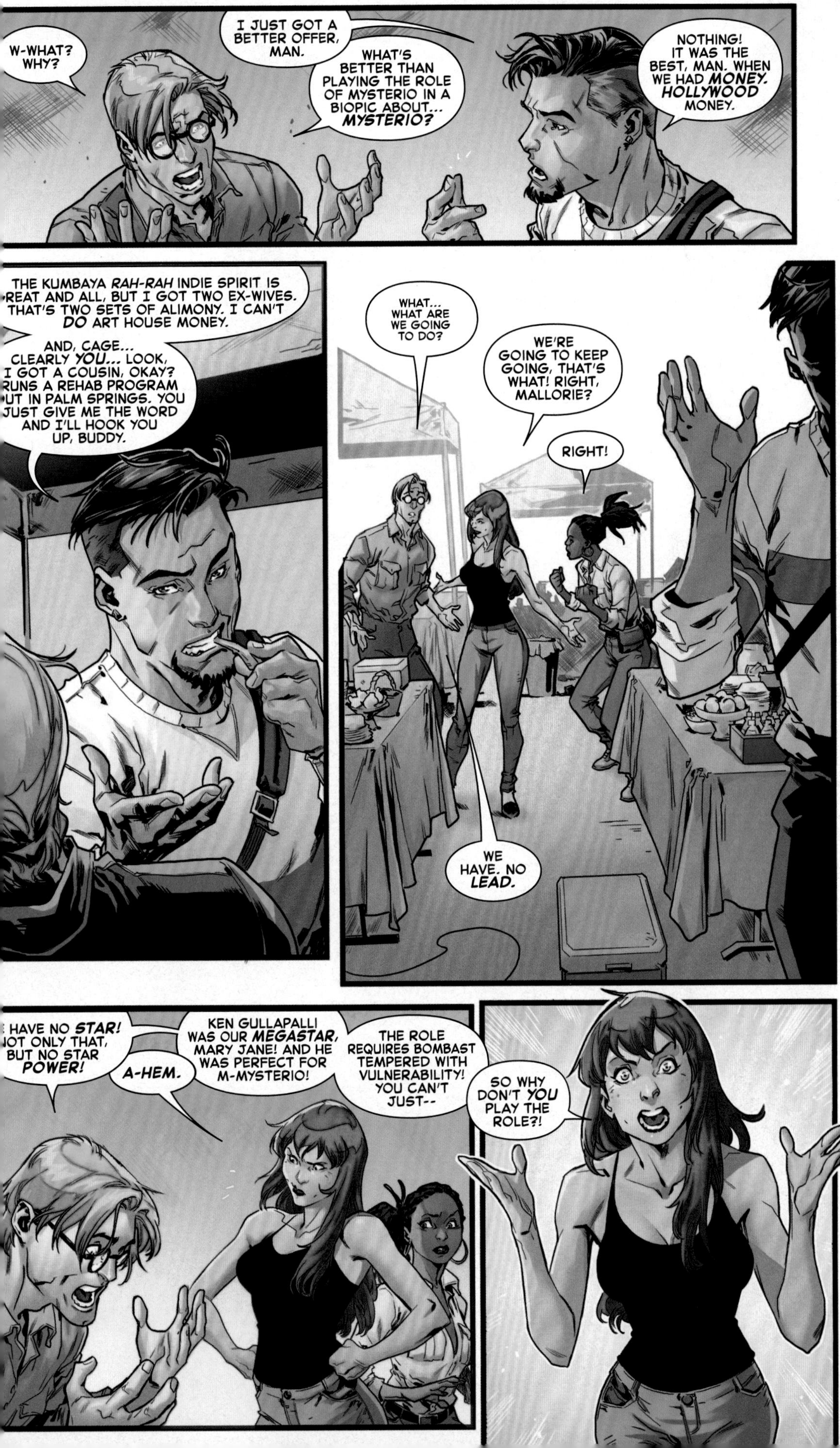
W-WHAT? WHY?
I JUST GOT A BETTER OFFER, MAN.
WHAT'S BETTER THAN PLAYING THE ROLE OF MYSTERIO IN A BIOPIC ABOUT... MYSTERIO?
NOTHING! IT WAS THE BEST, MAN. WHEN WE HAD MONEY. HOLLYWOOD MONEY.
THE KUMBAYA RAH-RAH INDIE SPIRIT IS REAT AND ALL, BUT I GOT TWO EX-WIVES. THAT'S TWO SETS OF ALIMONY. I CAN'T DO ART HOUSE MONEY.
AND, CAGE... CLEARLY YOU... LOOK, I GOT A COUSIN, OKAY? RUNS A REHAB PROGRAM UT IN PALM SPRINGS. YOU JUST GIVE ME THE WORD AND I'LL HOOK YOU UP, BUDDY.
WHAT... WHAT ARE WE GOING TO DO?
WE'RE GOING TO KEEP GOING, THAT'S WHAT! RIGHT, MALLORIE?
RIGHT!
WE HAVE. NO LEAD.
E HAVE NO STAR! OT ONLY THAT, BUT NO STAR POWER!
A-HEM.
KEN GULLAPALLI WAS OUR MEGASTAR, MARY JANE! AND HE WAS PERFECT FOR M-MYSTERIO!
THE ROLE REQUIRES BOMBAST TEMPERED WITH VULNERABILITY! YOU CAN'T JUST--
SO WHY DON'T YOU PLAY THE ROLE?!

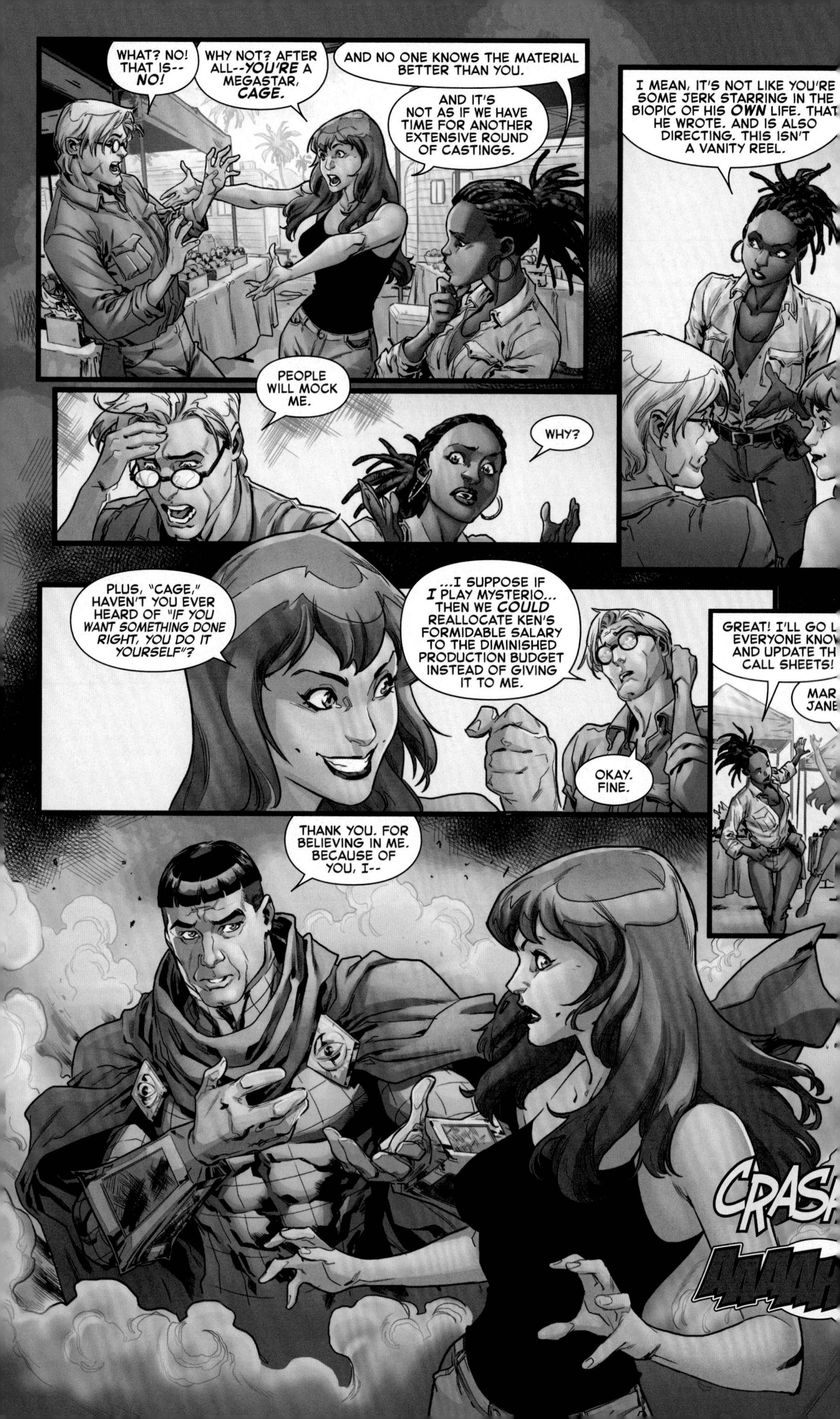

WHAT? NO! THAT IS-- NO!
WHY NOT? AFTER ALL--YOU'RE A MEGASTAR, CAGE.
AND NO ONE KNOWS THE MATERIAL BETTER THAN YOU.
AND IT'S NOT AS IF WE HAVE TIME FOR ANOTHER EXTENSIVE ROUND OF CASTINGS.
I MEAN, IT'S NOT LIKE YOU'RE SOME JERK STARRING IN THE BIOPIC OF HIS OWN LIFE. THAT HE WROTE. AND IS ALSO DIRECTING. THIS ISN'T A VANITY REEL.
PEOPLE WILL MOCK ME.
WHY?
PLUS, "CAGE," HAVEN'T YOU EVER HEARD OF "IF YOU WANT SOMETHING DONE RIGHT, YOU DO IT YOURSELF"?
...I SUPPOSE IF I PLAY MYSTERIO... THEN WE COULD REALLOCATE KEN'S FORMIDABLE SALARY TO THE DIMINISHED PRODUCTION BUDGET INSTEAD OF GIVING IT TO ME.
OKAY. FINE.
THANK YOU. FOR BELIEVING IN ME. BECAUSE OF YOU, I--

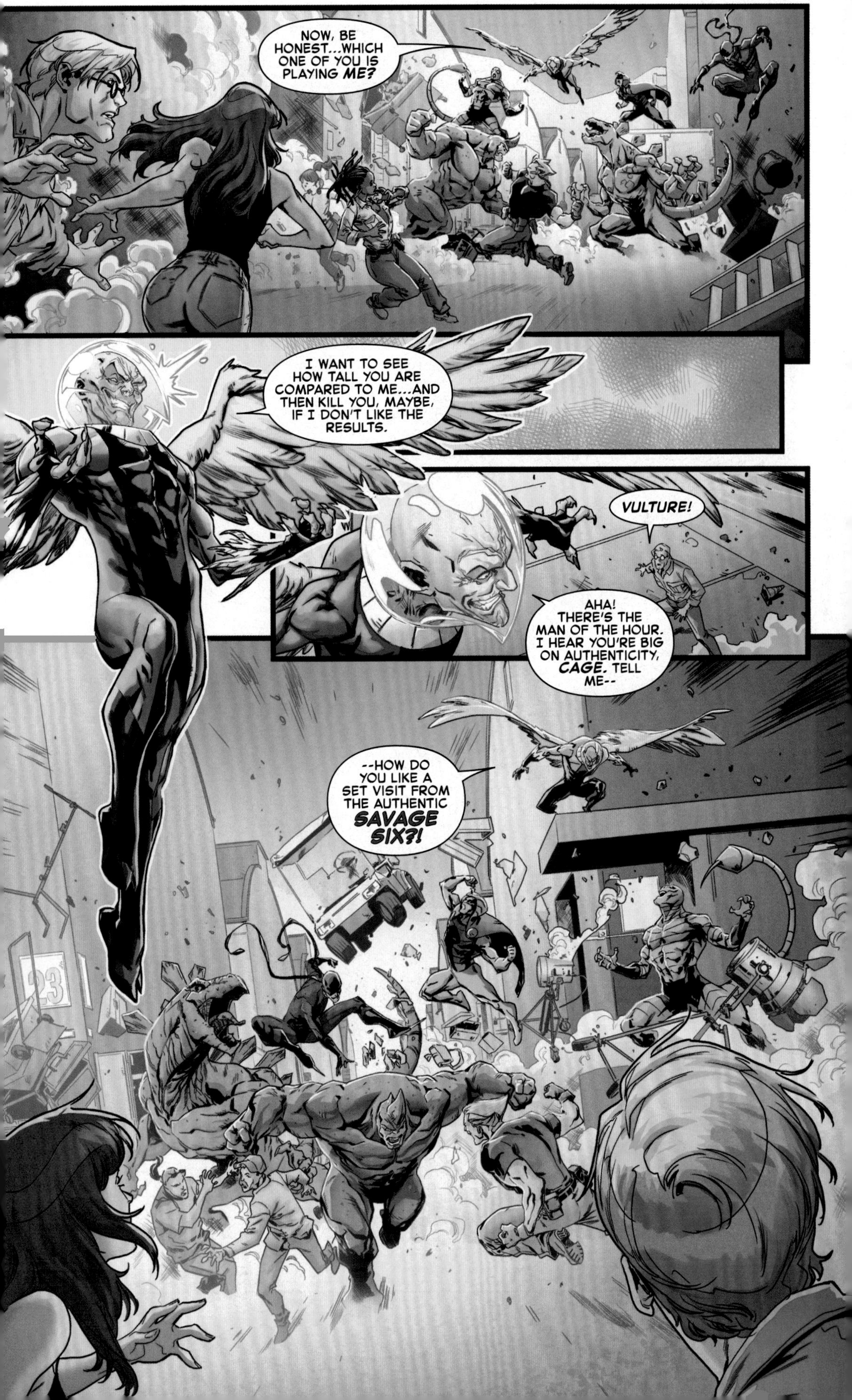

NOW, BE HONEST...WHICH ONE OF YOU IS PLAYING ME?
I WANT TO SEE HOW TALL YOU ARE COMPARED TO ME...AND THEN KILL YOU, MAYBE, IF I DON'T LIKE THE RESULTS.
VULTURE!
AHA! THERE'S THE MAN OF THE HOUR. I HEAR YOU'RE BIG ON AUTHENTICITY, CAGE. TELL ME--
--HOW DO YOU LIKE A SET VISIT FROM THE AUTHENTIC SAVAGE SIX?!
23

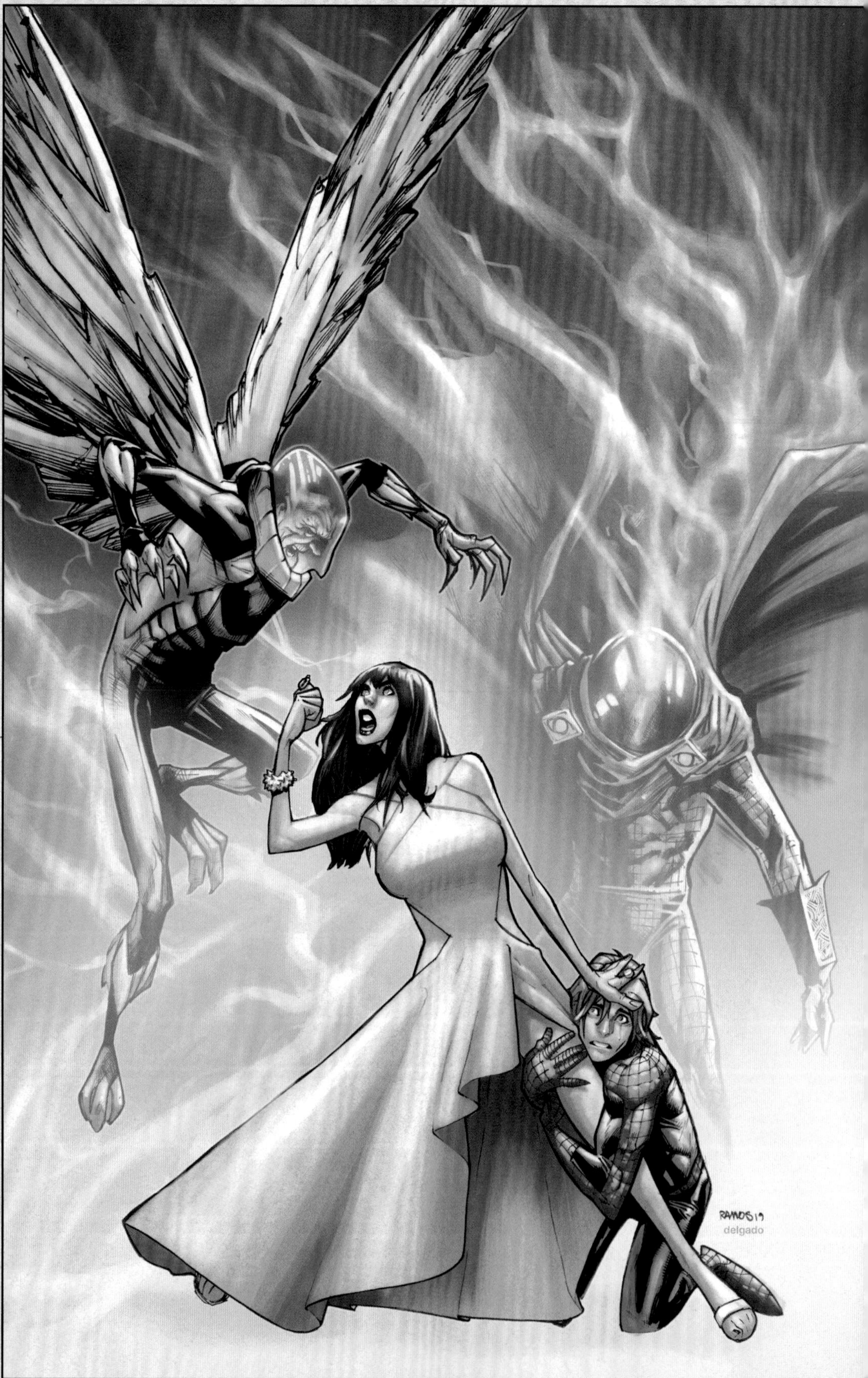
RAMOS 19
delgado

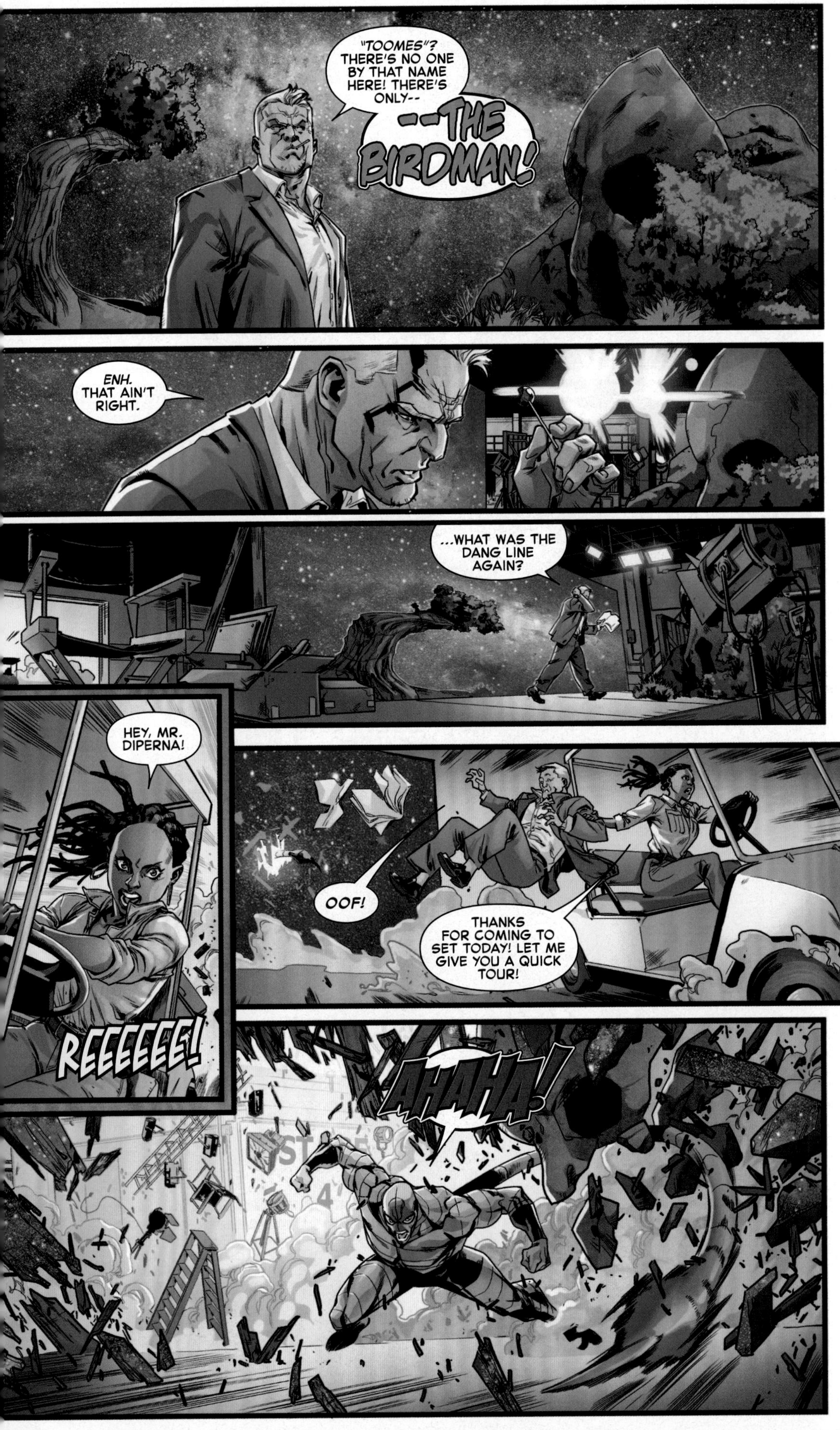
"TOOMES"? THERE'S NO ONE BY THAT NAME HERE! THERE'S ONLY--
--THE BIRDMAN!
ENH. THAT AIN'T RIGHT.
...WHAT WAS THE DANG LINE AGAIN?
HEY, MR. DIPERNA!
REEEEEEE!
OOF!
THANKS FOR COMING TO SET TODAY! LET ME GIVE YOU A QUICK TOUR!
AHAHA!

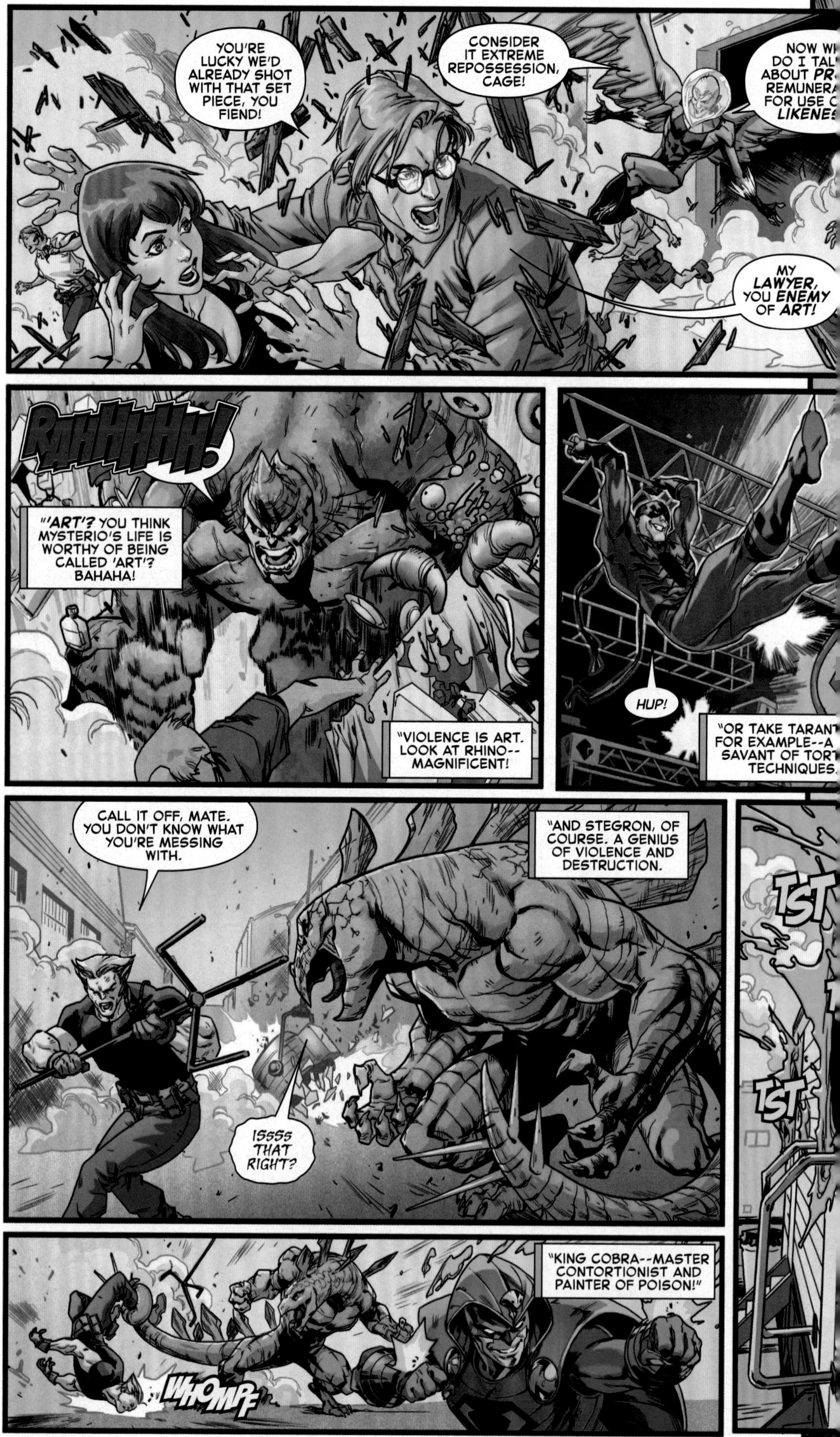

YOU'RE LUCKY WE'D ALREADY SHOT WITH THAT SET PIECE, YOU FIEND!
CONSIDER IT EXTREME REPOSSESSION, CAGE!
NOW WH DO I TAL ABOUT PR REMUNERA FOR USE O LIKENES
MY LAWYER, YOU ENEMY OF ART!
RAHHHHHH!
"'ART'? YOU THINK MYSTERIO'S LIFE IS WORTHY OF BEING CALLED 'ART'? BAHAHA!
"VIOLENCE IS ART. LOOK AT RHINO--MAGNIFICENT!
HUP!
"OR TAKE TARANT FOR EXAMPLE--A SAVANT OF TORT TECHNIQUES.
CALL IT OFF, MATE. YOU DON'T KNOW WHAT YOU'RE MESSING WITH.
"AND STEGRON, OF COURSE. A GENIUS OF VIOLENCE AND DESTRUCTION.
ISSSS THAT RIGHT?
TST
TST
"KING COBRA--MASTER CONTORTIONIST AND PAINTER OF POISON!"
WHOMPF

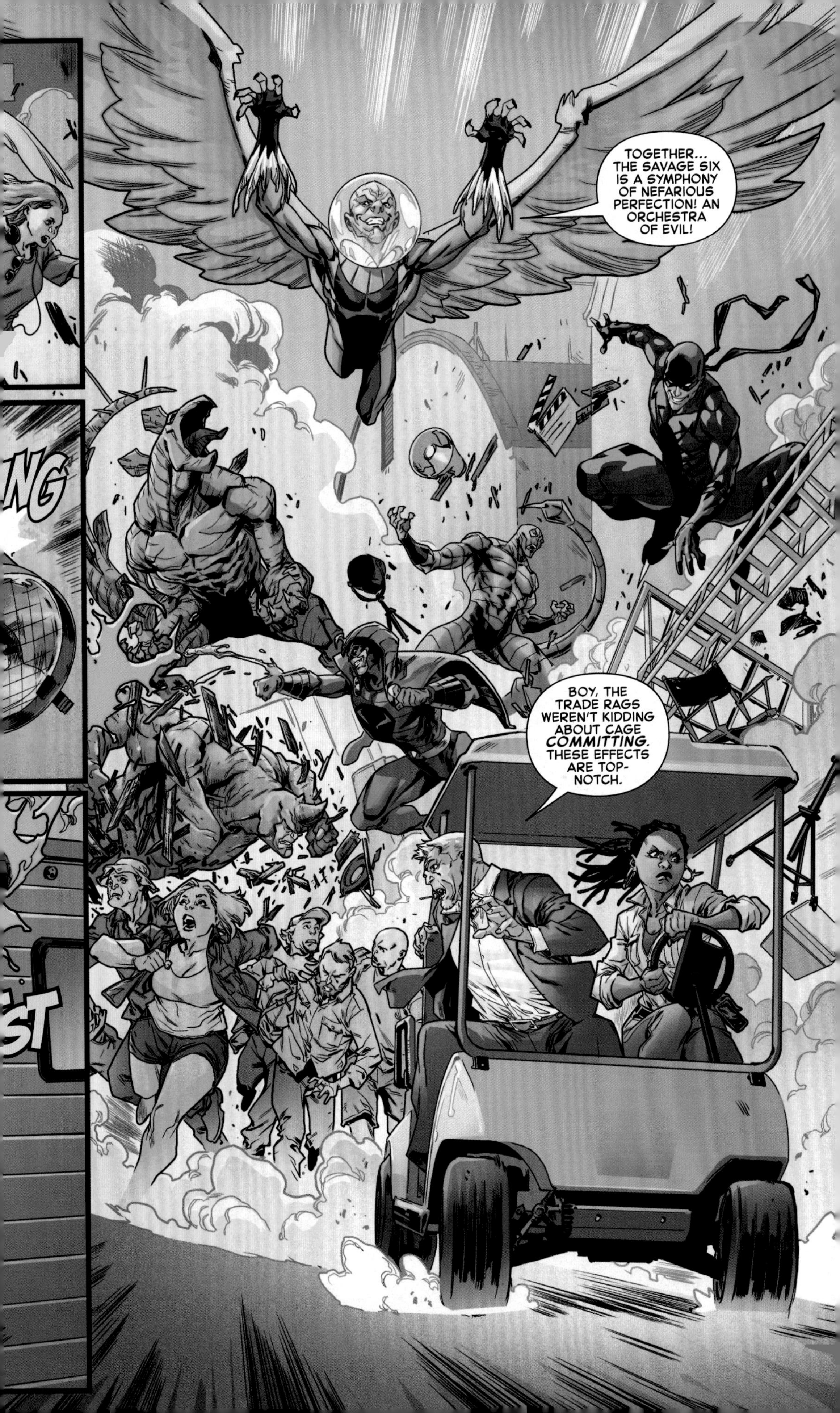
TOGETHER... THE SAVAGE SIX IS A SYMPHONY OF NEFARIOUS PERFECTION! AN ORCHESTRA OF EVIL!
BOY, THE TRADE RAGS WEREN'T KIDDING ABOUT CAGE COMMITTING. THESE EFFECTS ARE TOP-NOTCH.

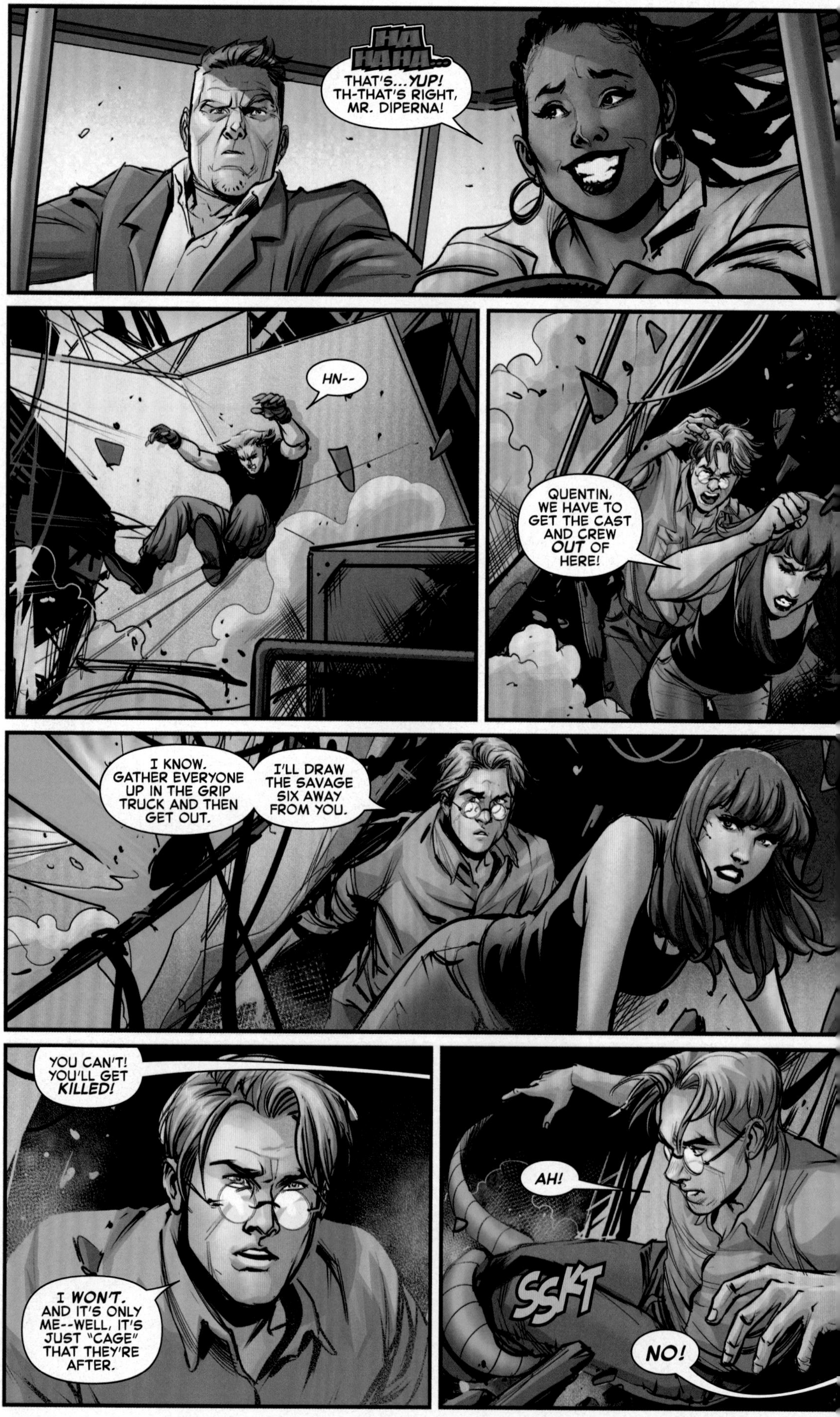
HA HAHA...
THAT'S...YUP! TH-THAT'S RIGHT, MR. DIPERNA!
HN--
QUENTIN, WE HAVE TO GET THE CAST AND CREW OUT OF HERE!
I KNOW. GATHER EVERYONE UP IN THE GRIP TRUCK AND THEN GET OUT.
I'LL DRAW THE SAVAGE SIX AWAY FROM YOU.
YOU CAN'T! YOU'LL GET KILLED!
I WON'T. AND IT'S ONLY ME--WELL, IT'S JUST "CAGE" THAT THEY'RE AFTER.
AH!
SSKT
NO!

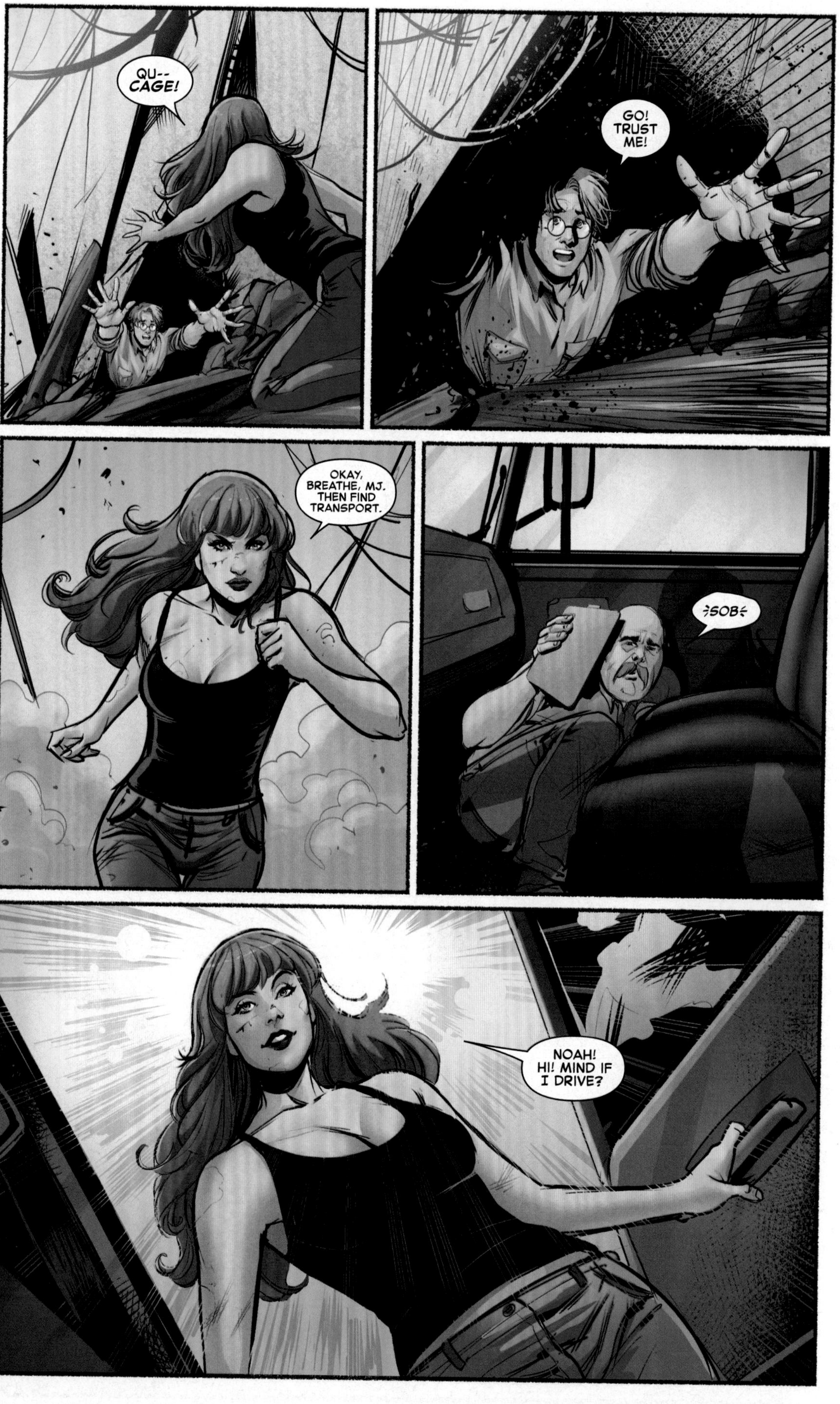
QU-- CAGE!
GO! TRUST ME!
OKAY, BREATHE, MJ. THEN FIND TRANSPORT.
SOB
NOAH! HI! MIND IF I DRIVE?

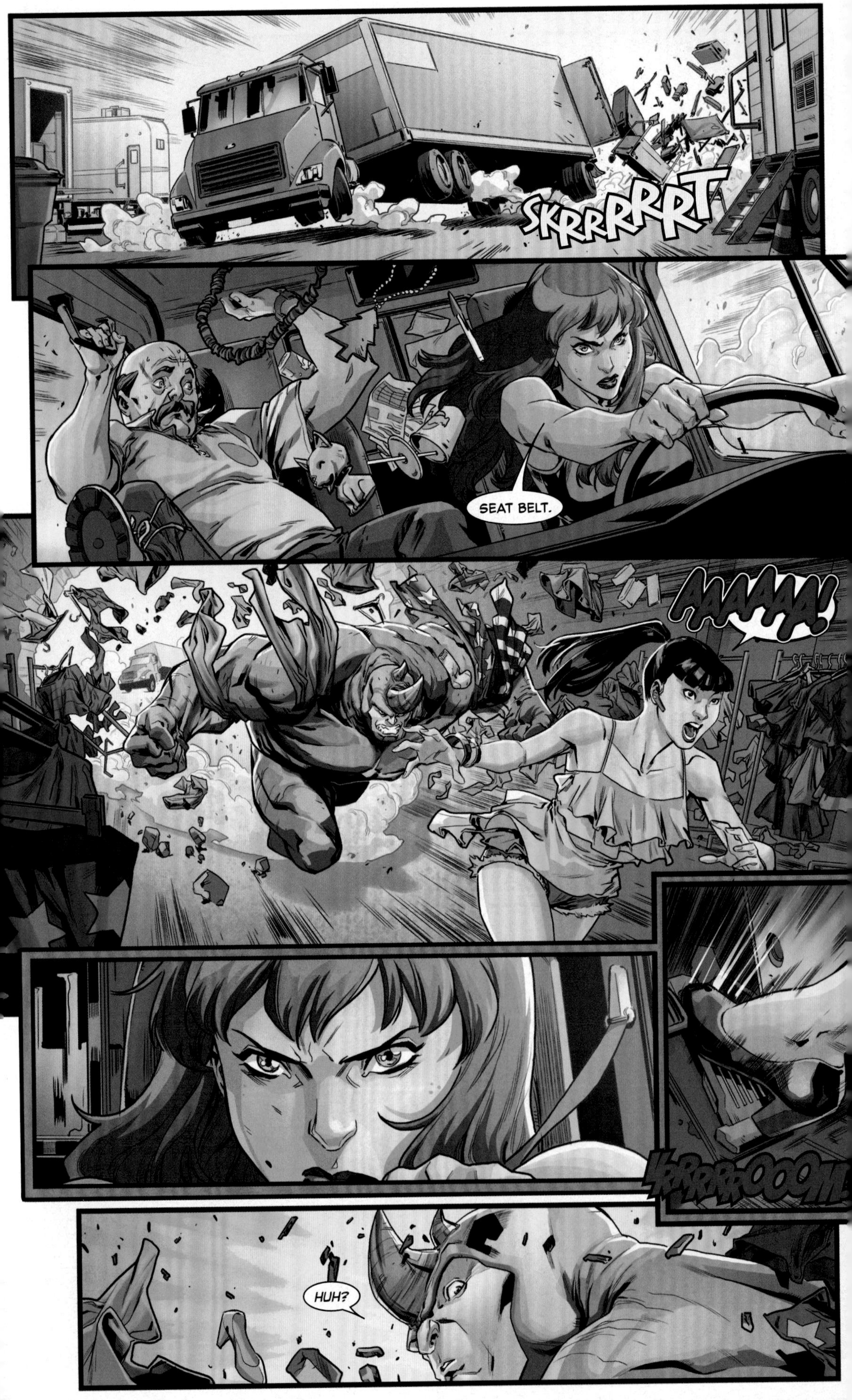

SKRRRRRT
SEAT BELT.
AAAAAA!
HRRRRROOOM
HUH?

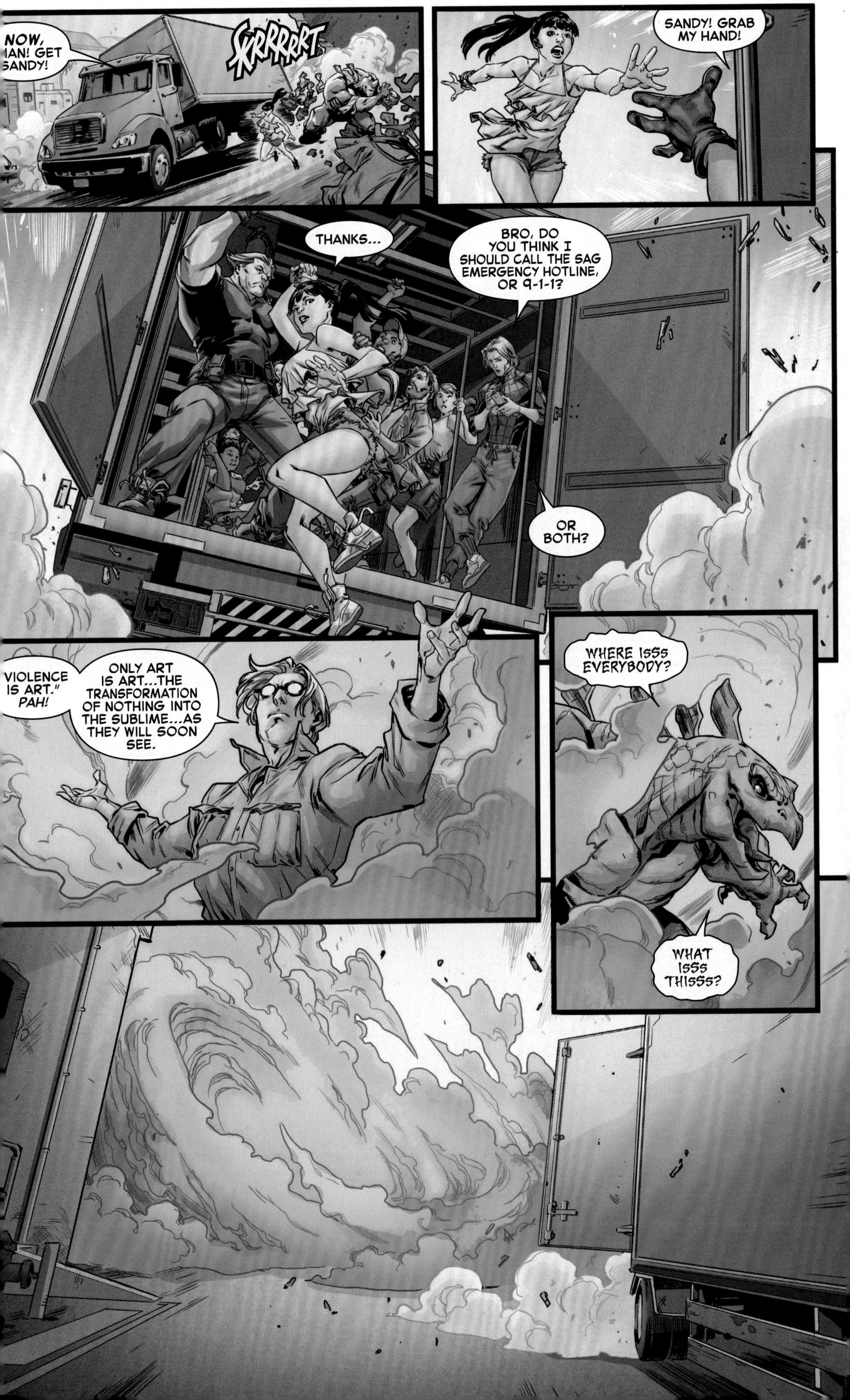
NOW, IAN! GET SANDY!
SKRRRRRT
SANDY! GRAB MY HAND!
THANKS...
BRO, DO YOU THINK I SHOULD CALL THE SAG EMERGENCY HOTLINE, OR 9-1-1?
OR BOTH?
VIOLENCE IS ART." PAH!
ONLY ART IS ART...THE TRANSFORMATION OF NOTHING INTO THE SUBLIME...AS THEY WILL SOON SEE.
WHERE ISSS EVERYBODY?
WHAT ISSS THISSS?

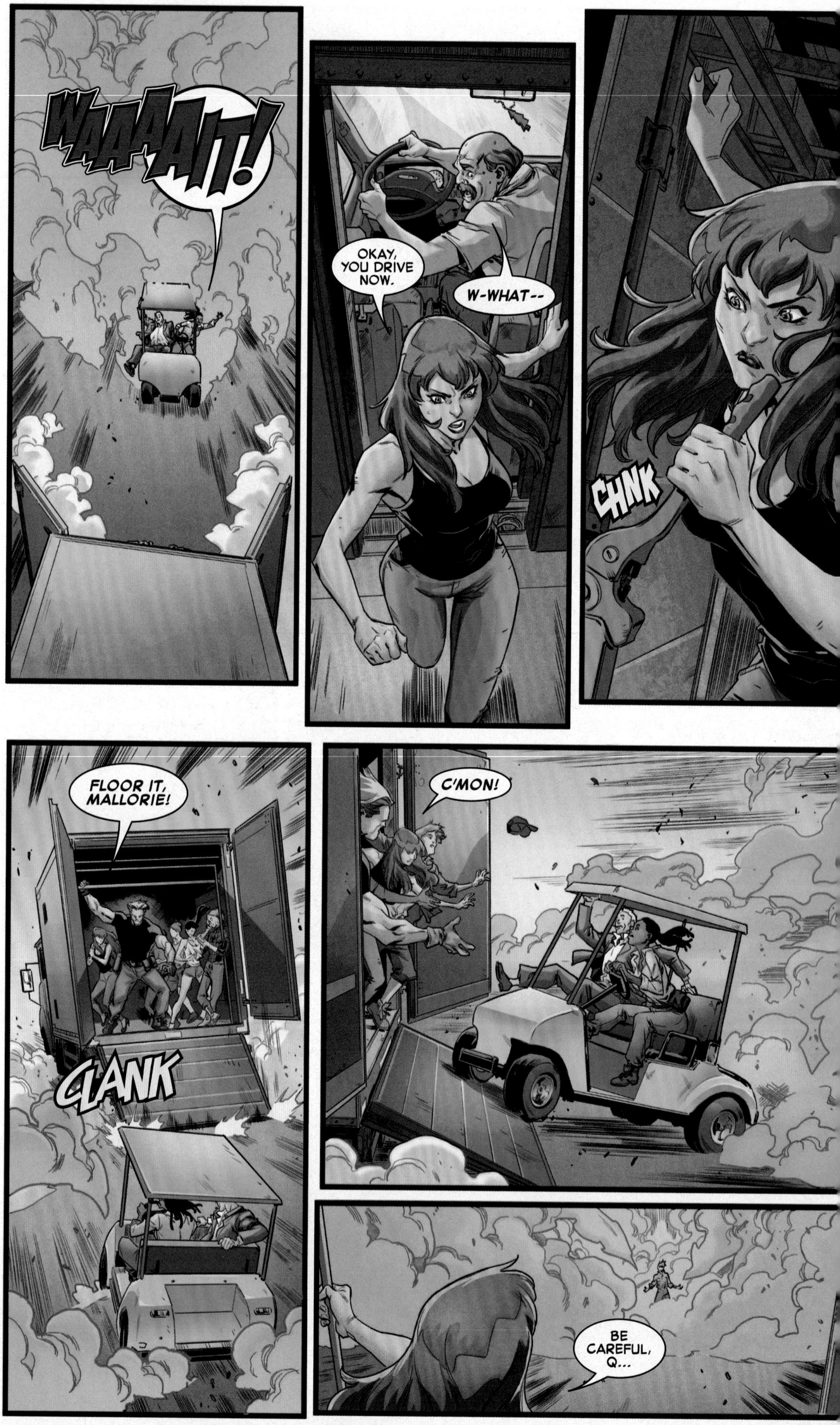
WAAAAAIT!
OKAY, YOU DRIVE NOW.
W-WHAT--
CHNK
FLOOR IT, MALLORIE!
CLANK
C'MON!
BE CAREFUL, Q...

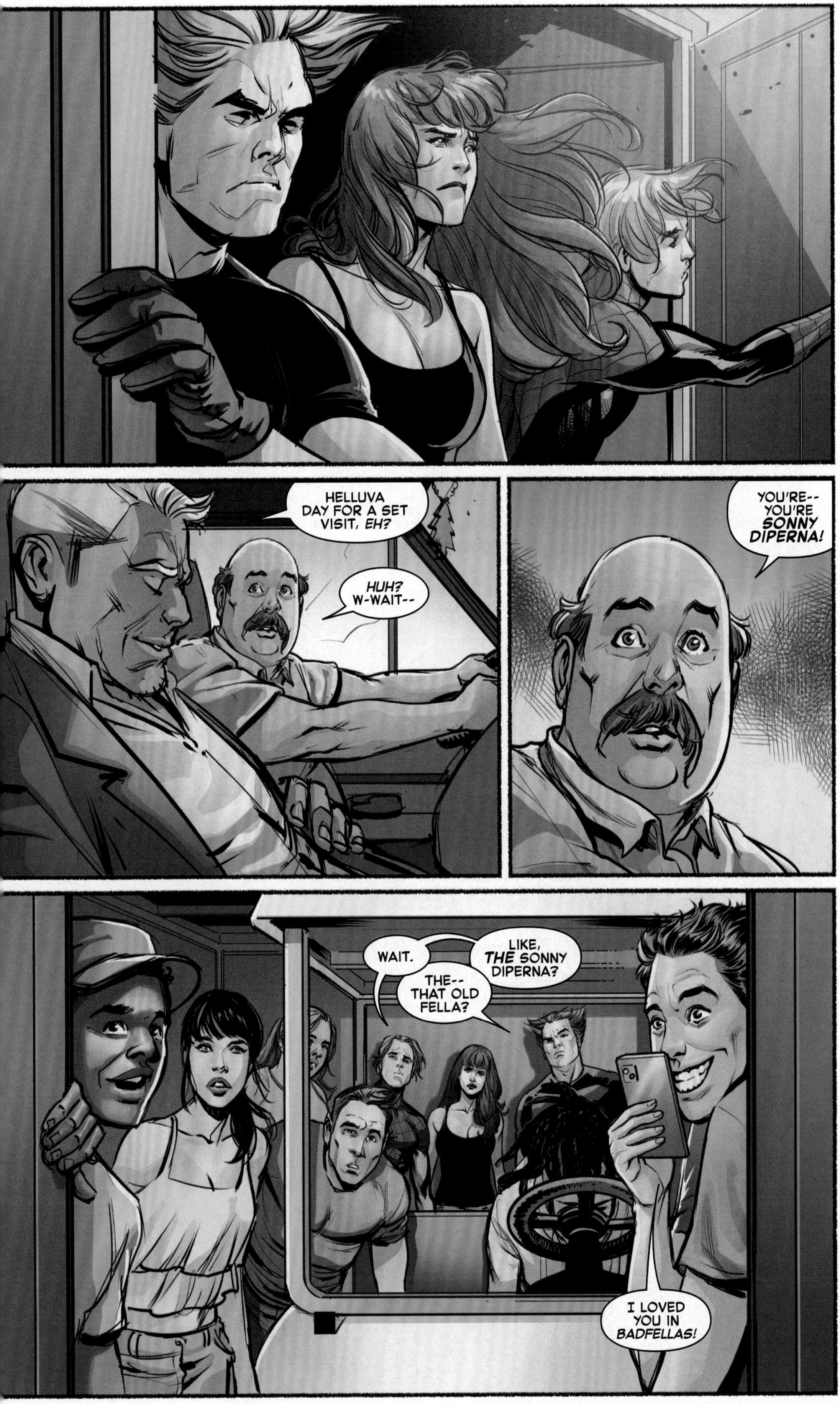
HELLUVA DAY FOR A SET VISIT, *EH?*
HUH? W-WAIT--
YOU'RE-- YOU'RE ***SONNY DIPERNA!***
WAIT.
LIKE, ***THE*** SONNY DIPERNA?
THE-- THAT OLD FELLA?
I LOVED YOU IN ***BADFELLAS!***

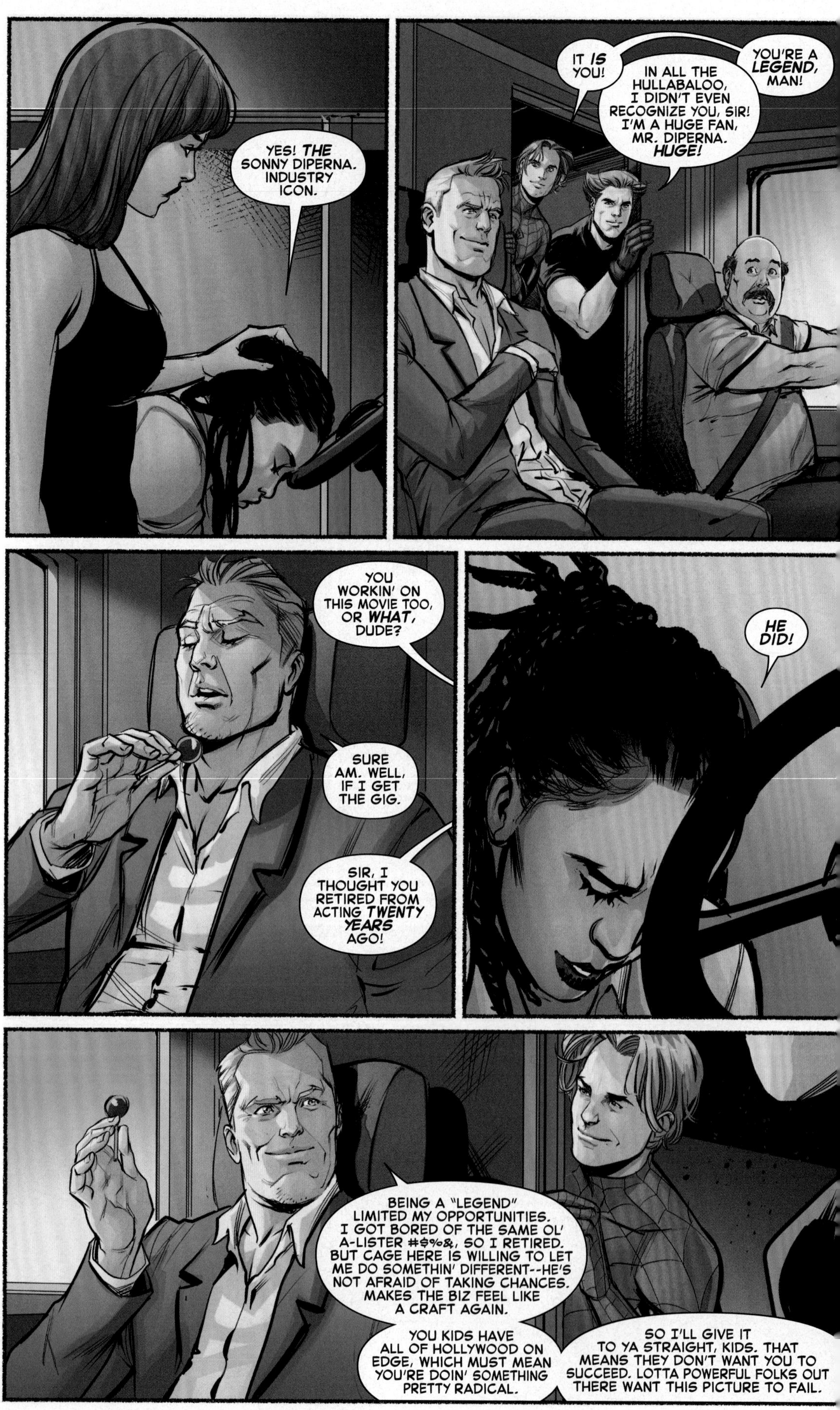
YES! THE SONNY DIPERNA. INDUSTRY ICON.
IT IS YOU!
IN ALL THE HULLABALOO, I DIDN'T EVEN RECOGNIZE YOU, SIR! I'M A HUGE FAN, MR. DIPERNA. HUGE!
YOU'RE A LEGEND, MAN!
YOU WORKIN' ON THIS MOVIE TOO, OR WHAT, DUDE?
SURE AM. WELL, IF I GET THE GIG.
SIR, I THOUGHT YOU RETIRED FROM ACTING TWENTY YEARS AGO!
HE DID!
BEING A "LEGEND" LIMITED MY OPPORTUNITIES. I GOT BORED OF THE SAME OL' A-LISTER #$%&, SO I RETIRED. BUT CAGE HERE IS WILLING TO LET ME DO SOMETHIN' DIFFERENT--HE'S NOT AFRAID OF TAKING CHANCES. MAKES THE BIZ FEEL LIKE A CRAFT AGAIN.
YOU KIDS HAVE ALL OF HOLLYWOOD ON EDGE, WHICH MUST MEAN YOU'RE DOIN' SOMETHING PRETTY RADICAL.
SO I'LL GIVE IT TO YA STRAIGHT, KIDS. THAT MEANS THEY DON'T WANT YOU TO SUCCEED. LOTTA POWERFUL FOLKS OUT THERE WANT THIS PICTURE TO FAIL.

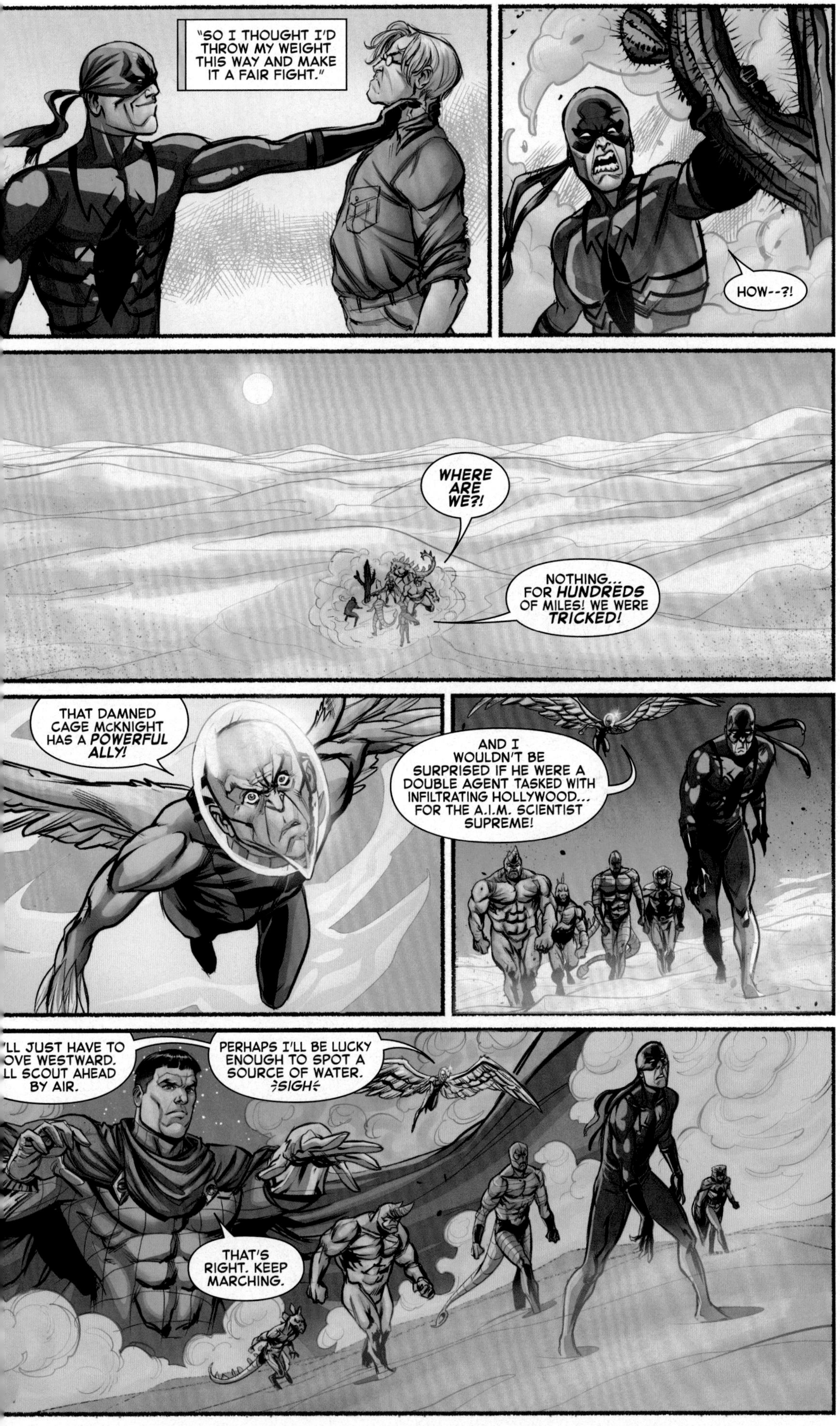
"SO I THOUGHT I'D THROW MY WEIGHT THIS WAY AND MAKE IT A FAIR FIGHT."
HOW--?!
WHERE ARE WE?!
NOTHING... FOR HUNDREDS OF MILES! WE WERE TRICKED!
THAT DAMNED CAGE McKNIGHT HAS A POWERFUL ALLY!
AND I WOULDN'T BE SURPRISED IF HE WERE A DOUBLE AGENT TASKED WITH INFILTRATING HOLLYWOOD... FOR THE A.I.M. SCIENTIST SUPREME!
'LL JUST HAVE TO OVE WESTWARD. LL SCOUT AHEAD BY AIR.
PERHAPS I'LL BE LUCKY ENOUGH TO SPOT A SOURCE OF WATER. *SIGH*
THAT'S RIGHT. KEEP MARCHING.

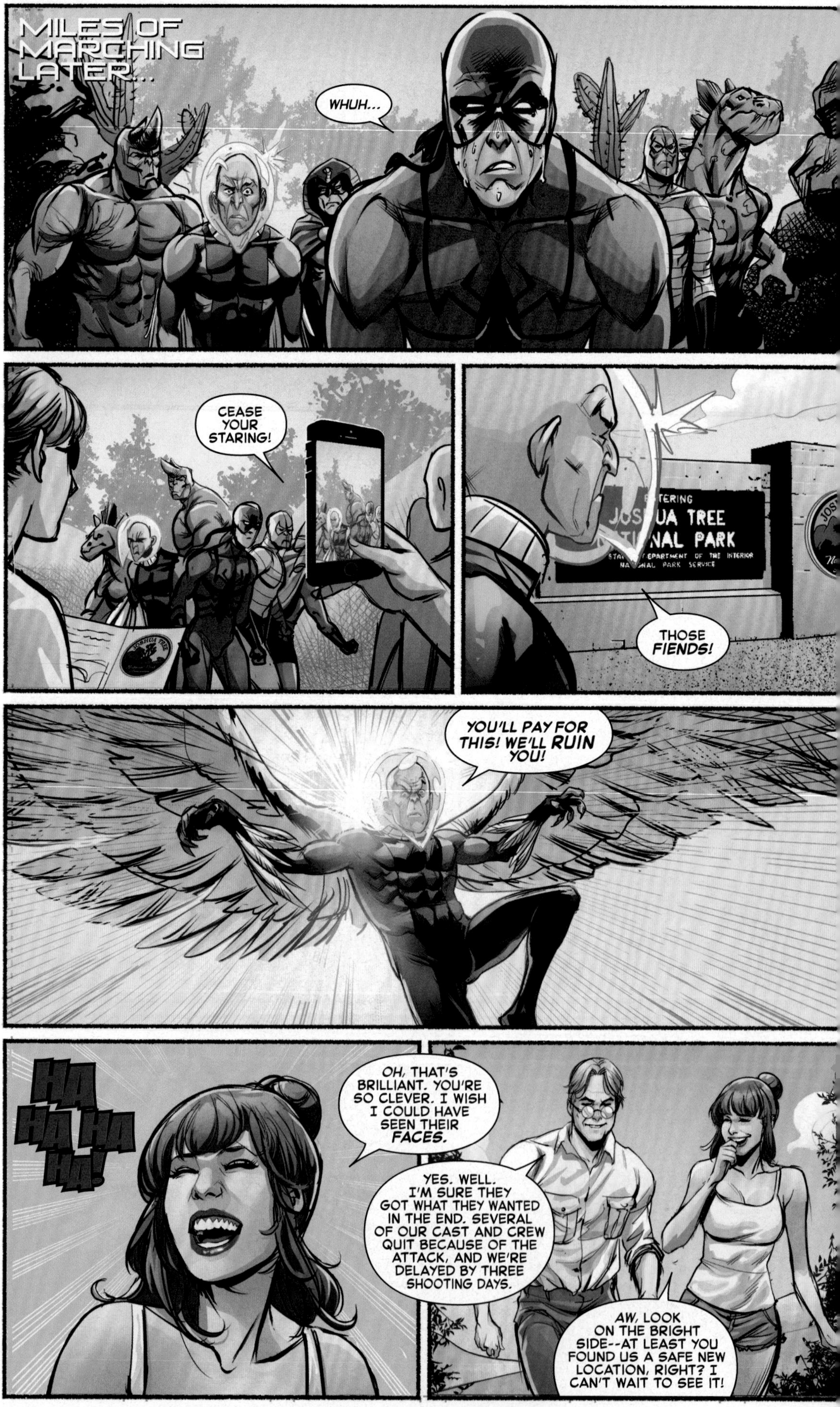
MILES OF MARCHING LATER...
WHUH...
CEASE YOUR STARING!
ENTERING JOSHUA TREE NATIONAL PARK
STATES DEPARTMENT OF THE INTERIOR
NATIONAL PARK SERVICE
THOSE FIENDS!
YOU'LL PAY FOR THIS! WE'LL RUIN YOU!
HA HA HA HA HA!
OH, THAT'S BRILLIANT. YOU'RE SO CLEVER. I WISH I COULD HAVE SEEN THEIR FACES.
YES. WELL. I'M SURE THEY GOT WHAT THEY WANTED IN THE END. SEVERAL OF OUR CAST AND CREW QUIT BECAUSE OF THE ATTACK, AND WE'RE DELAYED BY THREE SHOOTING DAYS.
AW, LOOK ON THE BRIGHT SIDE--AT LEAST YOU FOUND US A SAFE NEW LOCATION, RIGHT? I CAN'T WAIT TO SEE IT!

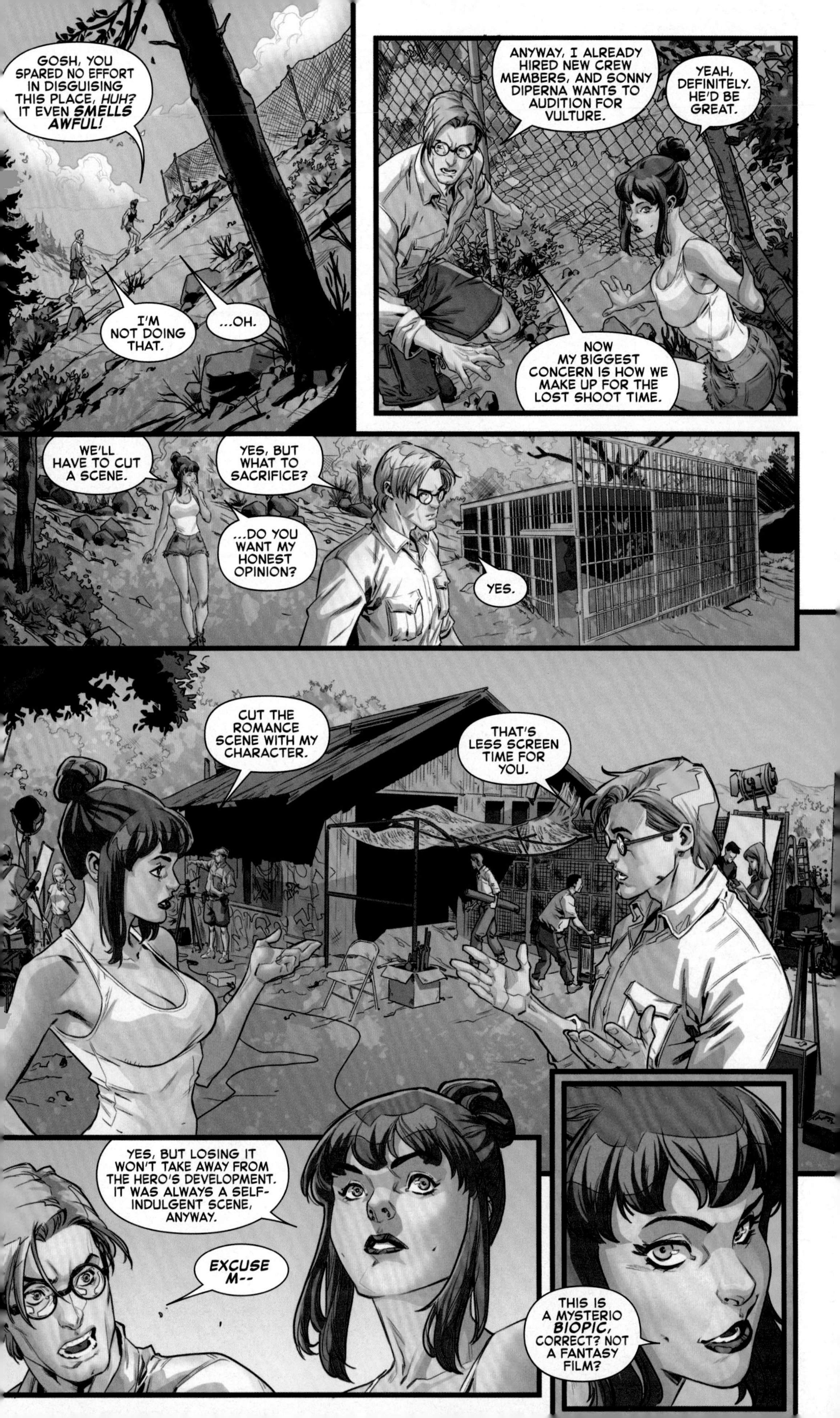
GOSH, YOU SPARED NO EFFORT IN DISGUISING THIS PLACE, *HUH?* IT EVEN *SMELLS AWFUL!*
I'M NOT DOING THAT.
...OH.
ANYWAY, I ALREADY HIRED NEW CREW MEMBERS, AND SONNY DIPERNA WANTS TO AUDITION FOR VULTURE.
YEAH, DEFINITELY. HE'D BE GREAT.
NOW MY BIGGEST CONCERN IS HOW WE MAKE UP FOR THE LOST SHOOT TIME.
WE'LL HAVE TO CUT A SCENE.
YES, BUT WHAT TO SACRIFICE?
...DO YOU WANT MY HONEST OPINION?
YES.
CUT THE ROMANCE SCENE WITH MY CHARACTER.
THAT'S LESS SCREEN TIME FOR YOU.
YES, BUT LOSING IT WON'T TAKE AWAY FROM THE HERO'S DEVELOPMENT. IT WAS ALWAYS A SELF-INDULGENT SCENE, ANYWAY.
EXCUSE M--
THIS IS A MYSTERIO *BIOPIC,* CORRECT? NOT A FANTASY FILM?

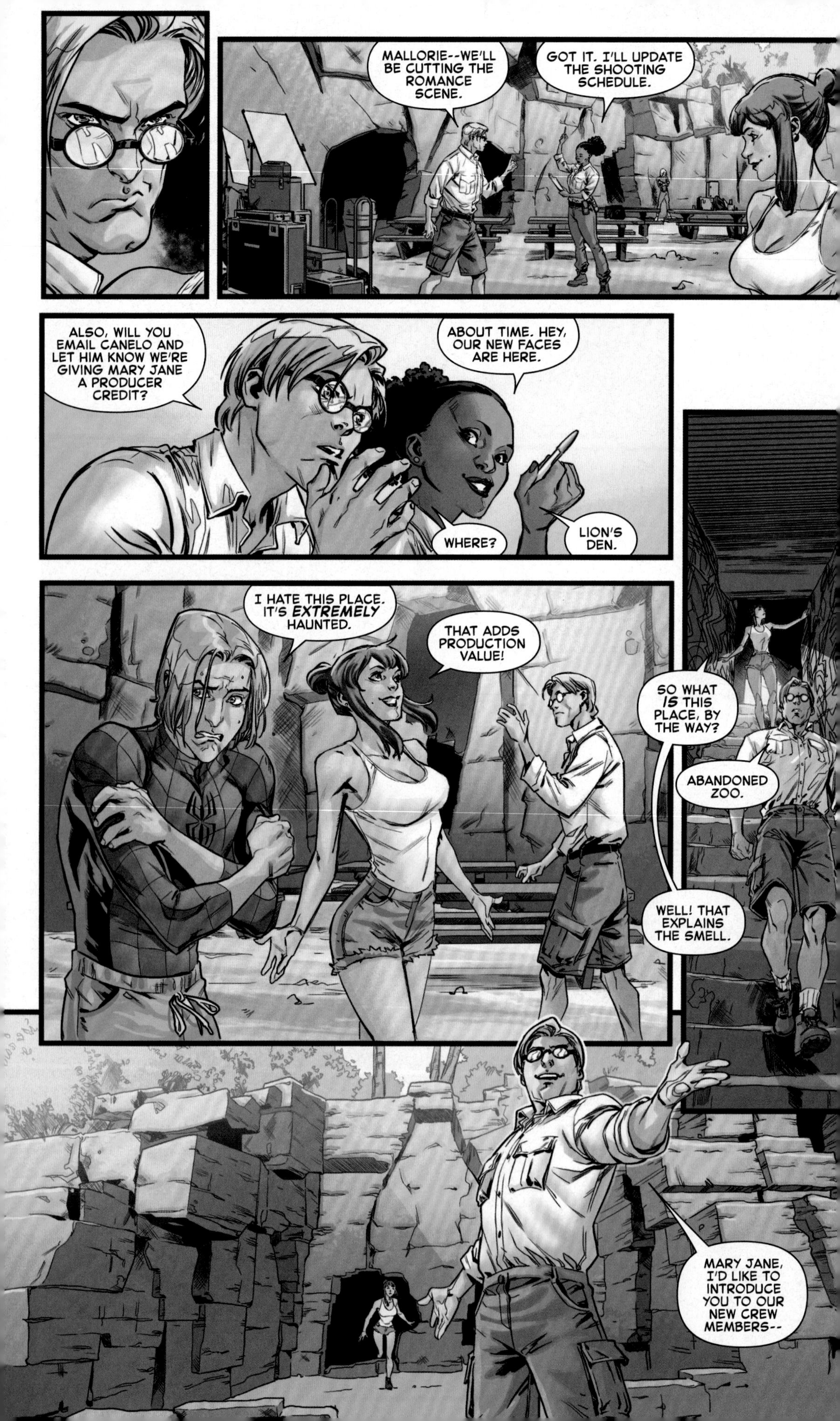

MALLORIE--WE'LL BE CUTTING THE ROMANCE SCENE.
GOT IT. I'LL UPDATE THE SHOOTING SCHEDULE.
ALSO, WILL YOU EMAIL CANELO AND LET HIM KNOW WE'RE GIVING MARY JANE A PRODUCER CREDIT?
ABOUT TIME. HEY, OUR NEW FACES ARE HERE.
WHERE?
LION'S DEN.
I HATE THIS PLACE. IT'S *EXTREMELY* HAUNTED.
THAT ADDS PRODUCTION VALUE!
SO WHAT *IS* THIS PLACE, BY THE WAY?
ABANDONED ZOO.
WELL! THAT EXPLAINS THE SMELL.
MARY JANE, I'D LIKE TO INTRODUCE YOU TO OUR NEW CREW MEMBERS--

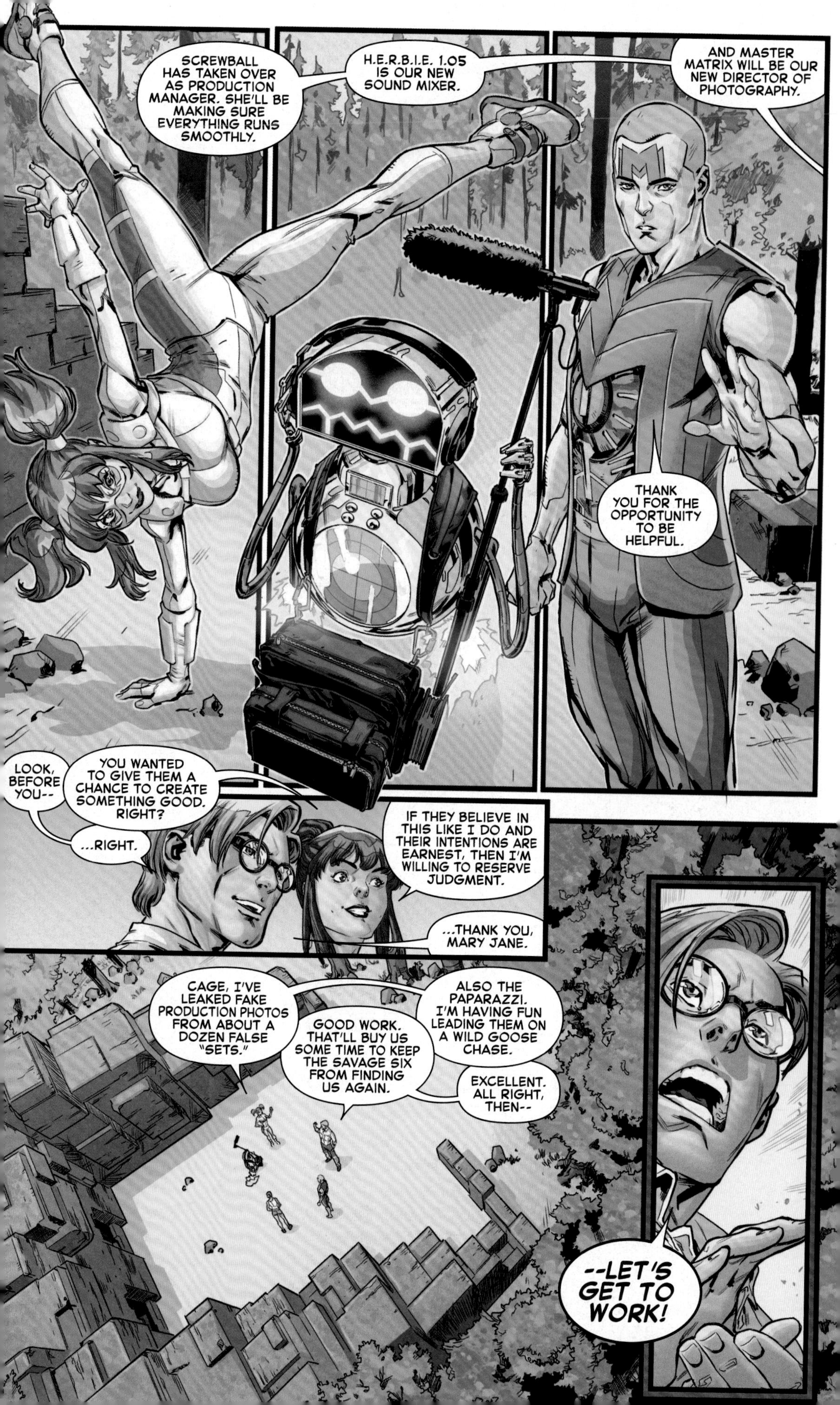
SCREWBALL HAS TAKEN OVER AS PRODUCTION MANAGER. SHE'LL BE MAKING SURE EVERYTHING RUNS SMOOTHLY.
H.E.R.B.I.E. 1.05 IS OUR NEW SOUND MIXER.
AND MASTER MATRIX WILL BE OUR NEW DIRECTOR OF PHOTOGRAPHY.
THANK YOU FOR THE OPPORTUNITY TO BE HELPFUL.
LOOK, BEFORE YOU--
YOU WANTED TO GIVE THEM A CHANCE TO CREATE SOMETHING GOOD. RIGHT?
...RIGHT.
IF THEY BELIEVE IN THIS LIKE I DO AND THEIR INTENTIONS ARE EARNEST, THEN I'M WILLING TO RESERVE JUDGMENT.
...THANK YOU, MARY JANE.
CAGE, I'VE LEAKED FAKE PRODUCTION PHOTOS FROM ABOUT A DOZEN FALSE "SETS."
GOOD WORK. THAT'LL BUY US SOME TIME TO KEEP THE SAVAGE SIX FROM FINDING US AGAIN.
ALSO THE PAPARAZZI. I'M HAVING FUN LEADING THEM ON A WILD GOOSE CHASE.
EXCELLENT. ALL RIGHT, THEN--
--LET'S GET TO WORK!

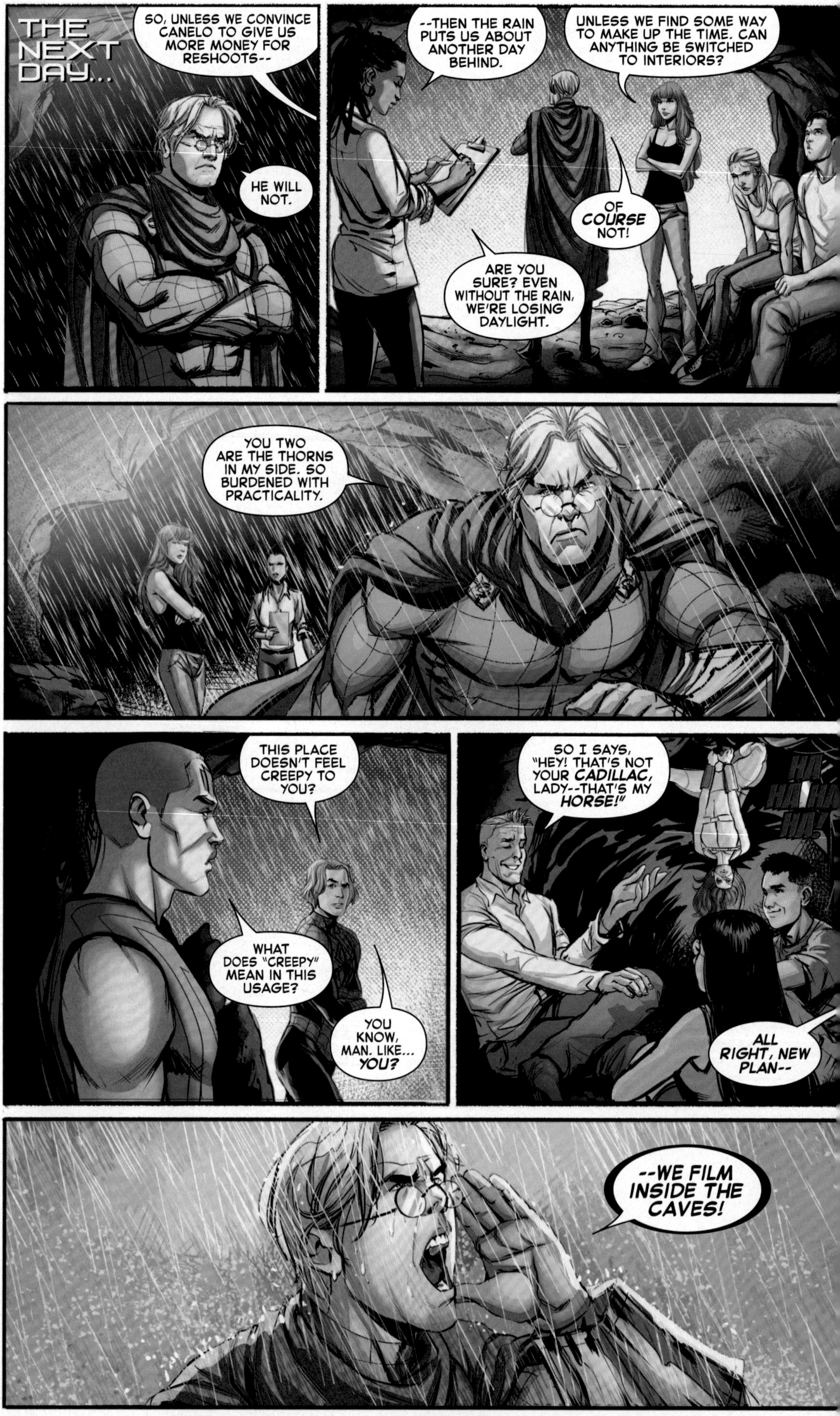
THE NEXT DAY...
SO, UNLESS WE CONVINCE CANELO TO GIVE US MORE MONEY FOR RESHOOTS--
HE WILL NOT.
--THEN THE RAIN PUTS US ABOUT ANOTHER DAY BEHIND.
UNLESS WE FIND SOME WAY TO MAKE UP THE TIME. CAN ANYTHING BE SWITCHED TO INTERIORS?
OF *COURSE* NOT!
ARE YOU SURE? EVEN WITHOUT THE RAIN, WE'RE LOSING DAYLIGHT.
YOU TWO ARE THE THORNS IN MY SIDE. SO BURDENED WITH PRACTICALITY.
THIS PLACE DOESN'T FEEL CREEPY TO YOU?
WHAT DOES "CREEPY" MEAN IN THIS USAGE?
YOU KNOW, MAN. LIKE... *YOU?*
SO I SAYS, "HEY! THAT'S NOT YOUR *CADILLAC,* LADY--THAT'S MY *HORSE!*"
HA HA HA HA!
ALL RIGHT, NEW PLAN--
--WE FILM INSIDE THE CAVES!

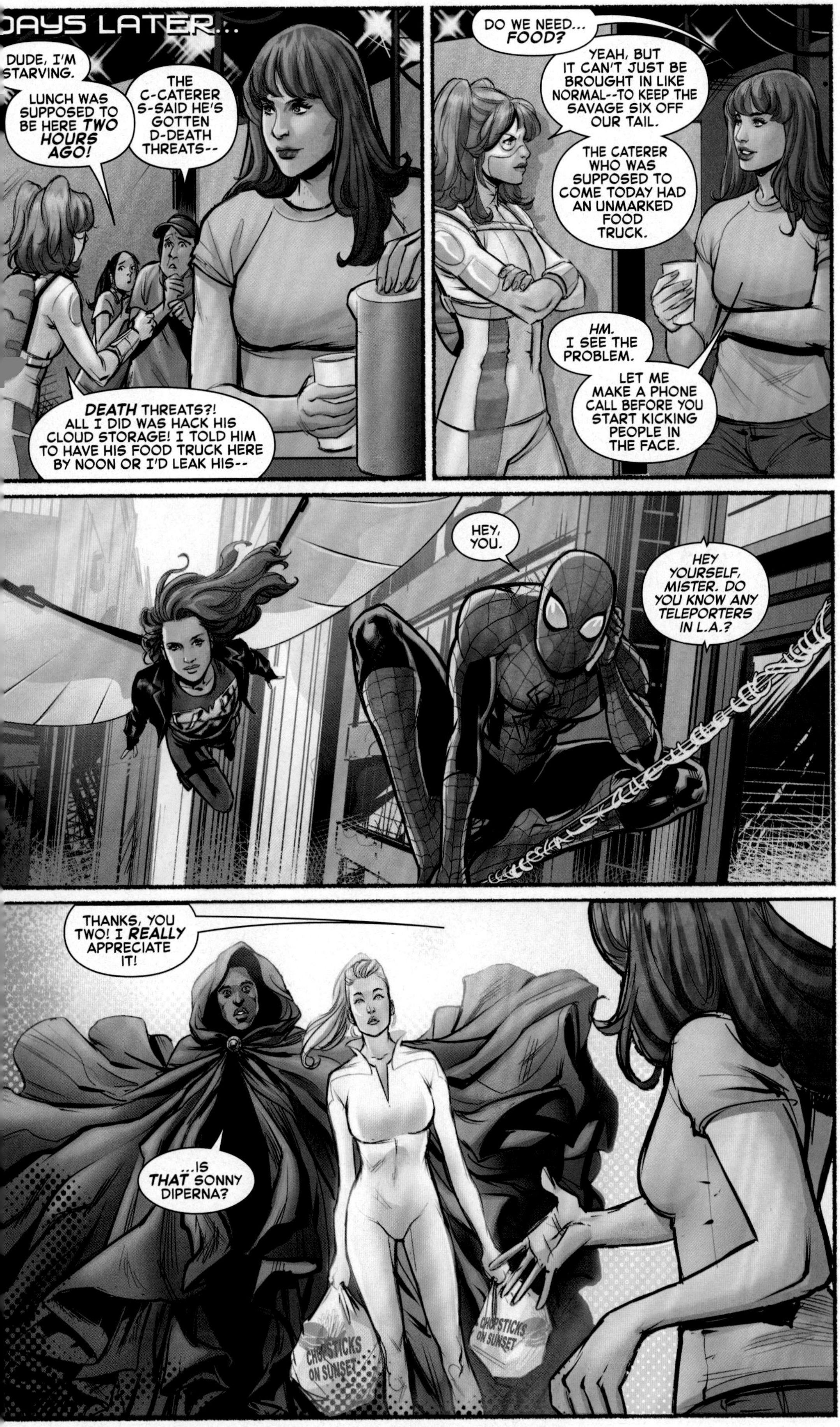
DAYS LATER...
DUDE, I'M STARVING.
LUNCH WAS SUPPOSED TO BE HERE TWO HOURS AGO!
THE C-CATERER S-SAID HE'S GOTTEN D-DEATH THREATS--
DEATH THREATS?! ALL I DID WAS HACK HIS CLOUD STORAGE! I TOLD HIM TO HAVE HIS FOOD TRUCK HERE BY NOON OR I'D LEAK HIS--
DO WE NEED... FOOD?
YEAH, BUT IT CAN'T JUST BE BROUGHT IN LIKE NORMAL--TO KEEP THE SAVAGE SIX OFF OUR TAIL.
THE CATERER WHO WAS SUPPOSED TO COME TODAY HAD AN UNMARKED FOOD TRUCK.
HM. I SEE THE PROBLEM.
LET ME MAKE A PHONE CALL BEFORE YOU START KICKING PEOPLE IN THE FACE.
HEY, YOU.
HEY YOURSELF, MISTER. DO YOU KNOW ANY TELEPORTERS IN L.A.?
THANKS, YOU TWO! I REALLY APPRECIATE IT!
...IS THAT SONNY DIPERNA?
CHOPSTICKS ON SUNSET
CHOPSTICKS ON SUNSET

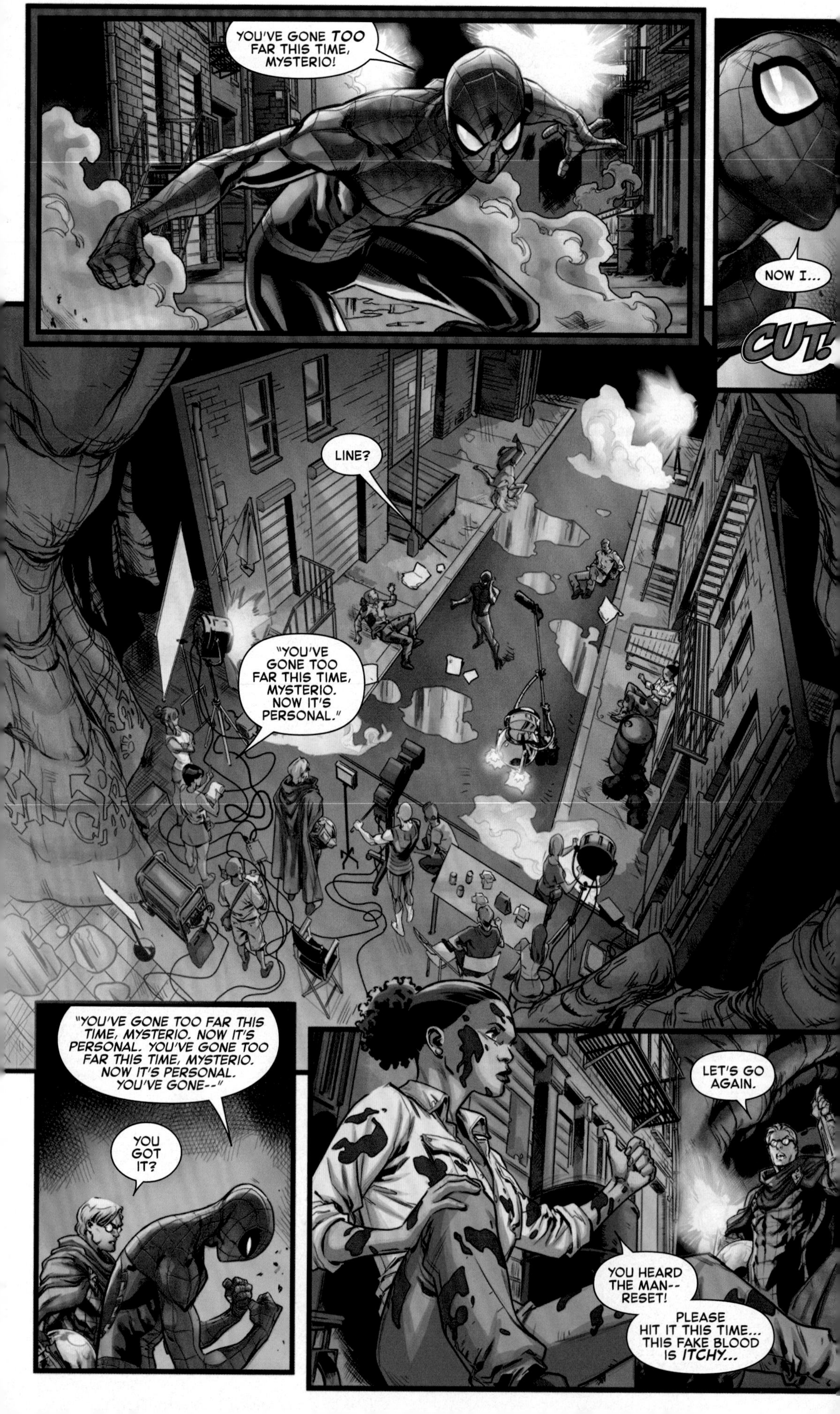
YOU'VE GONE TOO FAR THIS TIME, MYSTERIO!
NOW I...
CUT!
LINE?
"YOU'VE GONE TOO FAR THIS TIME, MYSTERIO. NOW IT'S PERSONAL."
"YOU'VE GONE TOO FAR THIS TIME, MYSTERIO. NOW IT'S PERSONAL. YOU'VE GONE TOO FAR THIS TIME, MYSTERIO. NOW IT'S PERSONAL. YOU'VE GONE--"
YOU GOT IT?
LET'S GO AGAIN.
YOU HEARD THE MAN-- RESET!
PLEASE HIT IT THIS TIME... THIS FAKE BLOOD IS ITCHY...

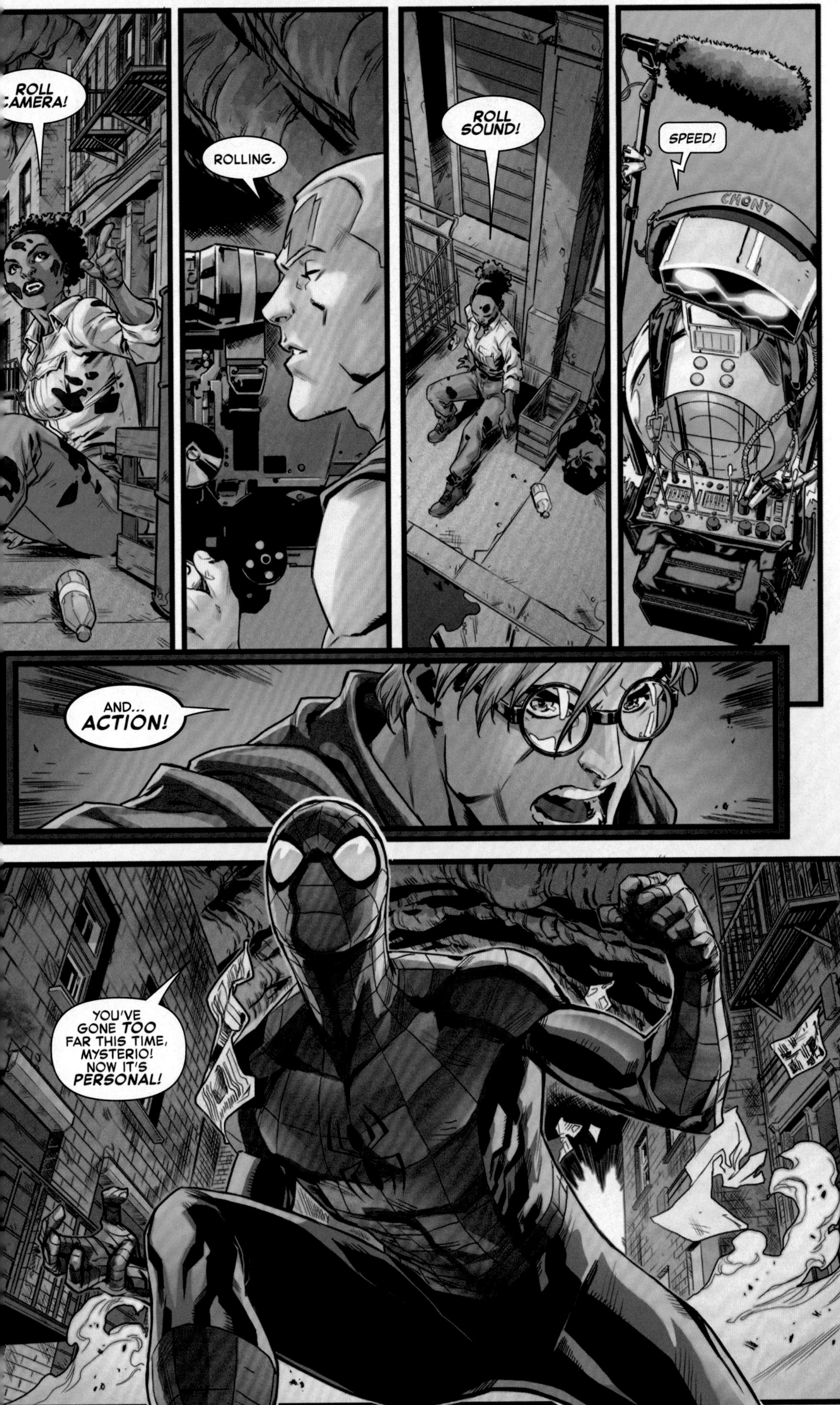
ROLL CAMERA!
ROLLING.
ROLL SOUND!
SPEED!
CHONY
AND... ACTION!
YOU'VE GONE TOO FAR THIS TIME, MYSTERIO! NOW IT'S PERSONAL!

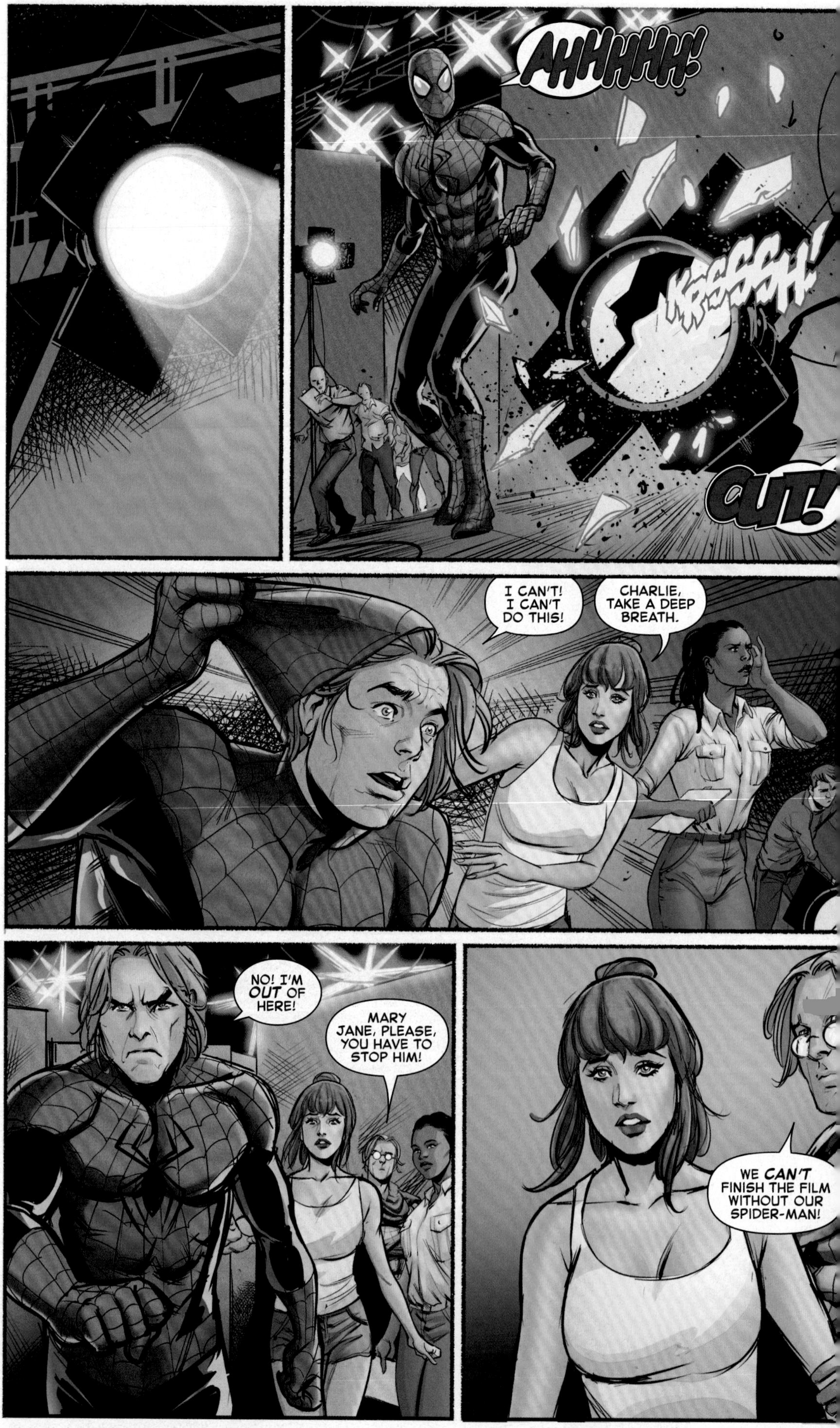
AHHHHH!
KRSSSH!
CUT!
I CAN'T! I CAN'T DO THIS!
CHARLIE, TAKE A DEEP BREATH.
NO! I'M OUT OF HERE!
MARY JANE, PLEASE, YOU HAVE TO STOP HIM!
WE CAN'T FINISH THE FILM WITHOUT OUR SPIDER-MAN!

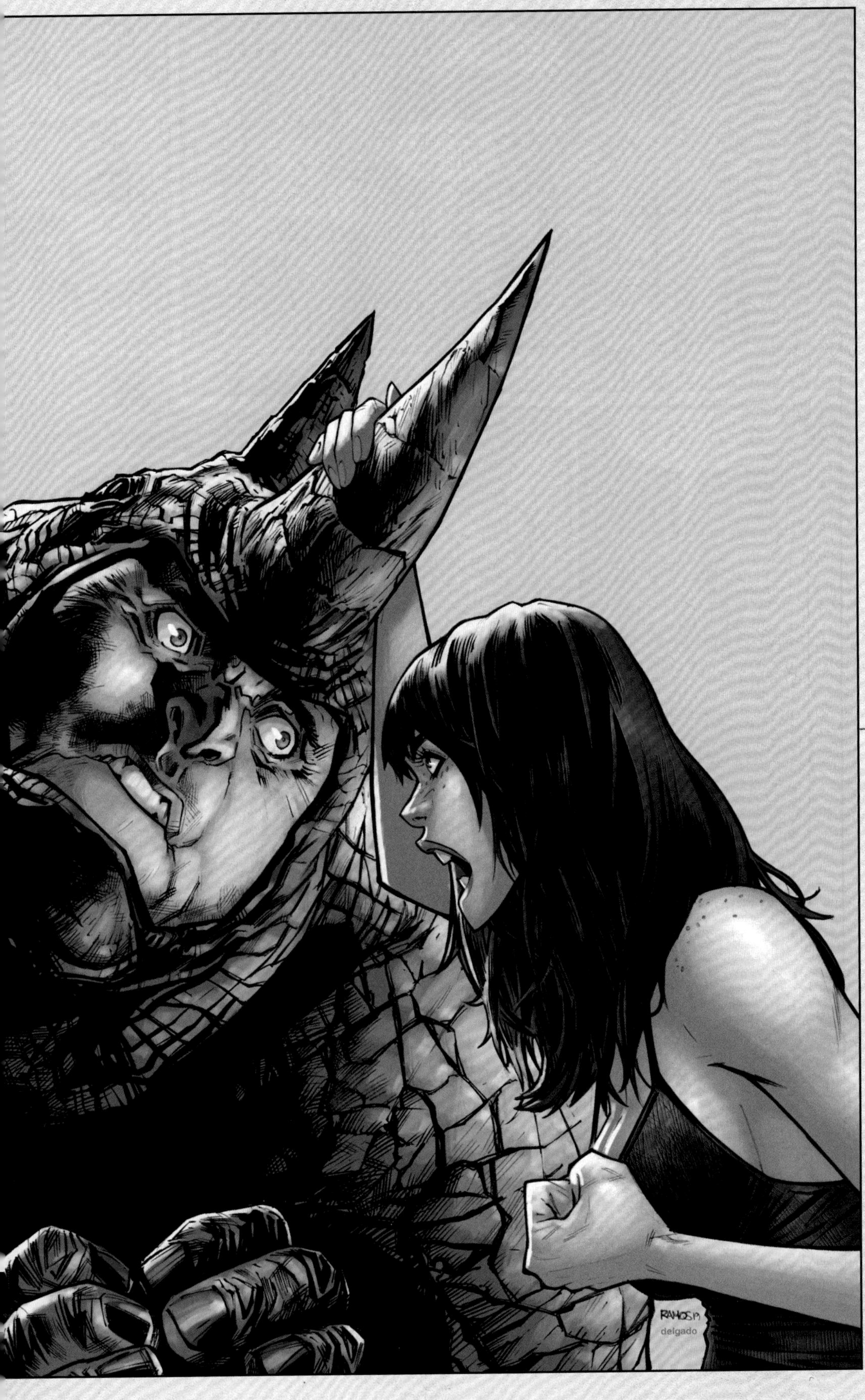
RAMOS'19
delgado

4

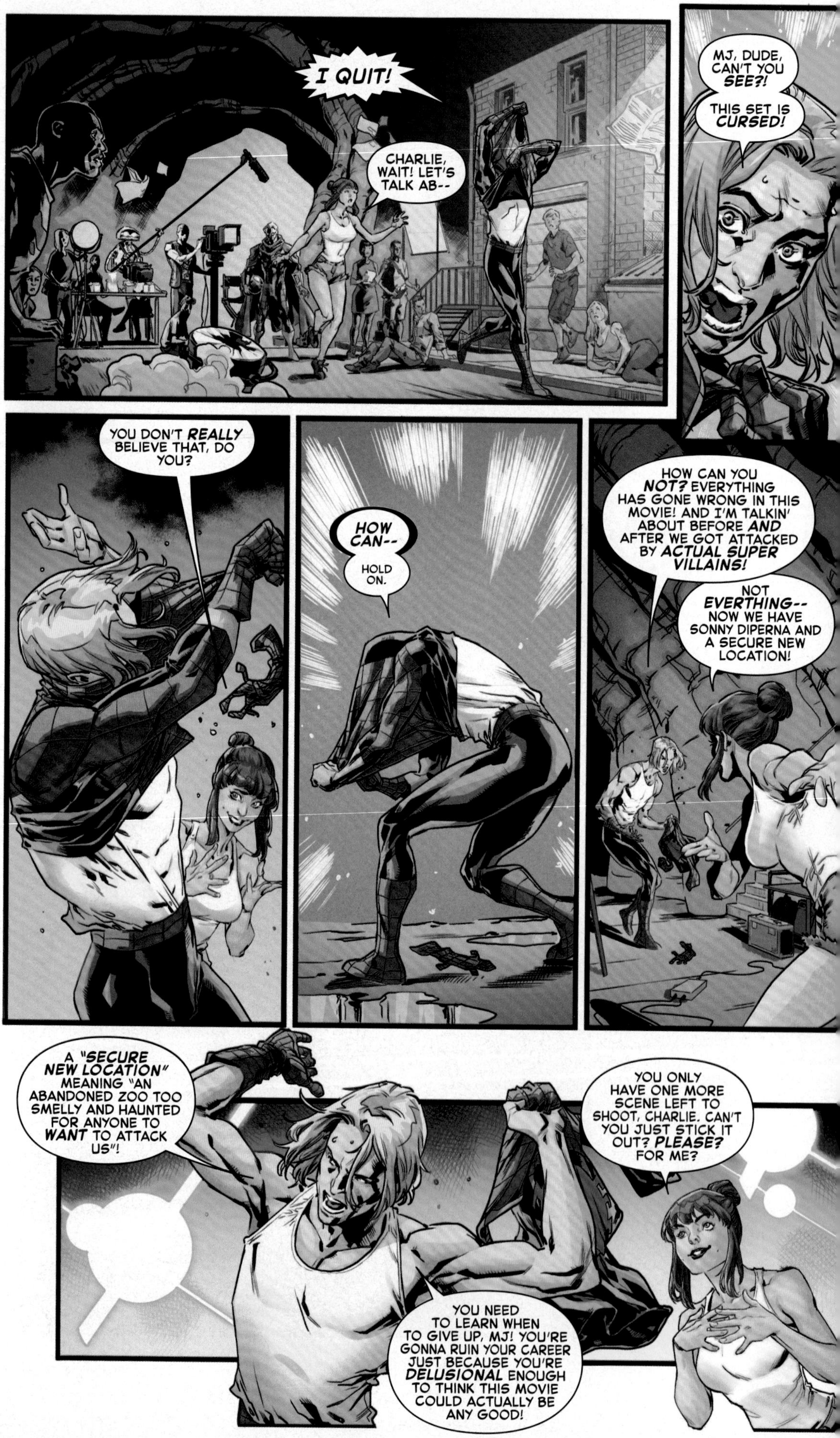

I QUIT!
CHARLIE, WAIT! LET'S TALK AB--
MJ, DUDE, CAN'T YOU SEE?!
THIS SET IS CURSED!
YOU DON'T REALLY BELIEVE THAT, DO YOU?
HOW CAN--
HOLD ON.
HOW CAN YOU NOT? EVERYTHING HAS GONE WRONG IN THIS MOVIE! AND I'M TALKIN' ABOUT BEFORE AND AFTER WE GOT ATTACKED BY ACTUAL SUPER VILLAINS!
NOT EVERTHING-- NOW WE HAVE SONNY DIPERNA AND A SECURE NEW LOCATION!
A "SECURE NEW LOCATION" MEANING "AN ABANDONED ZOO TOO SMELLY AND HAUNTED FOR ANYONE TO WANT TO ATTACK US"!
YOU ONLY HAVE ONE MORE SCENE LEFT TO SHOOT, CHARLIE. CAN'T YOU JUST STICK IT OUT? PLEASE? FOR ME?
YOU NEED TO LEARN WHEN TO GIVE UP, MJ! YOU'RE GONNA RUIN YOUR CAREER JUST BECAUSE YOU'RE DELUSIONAL ENOUGH TO THINK THIS MOVIE COULD ACTUALLY BE ANY GOOD!

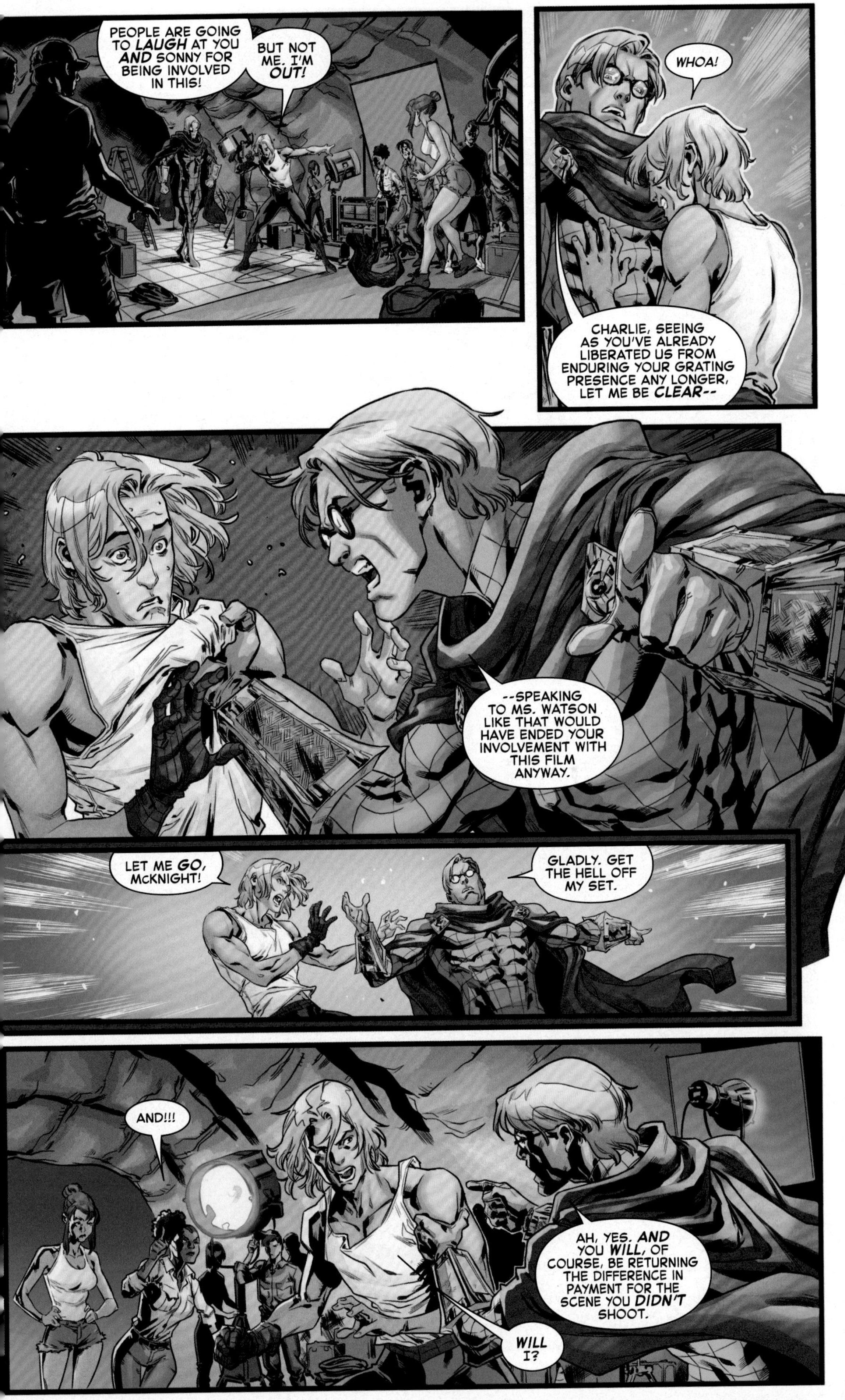

PEOPLE ARE GOING TO LAUGH AT YOU AND SONNY FOR BEING INVOLVED IN THIS!
BUT NOT ME. I'M OUT!
WHOA!
CHARLIE, SEEING AS YOU'VE ALREADY LIBERATED US FROM ENDURING YOUR GRATING PRESENCE ANY LONGER, LET ME BE CLEAR--
--SPEAKING TO MS. WATSON LIKE THAT WOULD HAVE ENDED YOUR INVOLVEMENT WITH THIS FILM ANYWAY.
LET ME GO, McKNIGHT!
GLADLY. GET THE HELL OFF MY SET.
AND!!!
AH, YES. AND YOU WILL, OF COURSE, BE RETURNING THE DIFFERENCE IN PAYMENT FOR THE SCENE YOU DIDN'T SHOOT.
WILL I?

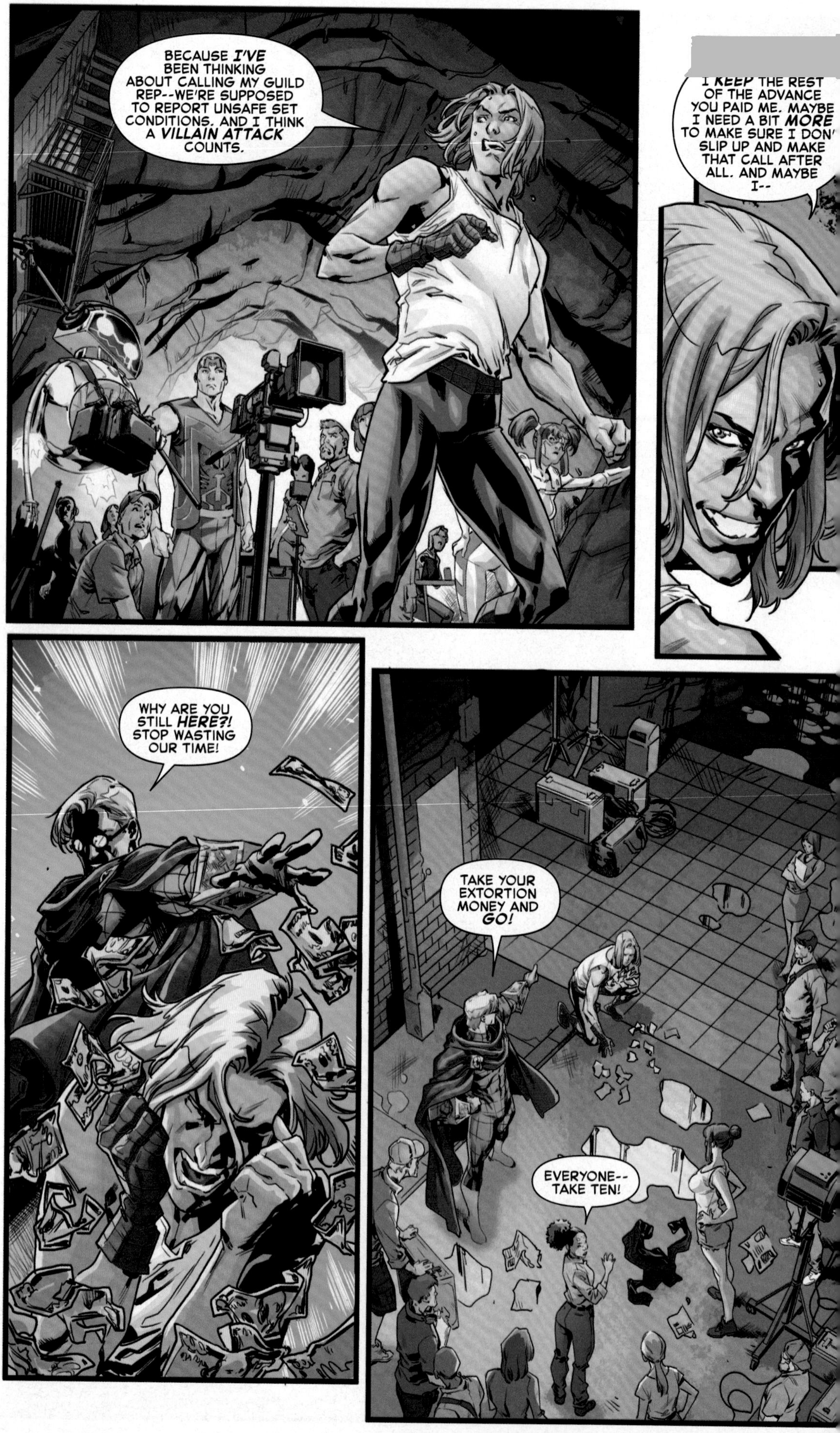
BECAUSE I'VE BEEN THINKING ABOUT CALLING MY GUILD REP--WE'RE SUPPOSED TO REPORT UNSAFE SET CONDITIONS. AND I THINK A VILLAIN ATTACK COUNTS.
I KEEP THE REST OF THE ADVANCE YOU PAID ME. MAYBE I NEED A BIT MORE TO MAKE SURE I DON' SLIP UP AND MAKE THAT CALL AFTER ALL. AND MAYBE I--
WHY ARE YOU STILL HERE?! STOP WASTING OUR TIME!
TAKE YOUR EXTORTION MONEY AND GO!
EVERYONE-- TAKE TEN!

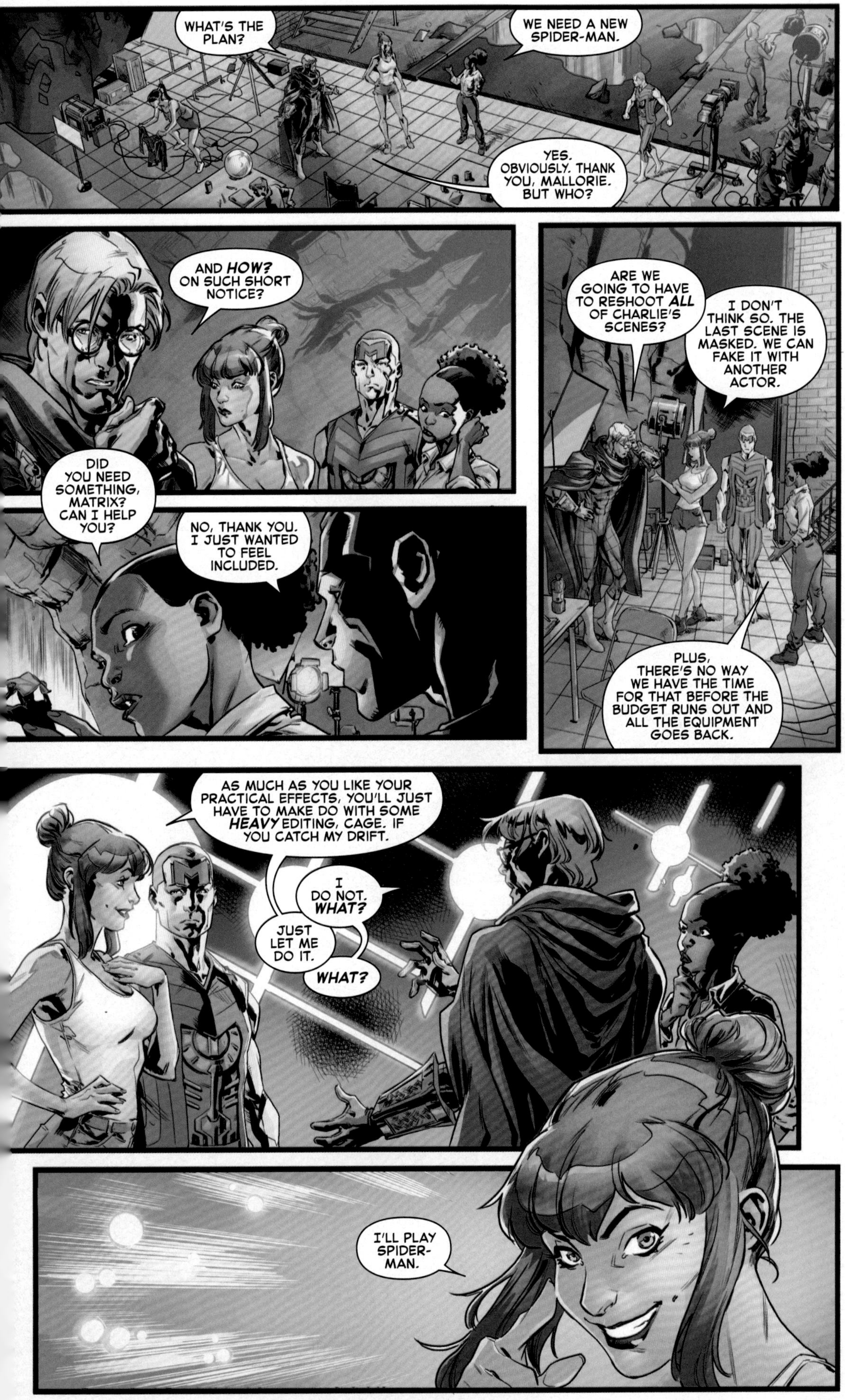
WHAT'S THE PLAN?
WE NEED A NEW SPIDER-MAN.
YES. OBVIOUSLY. THANK YOU, MALLORIE. BUT WHO?
AND HOW? ON SUCH SHORT NOTICE?
DID YOU NEED SOMETHING, MATRIX? CAN I HELP YOU?
NO, THANK YOU. I JUST WANTED TO FEEL INCLUDED.
ARE WE GOING TO HAVE TO RESHOOT ALL OF CHARLIE'S SCENES?
I DON'T THINK SO. THE LAST SCENE IS MASKED. WE CAN FAKE IT WITH ANOTHER ACTOR.
PLUS, THERE'S NO WAY WE HAVE THE TIME FOR THAT BEFORE THE BUDGET RUNS OUT AND ALL THE EQUIPMENT GOES BACK.
AS MUCH AS YOU LIKE YOUR PRACTICAL EFFECTS, YOU'LL JUST HAVE TO MAKE DO WITH SOME HEAVY EDITING, CAGE. IF YOU CATCH MY DRIFT.
I DO NOT. WHAT?
JUST LET ME DO IT.
WHAT?
I'LL PLAY SPIDER-MAN.

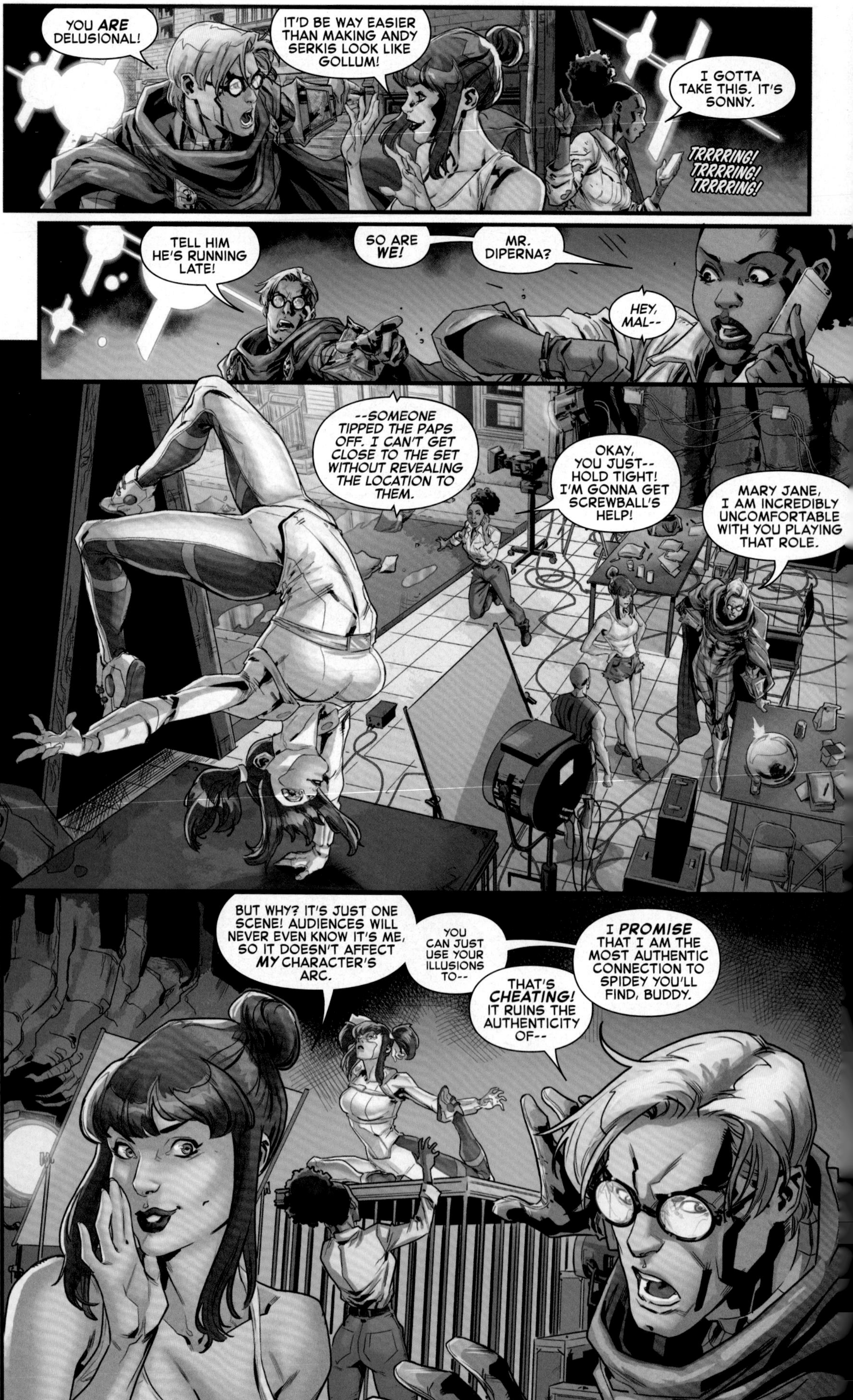
YOU ARE DELUSIONAL!
IT'D BE WAY EASIER THAN MAKING ANDY SERKIS LOOK LIKE GOLLUM!
I GOTTA TAKE THIS. IT'S SONNY.
TRRRRING! TRRRRING! TRRRRING!
TELL HIM HE'S RUNNING LATE!
SO ARE WE!
MR. DIPERNA?
HEY, MAL--
--SOMEONE TIPPED THE PAPS OFF. I CAN'T GET CLOSE TO THE SET WITHOUT REVEALING THE LOCATION TO THEM.
OKAY, YOU JUST-- HOLD TIGHT! I'M GONNA GET SCREWBALL'S HELP!
MARY JANE, I AM INCREDIBLY UNCOMFORTABLE WITH YOU PLAYING THAT ROLE.
BUT WHY? IT'S JUST ONE SCENE! AUDIENCES WILL NEVER EVEN KNOW IT'S ME, SO IT DOESN'T AFFECT MY CHARACTER'S ARC.
YOU CAN JUST USE YOUR ILLUSIONS TO--
THAT'S CHEATING! IT RUINS THE AUTHENTICITY OF--
I PROMISE THAT I AM THE MOST AUTHENTIC CONNECTION TO SPIDEY YOU'LL FIND, BUDDY.

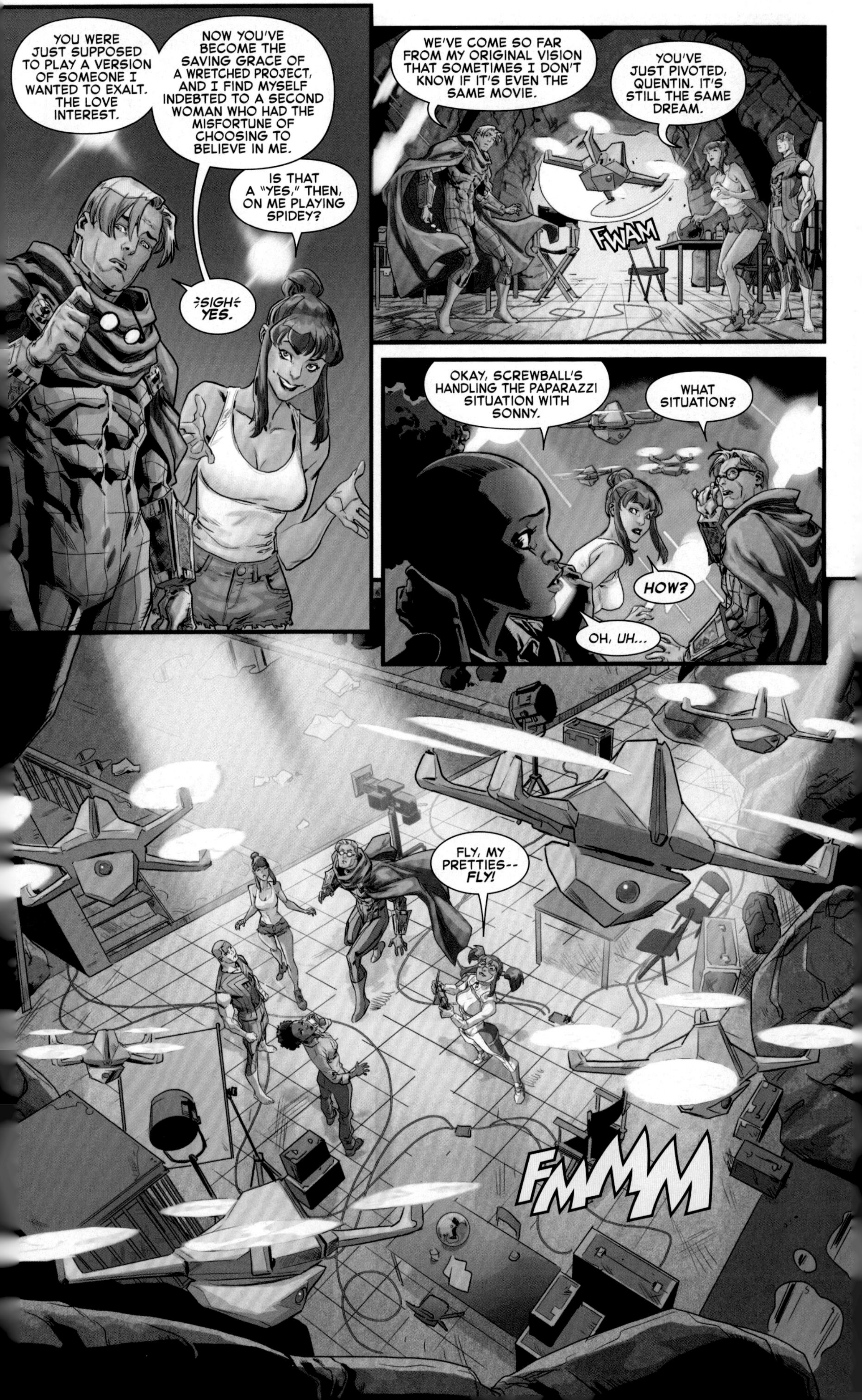
YOU WERE JUST SUPPOSED TO PLAY A VERSION OF SOMEONE I WANTED TO EXALT. THE LOVE INTEREST.
NOW YOU'VE BECOME THE SAVING GRACE OF A WRETCHED PROJECT, AND I FIND MYSELF INDEBTED TO A SECOND WOMAN WHO HAD THE MISFORTUNE OF CHOOSING TO BELIEVE IN ME.
IS THAT A "YES," THEN, ON ME PLAYING SPIDEY?
SIGH YES.
WE'VE COME SO FAR FROM MY ORIGINAL VISION THAT SOMETIMES I DON'T KNOW IF IT'S EVEN THE SAME MOVIE.
YOU'VE JUST PIVOTED, QUENTIN. IT'S STILL THE SAME DREAM.
FWAM
OKAY, SCREWBALL'S HANDLING THE PAPARAZZI SITUATION WITH SONNY.
WHAT SITUATION?
HOW?
OH, UH...
FLY, MY PRETTIES-- FLY!
FMMM

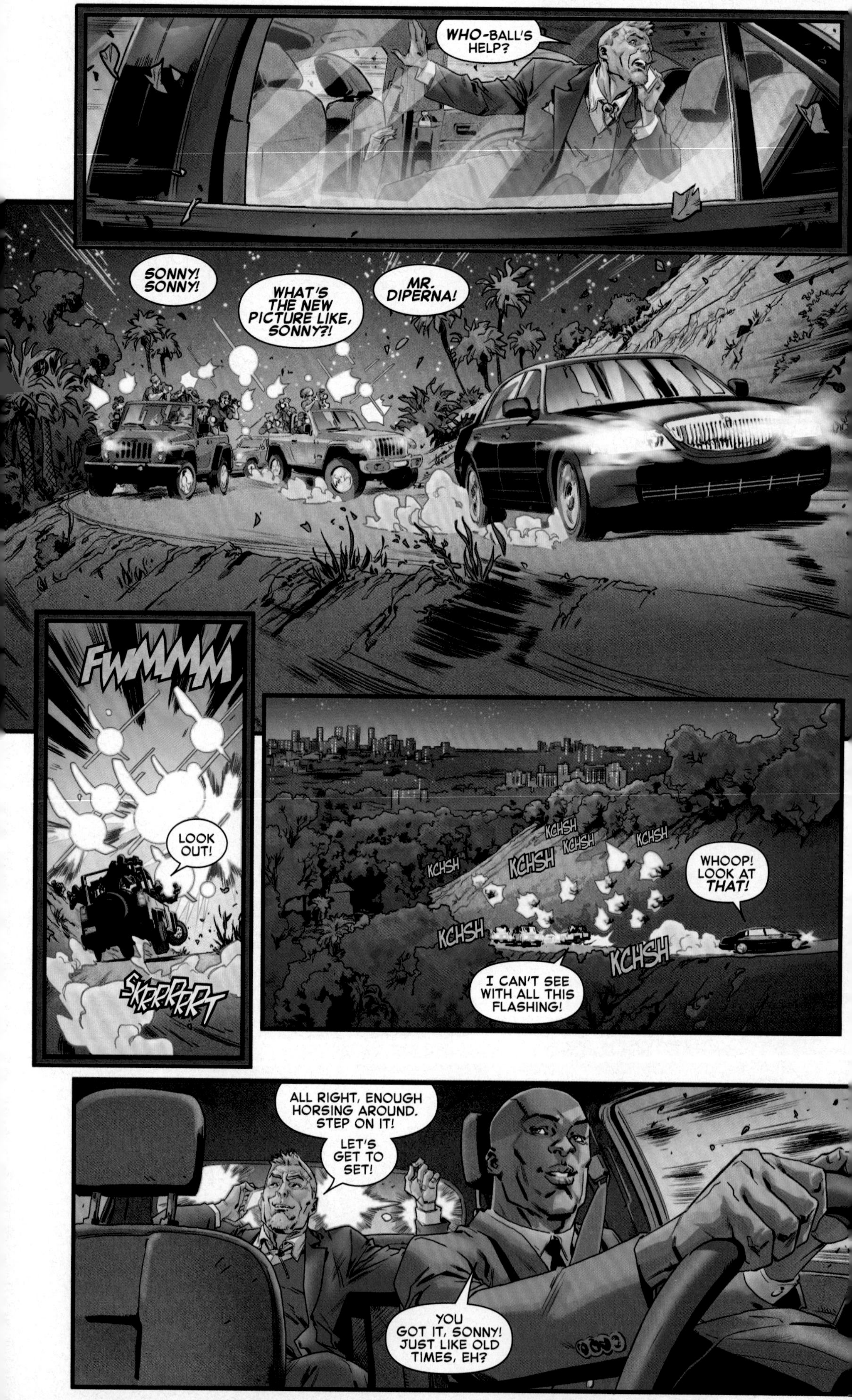
WHO-BALL'S HELP?
SONNY! SONNY!
WHAT'S THE NEW PICTURE LIKE, SONNY?!
MR. DIPERNA!
FWMMM
LOOK OUT!
SKRRRRRT
KCHSH
KCHSH
KCHSH
KCHSH
KCHSH
KCHSH
KCHSH
WHOOP! LOOK AT THAT!
I CAN'T SEE WITH ALL THIS FLASHING!
ALL RIGHT, ENOUGH HORSING AROUND. STEP ON IT!
LET'S GET TO SET!
YOU GOT IT, SONNY! JUST LIKE OLD TIMES, EH?

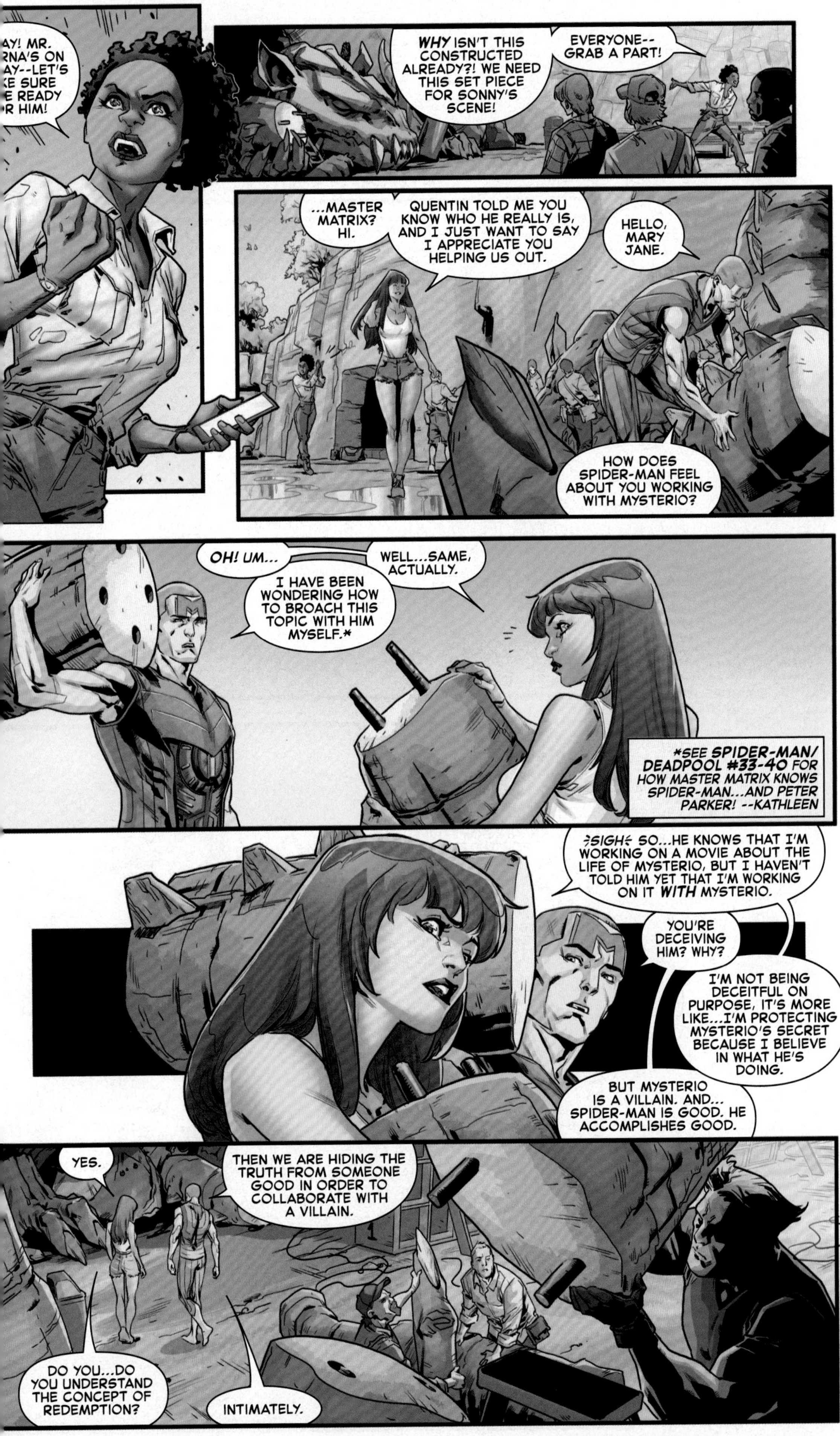
AY! MR.
RNA'S ON
AY--LET'S
KE SURE
E READY
R HIM!
WHY ISN'T THIS CONSTRUCTED ALREADY?! WE NEED THIS SET PIECE FOR SONNY'S SCENE!
EVERYONE-- GRAB A PART!
...MASTER MATRIX? HI.
QUENTIN TOLD ME YOU KNOW WHO HE REALLY IS, AND I JUST WANT TO SAY I APPRECIATE YOU HELPING US OUT.
HELLO, MARY JANE.
HOW DOES SPIDER-MAN FEEL ABOUT YOU WORKING WITH MYSTERIO?
OH! UM...
WELL...SAME, ACTUALLY.
I HAVE BEEN WONDERING HOW TO BROACH THIS TOPIC WITH HIM MYSELF.*
*SEE SPIDER-MAN/ DEADPOOL #33-40 FOR HOW MASTER MATRIX KNOWS SPIDER-MAN...AND PETER PARKER! --KATHLEEN
SIGH SO...HE KNOWS THAT I'M WORKING ON A MOVIE ABOUT THE LIFE OF MYSTERIO, BUT I HAVEN'T TOLD HIM YET THAT I'M WORKING ON IT WITH MYSTERIO.
YOU'RE DECEIVING HIM? WHY?
I'M NOT BEING DECEITFUL ON PURPOSE, IT'S MORE LIKE...I'M PROTECTING MYSTERIO'S SECRET BECAUSE I BELIEVE IN WHAT HE'S DOING.
BUT MYSTERIO IS A VILLAIN. AND... SPIDER-MAN IS GOOD. HE ACCOMPLISHES GOOD.
YES.
THEN WE ARE HIDING THE TRUTH FROM SOMEONE GOOD IN ORDER TO COLLABORATE WITH A VILLAIN.
DO YOU...DO YOU UNDERSTAND THE CONCEPT OF REDEMPTION?
INTIMATELY.

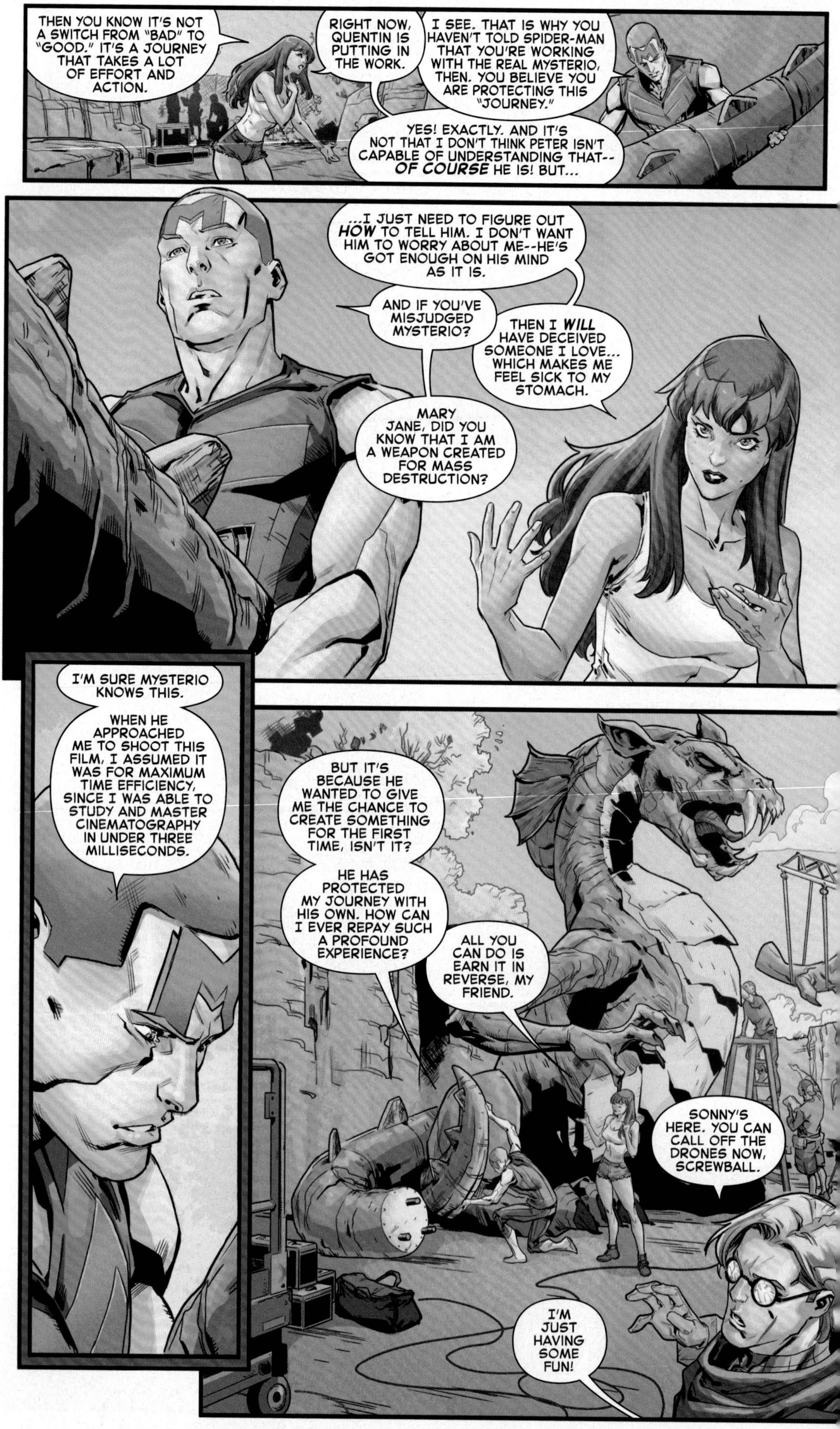
THEN YOU KNOW IT'S NOT A SWITCH FROM "BAD" TO "GOOD." IT'S A JOURNEY THAT TAKES A LOT OF EFFORT AND ACTION.
RIGHT NOW, QUENTIN IS PUTTING IN THE WORK.
I SEE. THAT IS WHY YOU HAVEN'T TOLD SPIDER-MAN THAT YOU'RE WORKING WITH THE REAL MYSTERIO, THEN. YOU BELIEVE YOU ARE PROTECTING THIS "JOURNEY."
YES! EXACTLY. AND IT'S NOT THAT I DON'T THINK PETER ISN'T CAPABLE OF UNDERSTANDING THAT-- *OF COURSE* HE IS! BUT...
...I JUST NEED TO FIGURE OUT *HOW* TO TELL HIM. I DON'T WANT HIM TO WORRY ABOUT ME--HE'S GOT ENOUGH ON HIS MIND AS IT IS.
AND IF YOU'VE MISJUDGED MYSTERIO?
THEN I *WILL* HAVE DECEIVED SOMEONE I LOVE... WHICH MAKES ME FEEL SICK TO MY STOMACH.
MARY JANE, DID YOU KNOW THAT I AM A WEAPON CREATED FOR MASS DESTRUCTION?
I'M SURE MYSTERIO KNOWS THIS.
WHEN HE APPROACHED ME TO SHOOT THIS FILM, I ASSUMED IT WAS FOR MAXIMUM TIME EFFICIENCY, SINCE I WAS ABLE TO STUDY AND MASTER CINEMATOGRAPHY IN UNDER THREE MILLISECONDS.
BUT IT'S BECAUSE HE WANTED TO GIVE ME THE CHANCE TO CREATE SOMETHING FOR THE FIRST TIME, ISN'T IT?
HE HAS PROTECTED MY JOURNEY WITH HIS OWN. HOW CAN I EVER REPAY SUCH A PROFOUND EXPERIENCE?
ALL YOU CAN DO IS EARN IT IN REVERSE, MY FRIEND.
SONNY'S HERE. YOU CAN CALL OFF THE DRONES NOW, SCREWBALL.
I'M JUST HAVING SOME FUN!

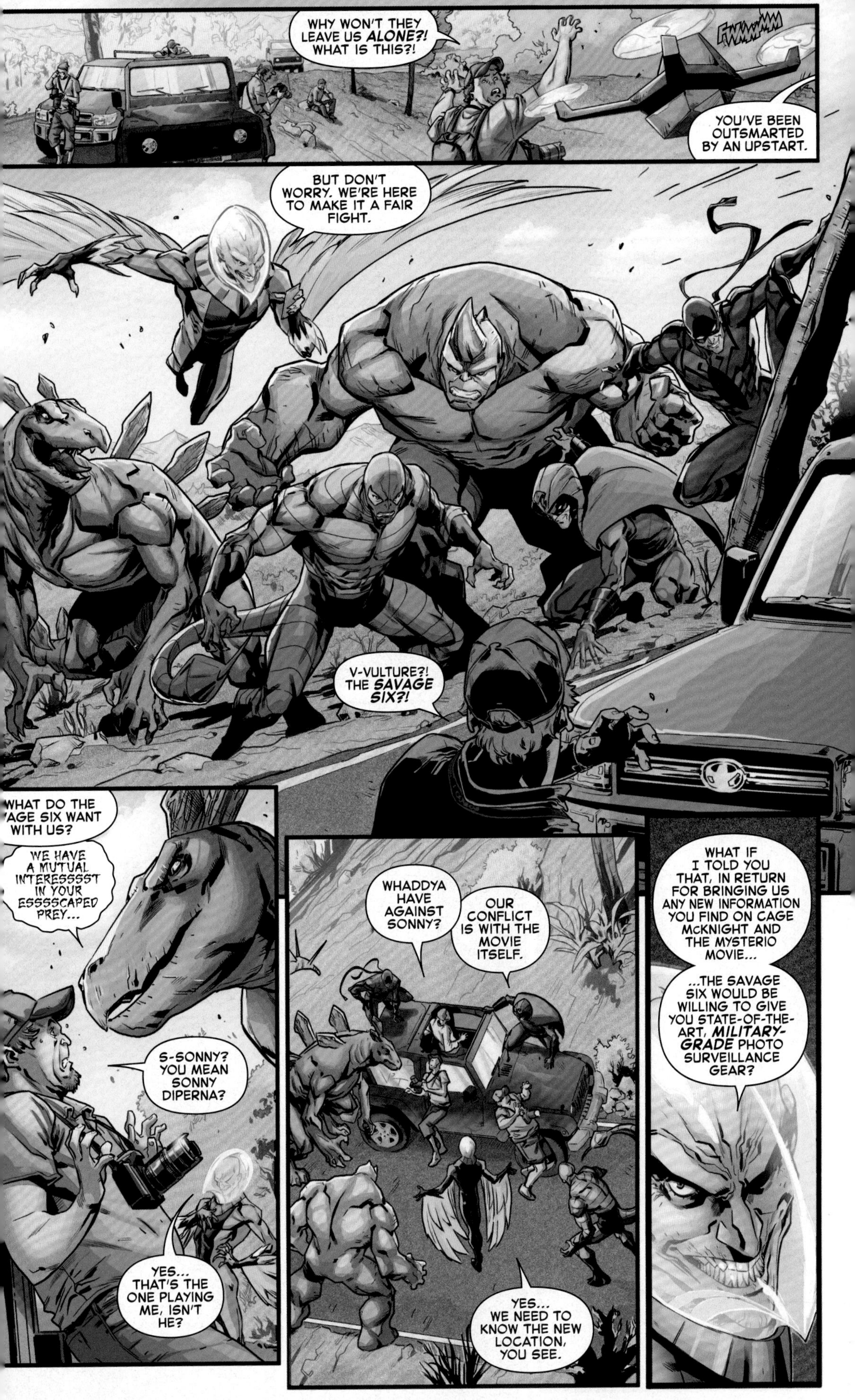
WHY WON'T THEY LEAVE US ALONE?! WHAT IS THIS?!
FWMMMM
YOU'VE BEEN OUTSMARTED BY AN UPSTART.
BUT DON'T WORRY. WE'RE HERE TO MAKE IT A FAIR FIGHT.
V-VULTURE?! THE SAVAGE SIX?!
WHAT DO THE AGE SIX WANT WITH US?
WE HAVE A MUTUAL INTERESSSST IN YOUR ESSSSCAPED PREY...
S-SONNY? YOU MEAN SONNY DIPERNA?
YES... THAT'S THE ONE PLAYING ME, ISN'T HE?
WHADDYA HAVE AGAINST SONNY?
OUR CONFLICT IS WITH THE MOVIE ITSELF.
YES... WE NEED TO KNOW THE NEW LOCATION, YOU SEE.
WHAT IF I TOLD YOU THAT, IN RETURN FOR BRINGING US ANY NEW INFORMATION YOU FIND ON CAGE McKNIGHT AND THE MYSTERIO MOVIE...
...THE SAVAGE SIX WOULD BE WILLING TO GIVE YOU STATE-OF-THE-ART, MILITARY-GRADE PHOTO SURVEILLANCE GEAR?

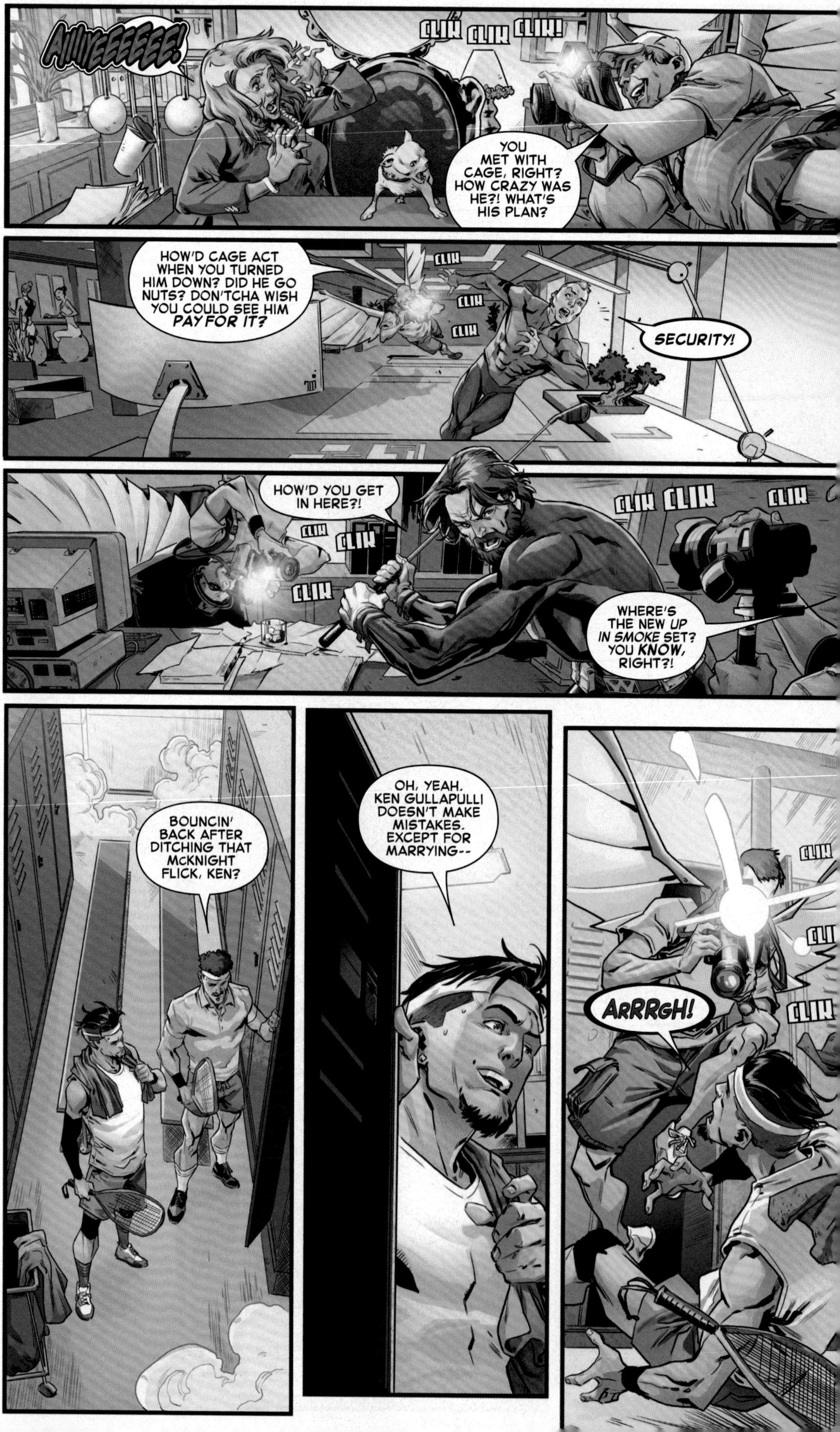
AIIIYEEEEEE!
CLIK CLIK CLIK!
YOU MET WITH CAGE, RIGHT? HOW CRAZY WAS HE?! WHAT'S HIS PLAN?
HOW'D CAGE ACT WHEN YOU TURNED HIM DOWN? DID HE GO NUTS? DON'TCHA WISH YOU COULD SEE HIM PAY FOR IT?
CLIK
CLIK
CLIK
SECURITY!
HOW'D YOU GET IN HERE?!
CLIK CLIK
CLIK
CLIK CLIK
CLIK
WHERE'S THE NEW UP IN SMOKE SET? YOU KNOW, RIGHT?!
BOUNCIN' BACK AFTER DITCHING THAT McKNIGHT FLICK, KEN?
OH, YEAH. KEN GULLAPULLI DOESN'T MAKE MISTAKES. EXCEPT FOR MARRYING--
CLIK
ARRRGH!
CLIK

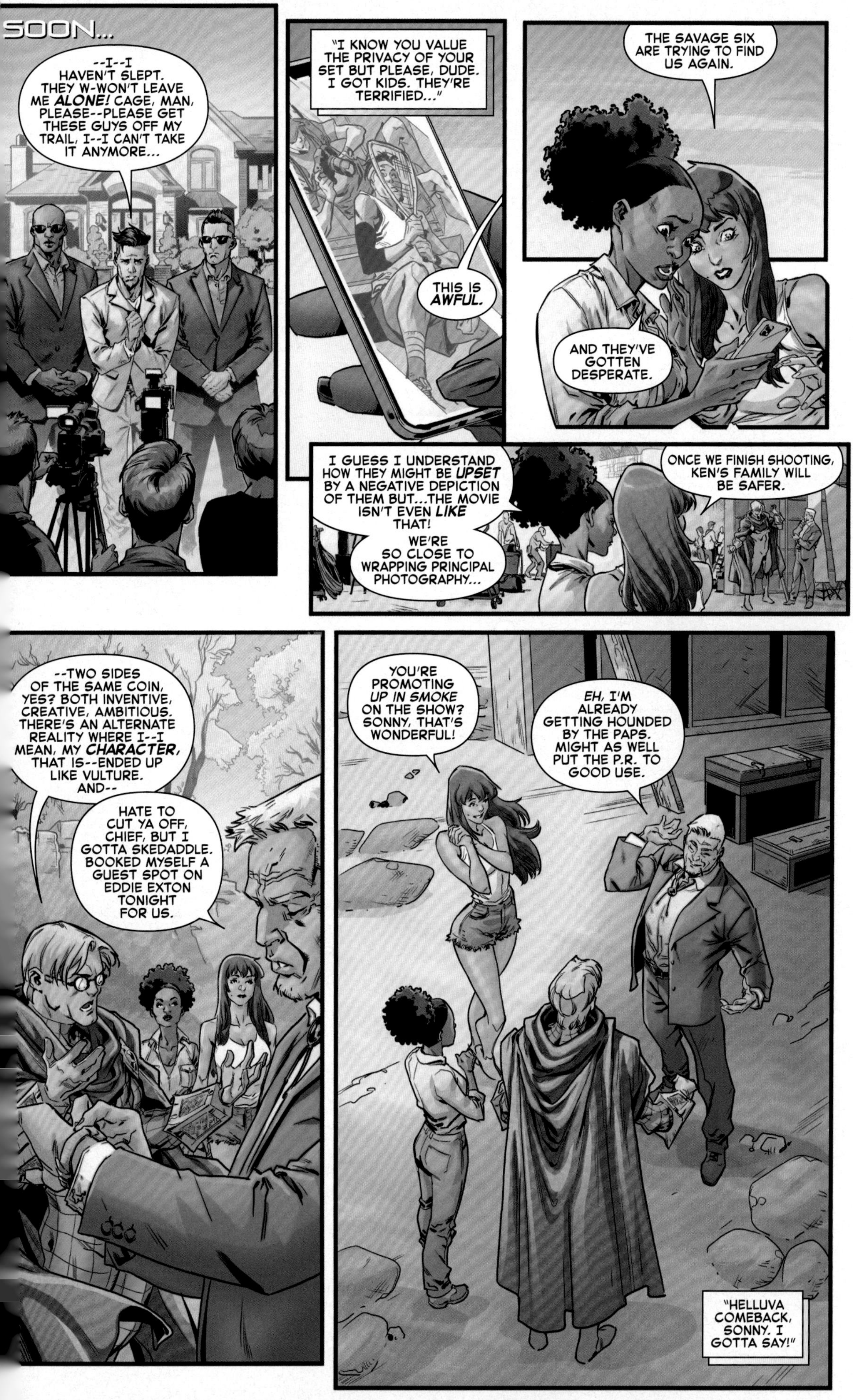
SOON...
--I--I HAVEN'T SLEPT. THEY W-WON'T LEAVE ME ALONE! CAGE, MAN, PLEASE--PLEASE GET THESE GUYS OFF MY TRAIL, I--I CAN'T TAKE IT ANYMORE...
"I KNOW YOU VALUE THE PRIVACY OF YOUR SET BUT PLEASE, DUDE. I GOT KIDS. THEY'RE TERRIFIED..."
THIS IS AWFUL.
THE SAVAGE SIX ARE TRYING TO FIND US AGAIN.
AND THEY'VE GOTTEN DESPERATE.
I GUESS I UNDERSTAND HOW THEY MIGHT BE UPSET BY A NEGATIVE DEPICTION OF THEM BUT...THE MOVIE ISN'T EVEN LIKE THAT!
WE'RE SO CLOSE TO WRAPPING PRINCIPAL PHOTOGRAPHY...
ONCE WE FINISH SHOOTING, KEN'S FAMILY WILL BE SAFER.
--TWO SIDES OF THE SAME COIN, YES? BOTH INVENTIVE, CREATIVE, AMBITIOUS. THERE'S AN ALTERNATE REALITY WHERE I--I MEAN, MY CHARACTER, THAT IS--ENDED UP LIKE VULTURE. AND--
HATE TO CUT YA OFF, CHIEF, BUT I GOTTA SKEDADDLE. BOOKED MYSELF A GUEST SPOT ON EDDIE EXTON TONIGHT FOR US.
YOU'RE PROMOTING UP IN SMOKE ON THE SHOW? SONNY, THAT'S WONDERFUL!
EH, I'M ALREADY GETTING HOUNDED BY THE PAPS. MIGHT AS WELL PUT THE P.R. TO GOOD USE.
"HELLUVA COMEBACK, SONNY. I GOTTA SAY!"

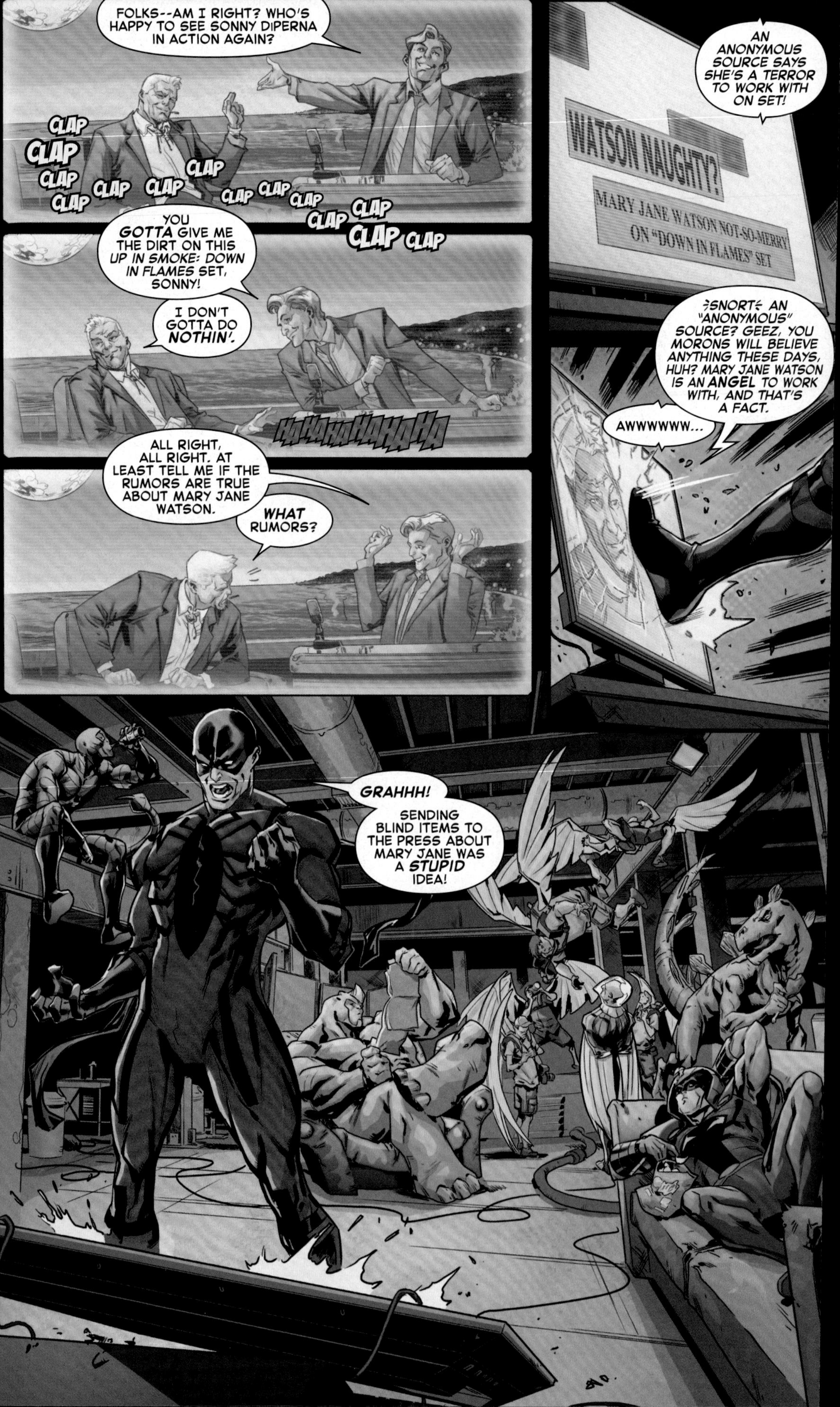

FOLKS--AM I RIGHT? WHO'S HAPPY TO SEE SONNY DIPERNA IN ACTION AGAIN?
CLAP CLAP CLAP CLAP CLAP CLAP CLAP CLAP CLAP CLAP CLAP CLAP CLAP CLAP
YOU GOTTA GIVE ME THE DIRT ON THIS UP IN SMOKE: DOWN IN FLAMES SET, SONNY!
I DON'T GOTTA DO NOTHIN'.
HAHAHAHAHAHAHA
ALL RIGHT, ALL RIGHT. AT LEAST TELL ME IF THE RUMORS ARE TRUE ABOUT MARY JANE WATSON.
WHAT RUMORS?
AN ANONYMOUS SOURCE SAYS SHE'S A TERROR TO WORK WITH ON SET!
WATSON NAUGHTY?
MARY JANE WATSON NOT-SO-MERRY ON "DOWN IN FLAMES" SET
⥽SNORT⥼ AN "ANONYMOUS" SOURCE? GEEZ, YOU MORONS WILL BELIEVE ANYTHING THESE DAYS, HUH? MARY JANE WATSON IS AN ANGEL TO WORK WITH, AND THAT'S A FACT.
AWWWWWW...
GRAHHH!
SENDING BLIND ITEMS TO THE PRESS ABOUT MARY JANE WAS A STUPID IDEA!

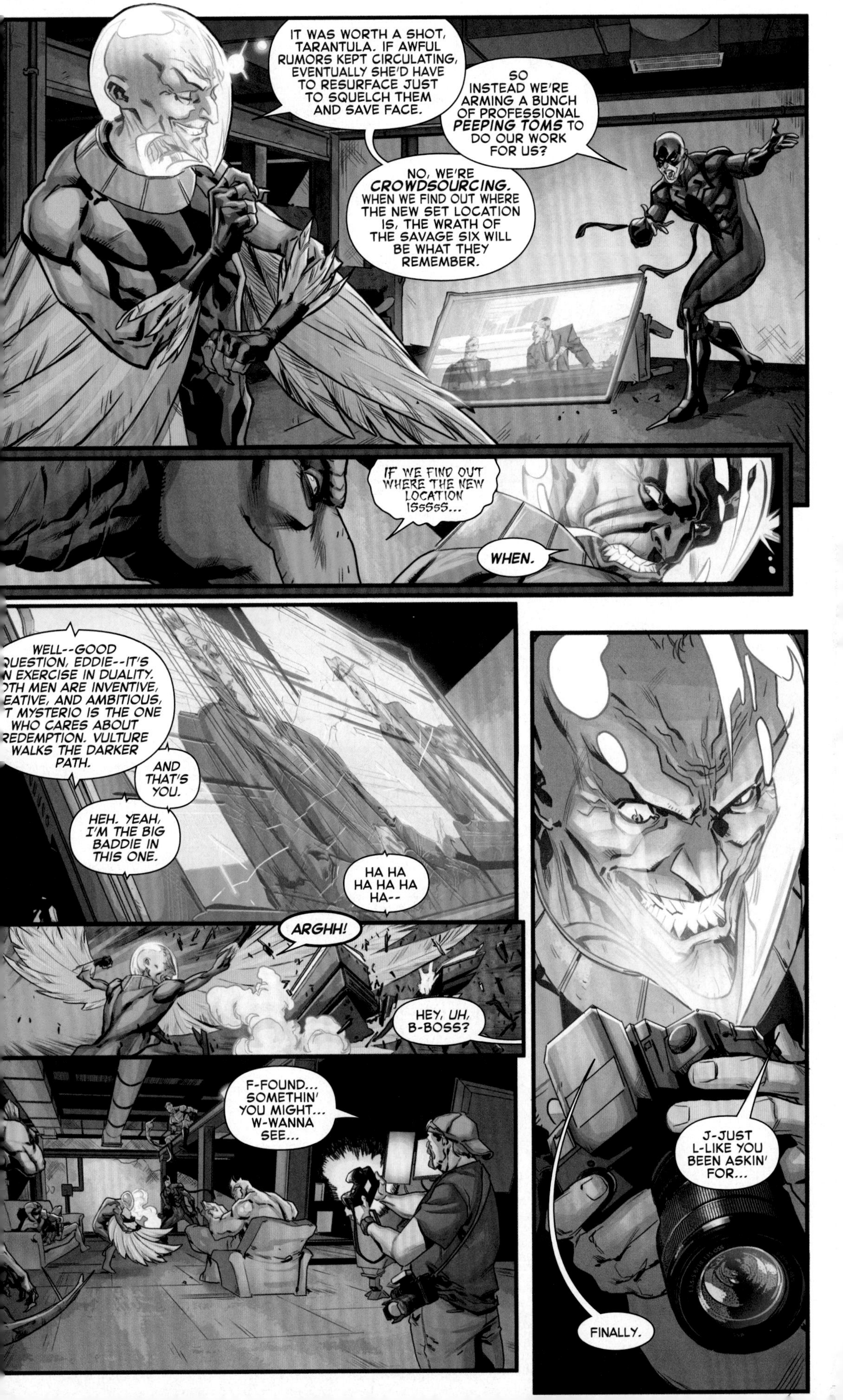
IT WAS WORTH A SHOT, TARANTULA. IF AWFUL RUMORS KEPT CIRCULATING, EVENTUALLY SHE'D HAVE TO RESURFACE JUST TO SQUELCH THEM AND SAVE FACE.
SO INSTEAD WE'RE ARMING A BUNCH OF PROFESSIONAL PEEPING TOMS TO DO OUR WORK FOR US?
NO, WE'RE CROWDSOURCING. WHEN WE FIND OUT WHERE THE NEW SET LOCATION IS, THE WRATH OF THE SAVAGE SIX WILL BE WHAT THEY REMEMBER.
IF WE FIND OUT WHERE THE NEW LOCATION ISSSSS...
WHEN.
WELL--GOOD QUESTION, EDDIE--IT'S AN EXERCISE IN DUALITY. BOTH MEN ARE INVENTIVE, CREATIVE, AND AMBITIOUS, BUT MYSTERIO IS THE ONE WHO CARES ABOUT REDEMPTION. VULTURE WALKS THE DARKER PATH.
AND THAT'S YOU.
HEH. YEAH, I'M THE BIG BADDIE IN THIS ONE.
HA HA HA HA HA HA--
ARGHH!
HEY, UH, B-BOSS?
F-FOUND... SOMETHIN' YOU MIGHT... W-WANNA SEE...
J-JUST L-LIKE YOU BEEN ASKIN' FOR...
FINALLY.

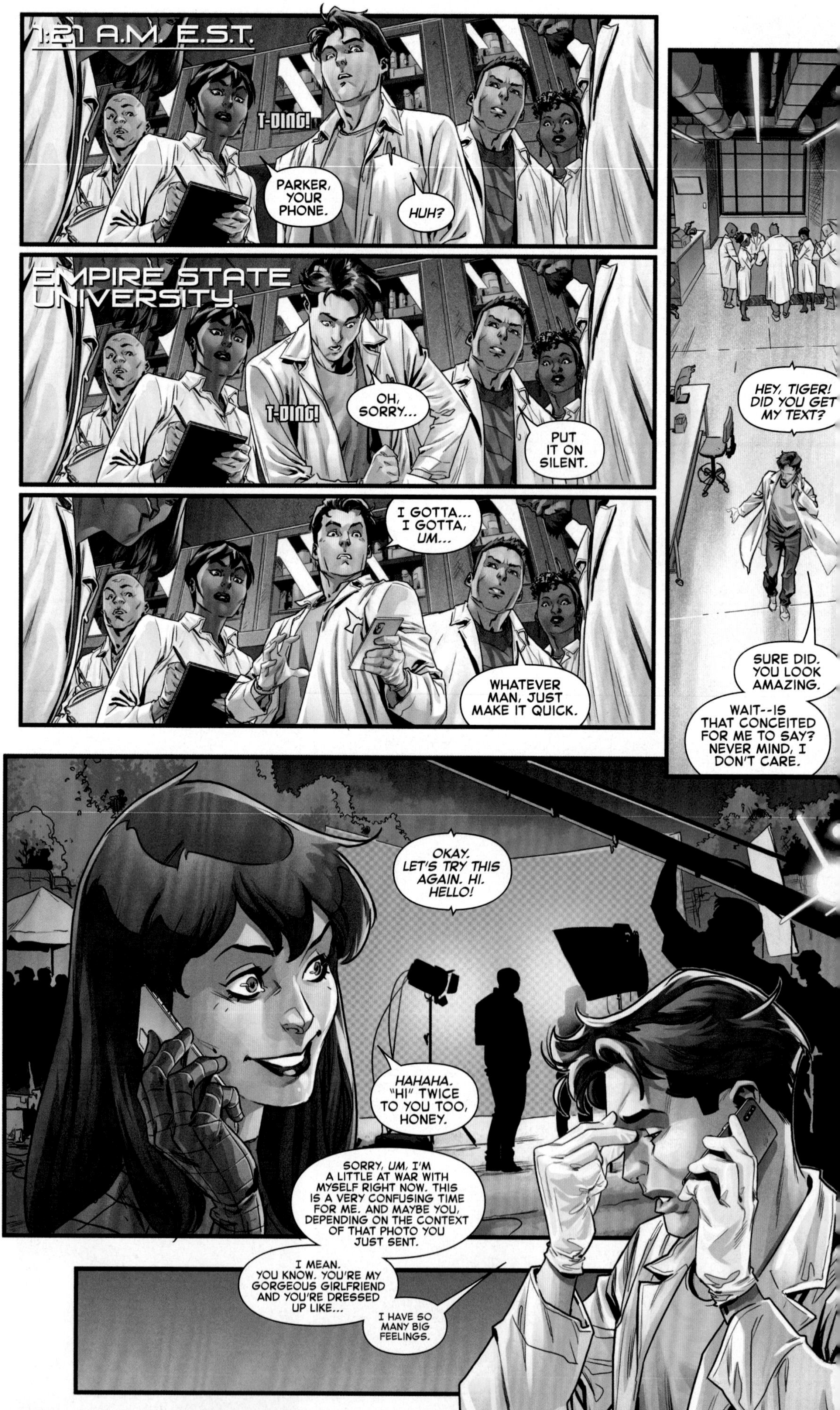

1:21 A.M. E.S.T.
T-DING!
PARKER, YOUR PHONE.
HUH?
EMPIRE STATE UNIVERSITY.
T-DING!
OH, SORRY...
PUT IT ON SILENT.
I GOTTA... I GOTTA, UM...
WHATEVER MAN, JUST MAKE IT QUICK.
HEY, TIGER! DID YOU GET MY TEXT?
SURE DID. YOU LOOK AMAZING.
WAIT--IS THAT CONCEITED FOR ME TO SAY? NEVER MIND, I DON'T CARE.
OKAY. LET'S TRY THIS AGAIN. HI. HELLO!
HAHAHA. "HI" TWICE TO YOU TOO, HONEY.
SORRY, UM, I'M A LITTLE AT WAR WITH MYSELF RIGHT NOW. THIS IS A VERY CONFUSING TIME FOR ME. AND MAYBE YOU, DEPENDING ON THE CONTEXT OF THAT PHOTO YOU JUST SENT.
I MEAN. YOU KNOW. YOU'RE MY GORGEOUS GIRLFRIEND AND YOU'RE DRESSED UP LIKE...
I HAVE SO MANY BIG FEELINGS.

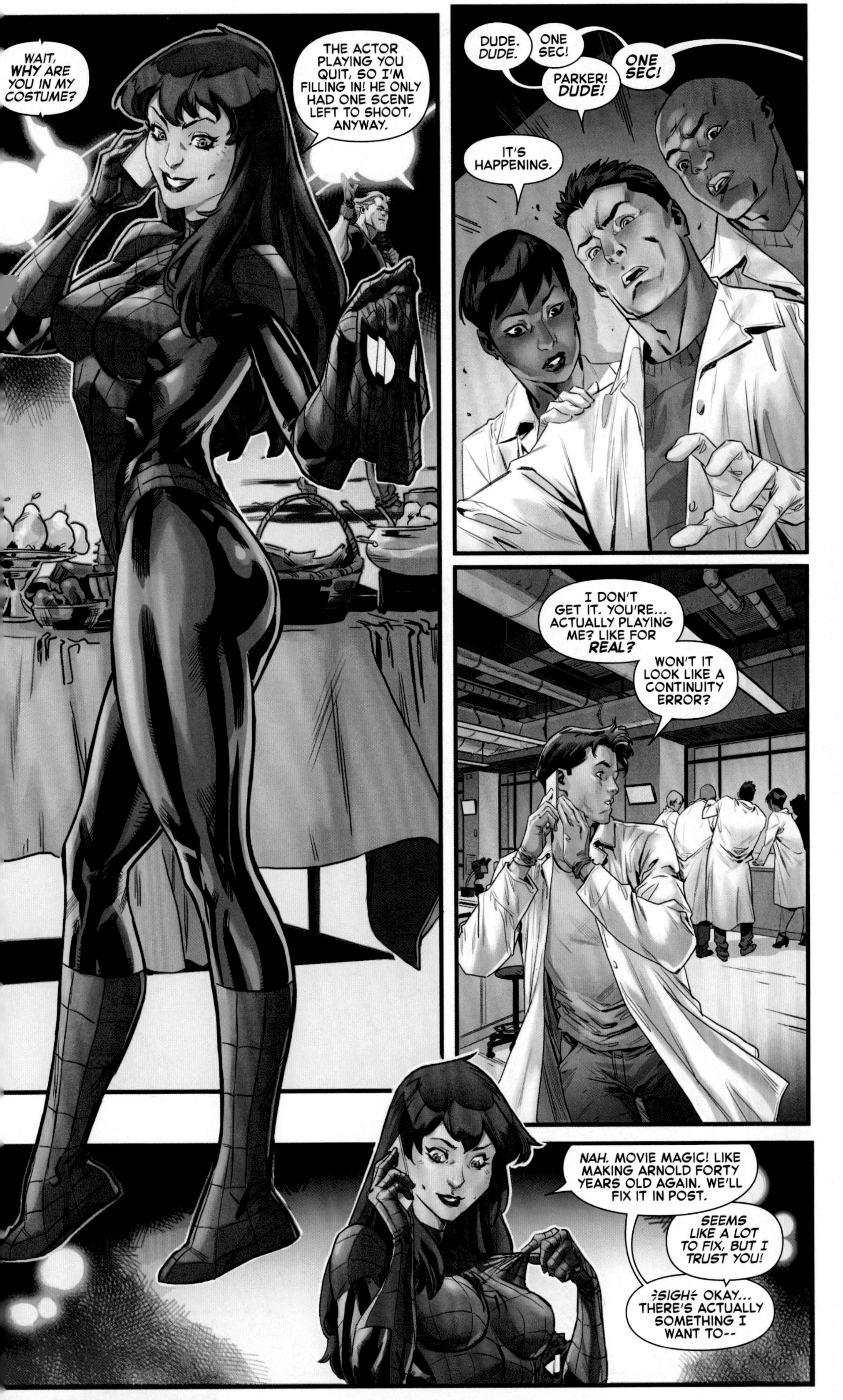
WAIT, WHY ARE YOU IN MY COSTUME?
THE ACTOR PLAYING YOU QUIT, SO I'M FILLING IN! HE ONLY HAD ONE SCENE LEFT TO SHOOT, ANYWAY.
DUDE. DUDE.
ONE SEC!
PARKER! DUDE!
ONE SEC!
IT'S HAPPENING.
I DON'T GET IT. YOU'RE... ACTUALLY PLAYING ME? LIKE FOR REAL?
WON'T IT LOOK LIKE A CONTINUITY ERROR?
NAH. MOVIE MAGIC! LIKE MAKING ARNOLD FORTY YEARS OLD AGAIN. WE'LL FIX IT IN POST.
SEEMS LIKE A LOT TO FIX, BUT I TRUST YOU!
SIGH OKAY... THERE'S ACTUALLY SOMETHING I WANT TO--

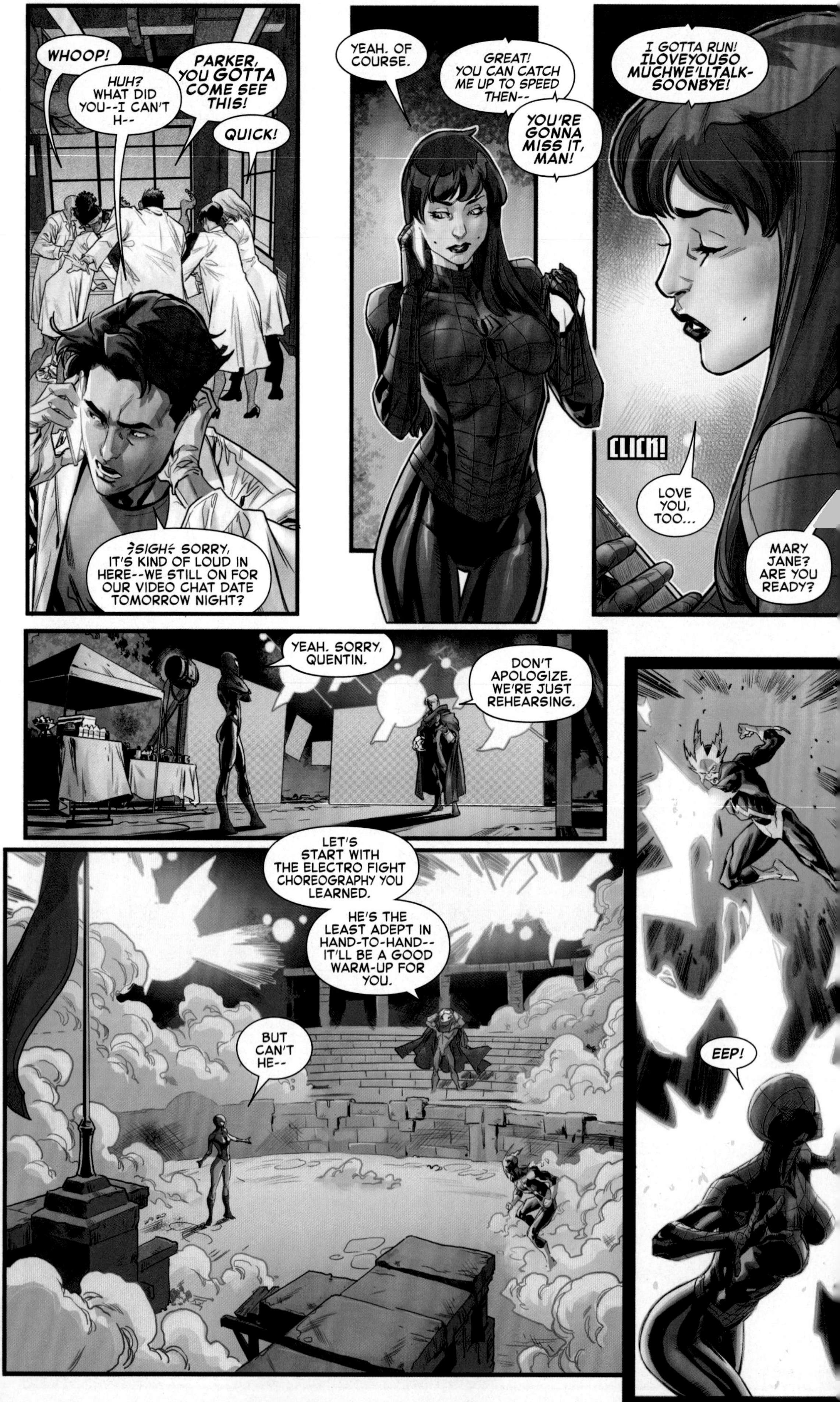
WHOOP!
HUH? WHAT DID YOU--I CAN'T H--
PARKER, YOU GOTTA COME SEE THIS!
QUICK!
SIGH SORRY, IT'S KIND OF LOUD IN HERE--WE STILL ON FOR OUR VIDEO CHAT DATE TOMORROW NIGHT?
YEAH. OF COURSE.
GREAT! YOU CAN CATCH ME UP TO SPEED THEN--
YOU'RE GONNA MISS IT, MAN!
I GOTTA RUN! ILOVEYOUSO MUCHWE'LLTALK-SOONBYE!
CLICK!
LOVE YOU, TOO...
MARY JANE? ARE YOU READY?
YEAH. SORRY, QUENTIN.
DON'T APOLOGIZE. WE'RE JUST REHEARSING.
LET'S START WITH THE ELECTRO FIGHT CHOREOGRAPHY YOU LEARNED.
HE'S THE LEAST ADEPT IN HAND-TO-HAND--IT'LL BE A GOOD WARM-UP FOR YOU.
BUT CAN'T HE--
EEP!

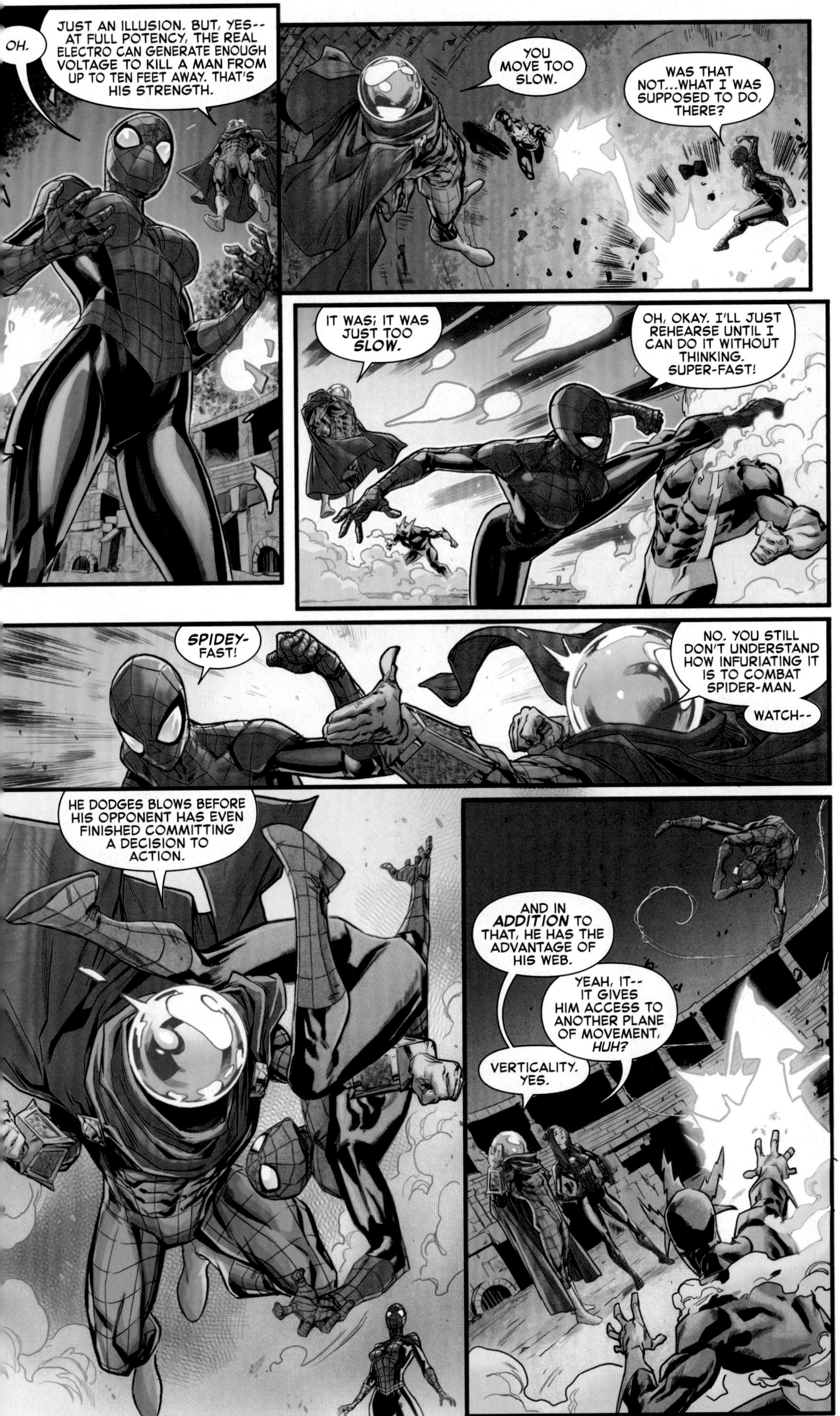
OH.
JUST AN ILLUSION. BUT, YES-- AT FULL POTENCY, THE REAL ELECTRO CAN GENERATE ENOUGH VOLTAGE TO KILL A MAN FROM UP TO TEN FEET AWAY. THAT'S HIS STRENGTH.
YOU MOVE TOO SLOW.
WAS THAT NOT...WHAT I WAS SUPPOSED TO DO, THERE?
IT WAS; IT WAS JUST TOO SLOW.
OH, OKAY. I'LL JUST REHEARSE UNTIL I CAN DO IT WITHOUT THINKING. SUPER-FAST!
SPIDEY-FAST!
NO. YOU STILL DON'T UNDERSTAND HOW INFURIATING IT IS TO COMBAT SPIDER-MAN.
WATCH--
HE DODGES BLOWS BEFORE HIS OPPONENT HAS EVEN FINISHED COMMITTING A DECISION TO ACTION.
AND IN ADDITION TO THAT, HE HAS THE ADVANTAGE OF HIS WEB.
YEAH, IT-- IT GIVES HIM ACCESS TO ANOTHER PLANE OF MOVEMENT, HUH?
VERTICALITY. YES.

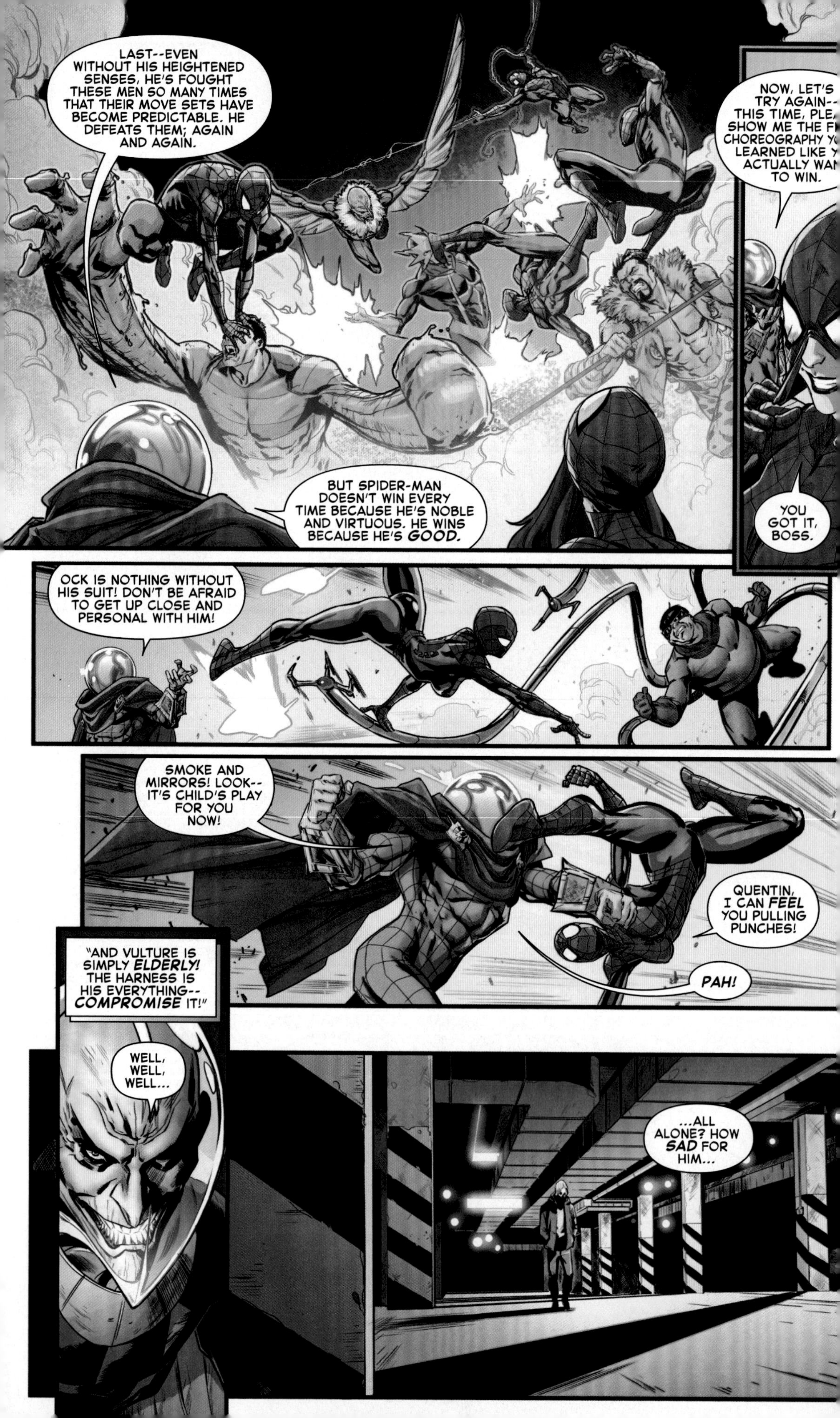
LAST--EVEN WITHOUT HIS HEIGHTENED SENSES, HE'S FOUGHT THESE MEN SO MANY TIMES THAT THEIR MOVE SETS HAVE BECOME PREDICTABLE. HE DEFEATS THEM; AGAIN AND AGAIN.
BUT SPIDER-MAN DOESN'T WIN EVERY TIME BECAUSE HE'S NOBLE AND VIRTUOUS. HE WINS BECAUSE HE'S GOOD.
NOW, LET'S TRY AGAIN--THIS TIME, PLE
SHOW ME THE F
CHOREOGRAPHY Y
LEARNED LIKE Y
ACTUALLY WA
TO WIN.
YOU GOT IT, BOSS.
OCK IS NOTHING WITHOUT HIS SUIT! DON'T BE AFRAID TO GET UP CLOSE AND PERSONAL WITH HIM!
SMOKE AND MIRRORS! LOOK--IT'S CHILD'S PLAY FOR YOU NOW!
QUENTIN, I CAN FEEL YOU PULLING PUNCHES!
PAH!
"AND VULTURE IS SIMPLY ELDERLY! THE HARNESS IS HIS EVERYTHING--COMPROMISE IT!"
WELL, WELL, WELL...
...ALL ALONE? HOW SAD FOR HIM...

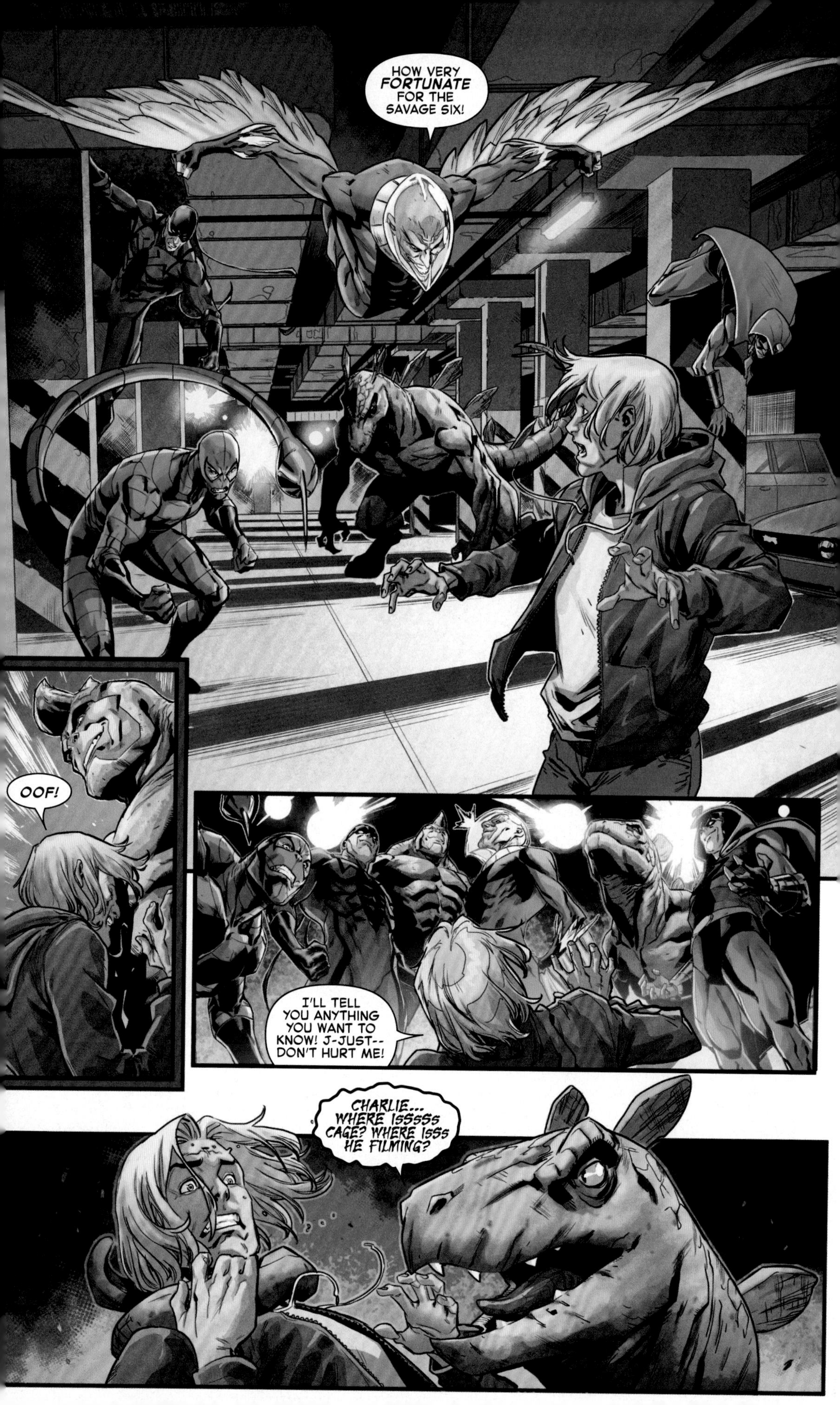

HOW VERY FORTUNATE FOR THE SAVAGE SIX!
OOF!
I'LL TELL YOU ANYTHING YOU WANT TO KNOW! J-JUST-- DON'T HURT ME!
CHARLIE... WHERE ISSSSS CAGE? WHERE ISSS HE FILMING?

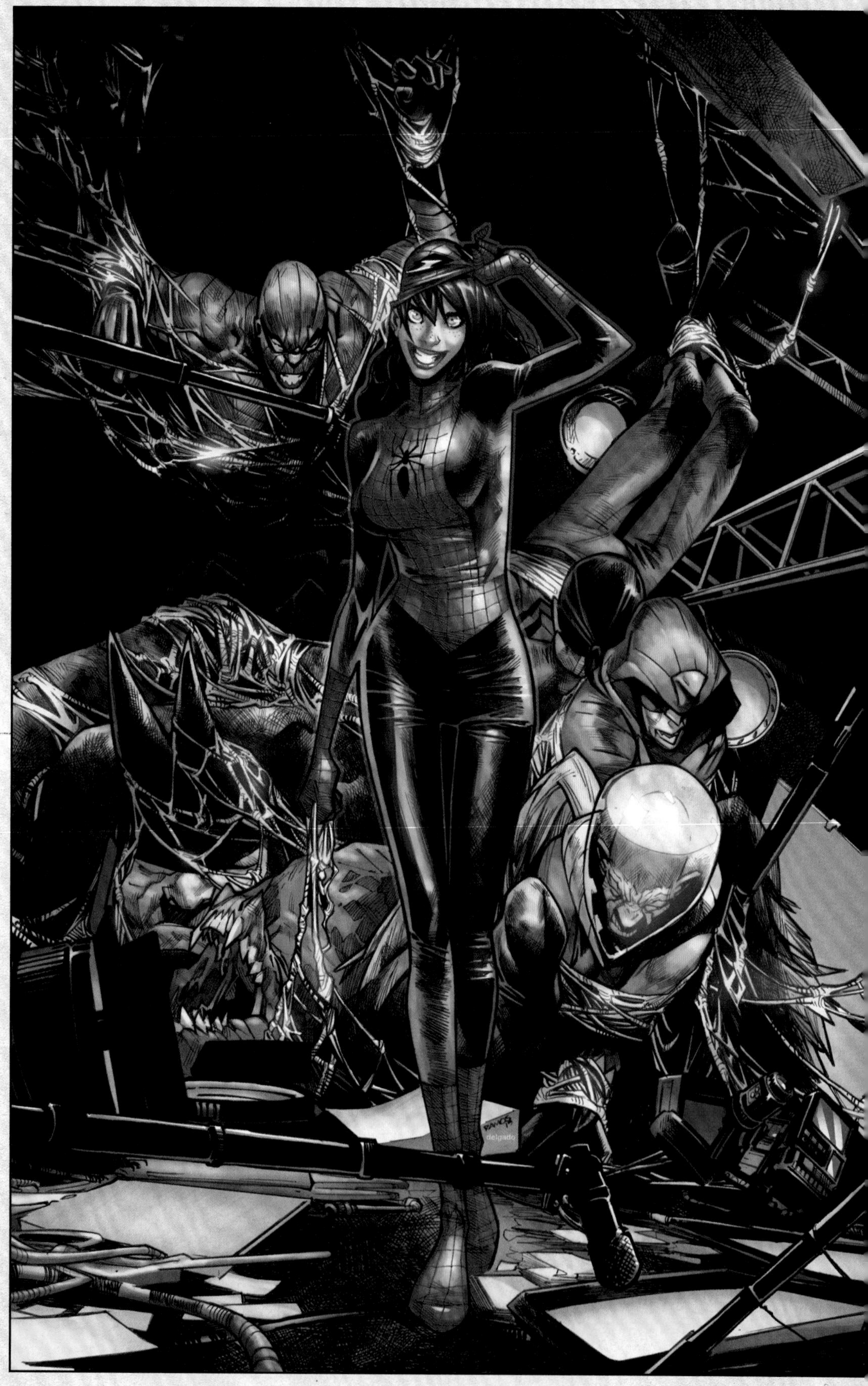

5

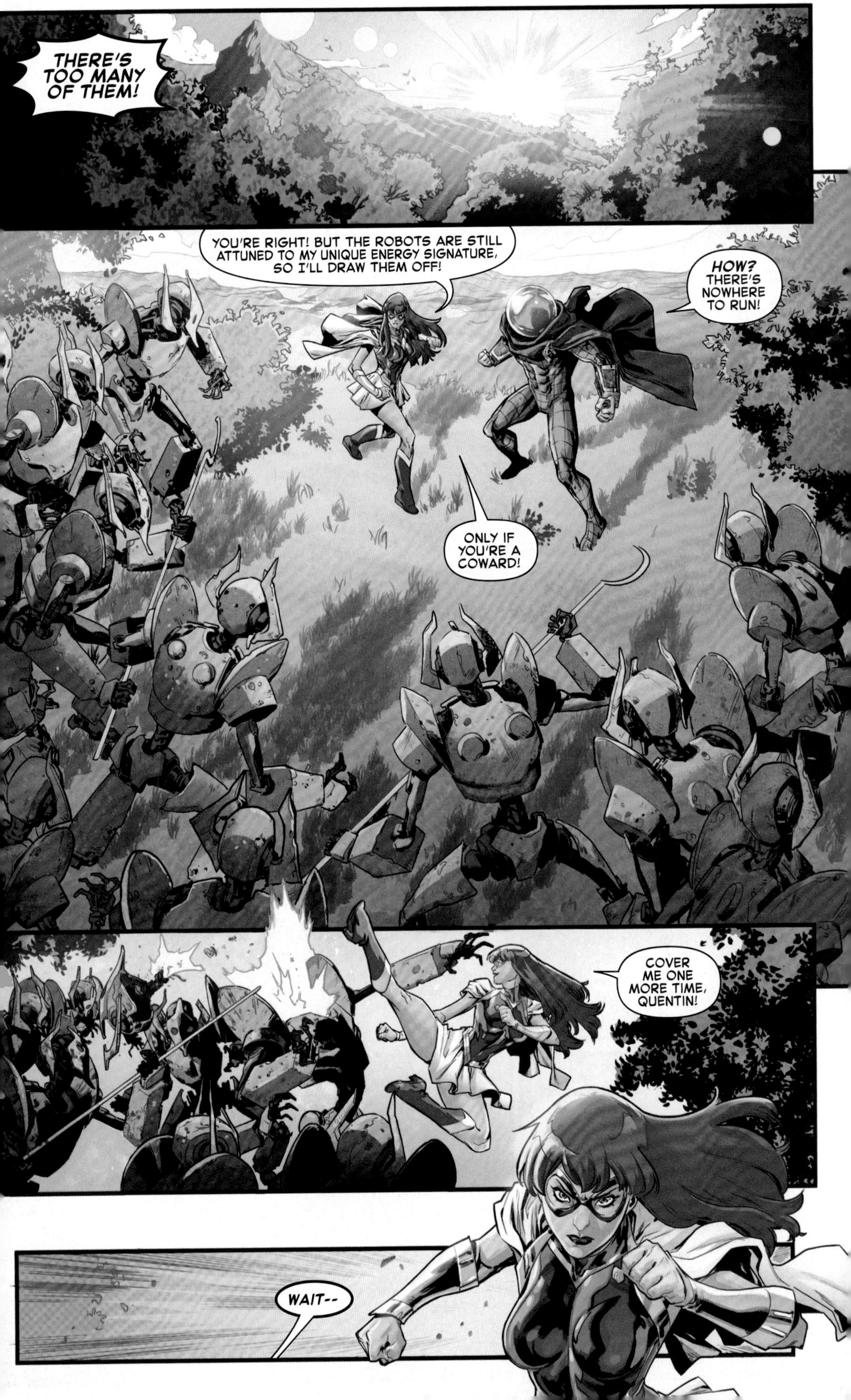
THERE'S TOO MANY OF THEM!
YOU'RE RIGHT! BUT THE ROBOTS ARE STILL ATTUNED TO MY UNIQUE ENERGY SIGNATURE, SO I'LL DRAW THEM OFF!
HOW? THERE'S NOWHERE TO RUN!
ONLY IF YOU'RE A COWARD!
COVER ME ONE MORE TIME, QUENTIN!
WAIT--

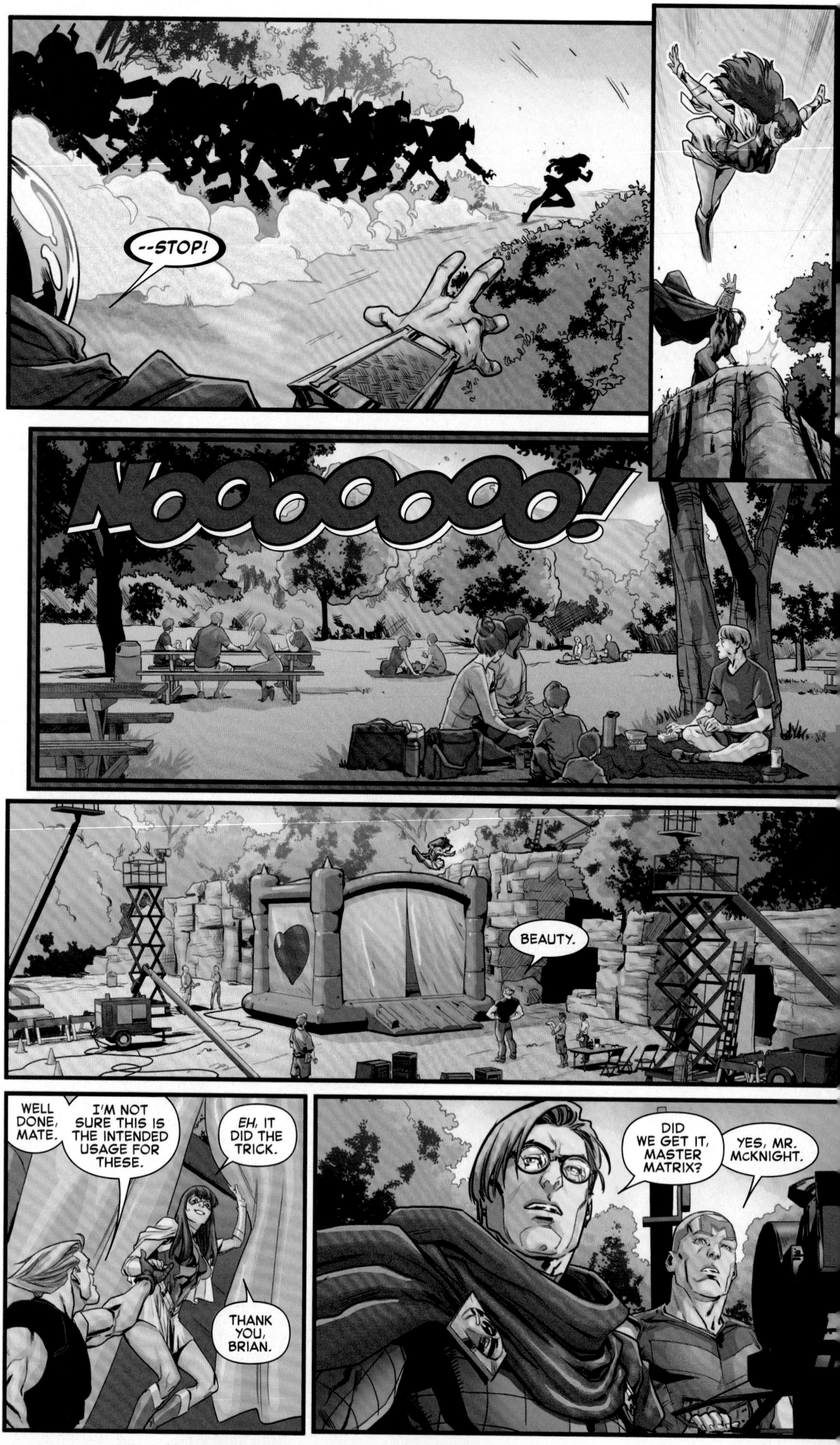
--STOP!
NOOOOOOO!
BEAUTY.
WELL DONE, MATE.
I'M NOT SURE THIS IS THE INTENDED USAGE FOR THESE.
EH, IT DID THE TRICK.
THANK YOU, BRIAN.
DID WE GET IT, MASTER MATRIX?
YES, MR. McKNIGHT.

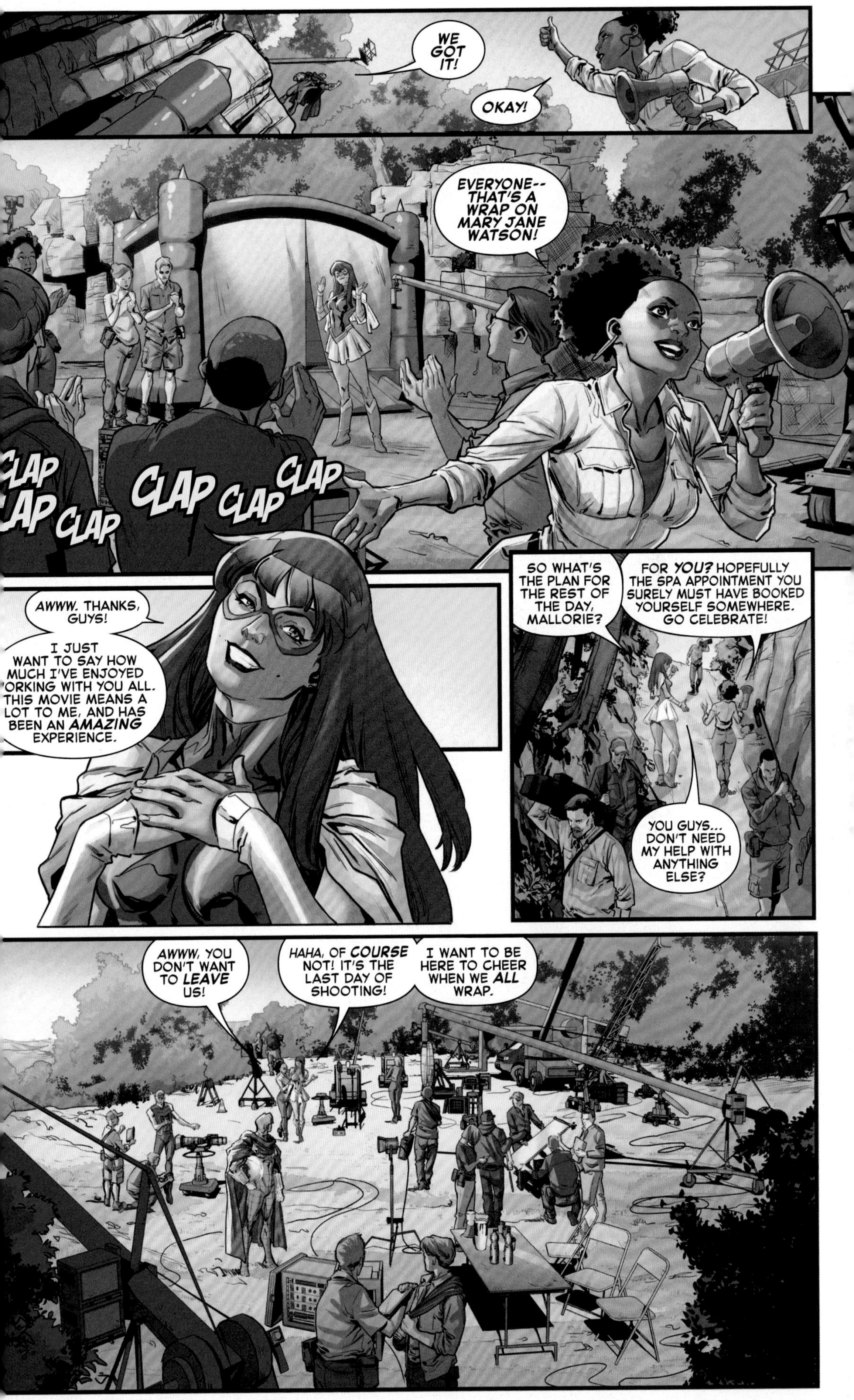

WE GOT IT!
OKAY!
EVERYONE-- THAT'S A WRAP ON MARY JANE WATSON!
CLAP CLAP CLAP CLAP CLAP CLAP
AWWW. THANKS, GUYS!
I JUST WANT TO SAY HOW MUCH I'VE ENJOYED WORKING WITH YOU ALL. THIS MOVIE MEANS A LOT TO ME, AND HAS BEEN AN AMAZING EXPERIENCE.
SO WHAT'S THE PLAN FOR THE REST OF THE DAY, MALLORIE?
FOR YOU? HOPEFULLY THE SPA APPOINTMENT YOU SURELY MUST HAVE BOOKED YOURSELF SOMEWHERE. GO CELEBRATE!
YOU GUYS... DON'T NEED MY HELP WITH ANYTHING ELSE?
AWWW, YOU DON'T WANT TO LEAVE US!
HAHA, OF COURSE NOT! IT'S THE LAST DAY OF SHOOTING!
I WANT TO BE HERE TO CHEER WHEN WE ALL WRAP.

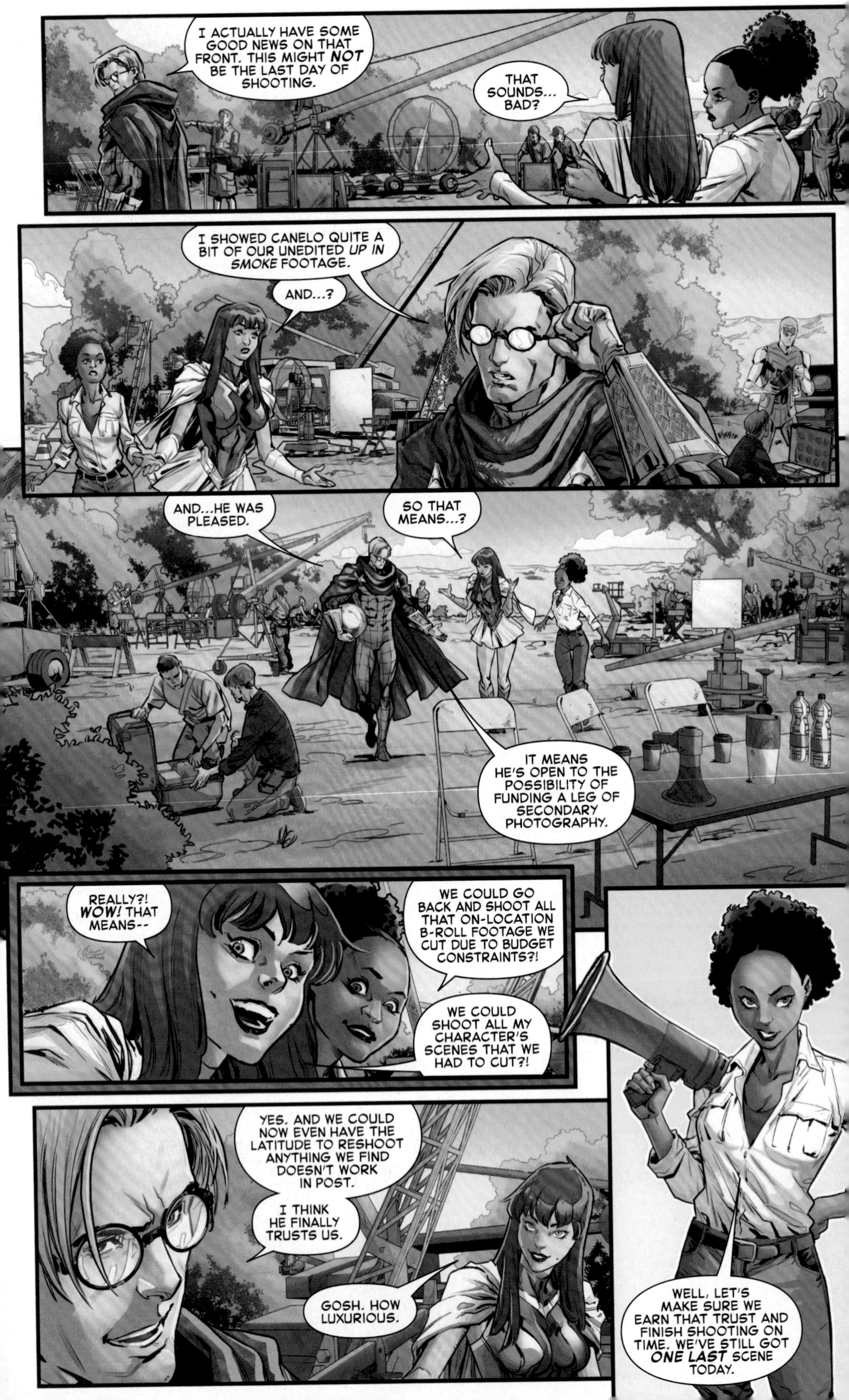
I ACTUALLY HAVE SOME GOOD NEWS ON THAT FRONT. THIS MIGHT NOT BE THE LAST DAY OF SHOOTING.
THAT SOUNDS... BAD?
I SHOWED CANELO QUITE A BIT OF OUR UNEDITED UP IN SMOKE FOOTAGE.
AND...?
AND...HE WAS PLEASED.
SO THAT MEANS...?
IT MEANS HE'S OPEN TO THE POSSIBILITY OF FUNDING A LEG OF SECONDARY PHOTOGRAPHY.
REALLY?! WOW! THAT MEANS--
WE COULD GO BACK AND SHOOT ALL THAT ON-LOCATION B-ROLL FOOTAGE WE CUT DUE TO BUDGET CONSTRAINTS?!
WE COULD SHOOT ALL MY CHARACTER'S SCENES THAT WE HAD TO CUT?!
YES. AND WE COULD NOW EVEN HAVE THE LATITUDE TO RESHOOT ANYTHING WE FIND DOESN'T WORK IN POST.
I THINK HE FINALLY TRUSTS US.
GOSH. HOW LUXURIOUS.
WELL, LET'S MAKE SURE WE EARN THAT TRUST AND FINISH SHOOTING ON TIME. WE'VE STILL GOT ONE LAST SCENE TODAY.

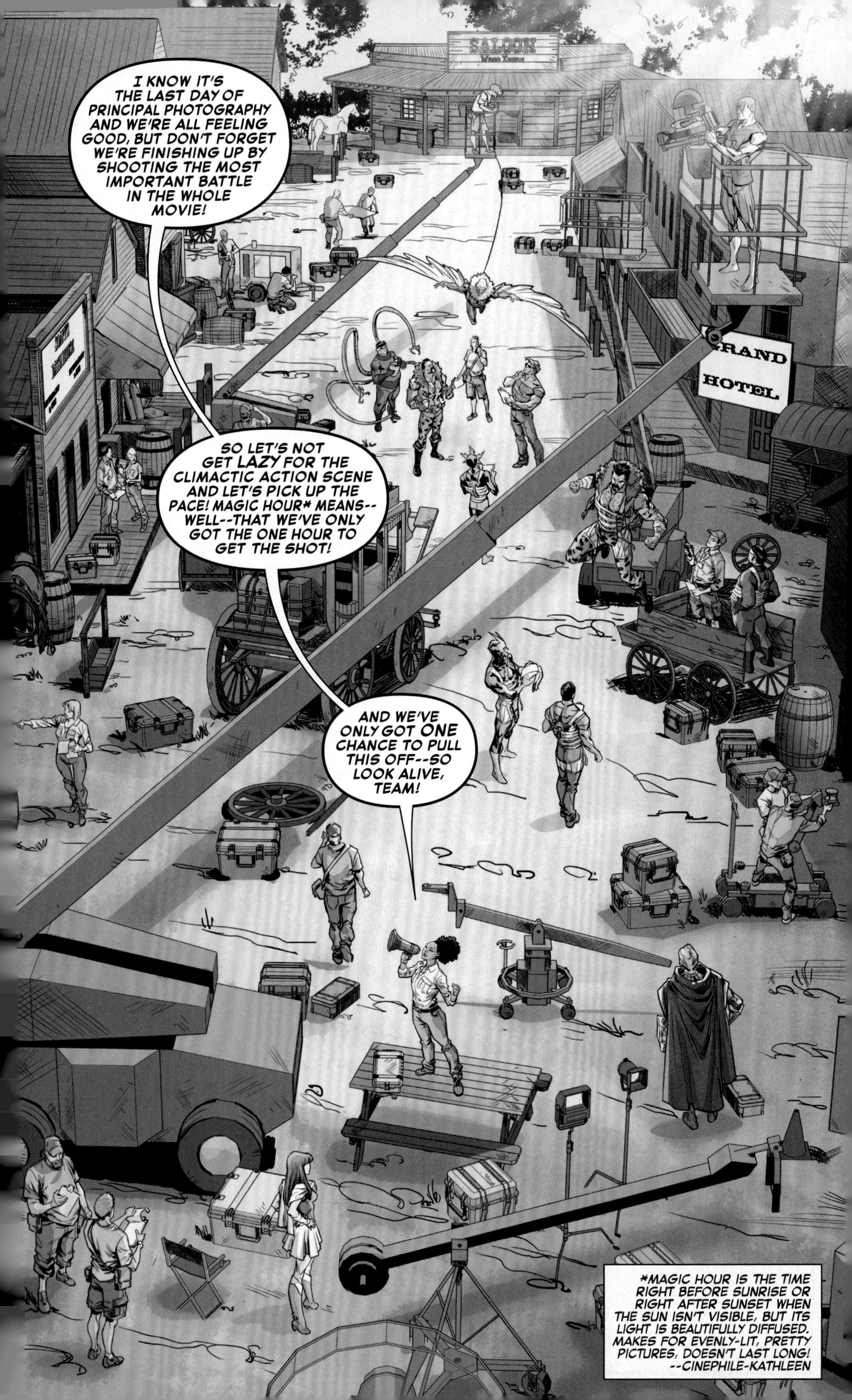
SALOON
I KNOW IT'S THE LAST DAY OF PRINCIPAL PHOTOGRAPHY AND WE'RE ALL FEELING GOOD, BUT DON'T FORGET WE'RE FINISHING UP BY SHOOTING THE MOST IMPORTANT BATTLE IN THE WHOLE MOVIE!
GRAND HOTEL
SO LET'S NOT GET LAZY FOR THE CLIMACTIC ACTION SCENE AND LET'S PICK UP THE PACE! MAGIC HOUR* MEANS-- WELL--THAT WE'VE ONLY GOT THE ONE HOUR TO GET THE SHOT!
AND WE'VE ONLY GOT ONE CHANCE TO PULL THIS OFF--SO LOOK ALIVE, TEAM!
*MAGIC HOUR IS THE TIME RIGHT BEFORE SUNRISE OR RIGHT AFTER SUNSET WHEN THE SUN ISN'T VISIBLE, BUT ITS LIGHT IS BEAUTIFULLY DIFFUSED. MAKES FOR EVENLY-LIT, PRETTY PICTURES, DOESN'T LAST LONG! --CINEPHILE-KATHLEEN

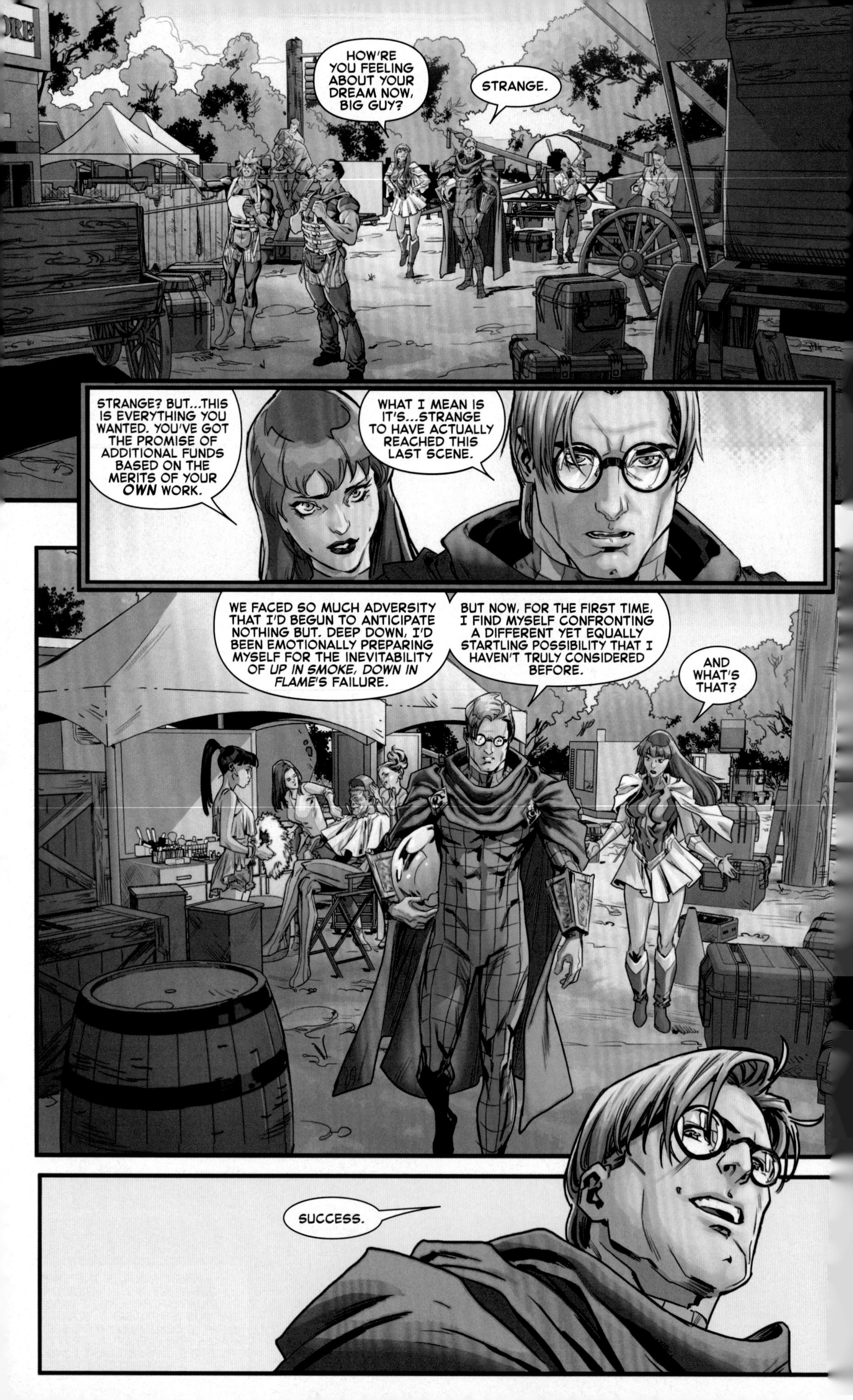
HOW'RE YOU FEELING ABOUT YOUR DREAM NOW, BIG GUY?
STRANGE.
STRANGE? BUT...THIS IS EVERYTHING YOU WANTED. YOU'VE GOT THE PROMISE OF ADDITIONAL FUNDS BASED ON THE MERITS OF YOUR *OWN* WORK.
WHAT I MEAN IS IT'S...STRANGE TO HAVE ACTUALLY REACHED THIS LAST SCENE.
WE FACED SO MUCH ADVERSITY THAT I'D BEGUN TO ANTICIPATE NOTHING BUT. DEEP DOWN, I'D BEEN EMOTIONALLY PREPARING MYSELF FOR THE INEVITABILITY OF *UP IN SMOKE, DOWN IN FLAME*'S FAILURE.
BUT NOW, FOR THE FIRST TIME, I FIND MYSELF CONFRONTING A DIFFERENT YET EQUALLY STARTLING POSSIBILITY THAT I HAVEN'T TRULY CONSIDERED BEFORE.
AND WHAT'S THAT?
SUCCESS.

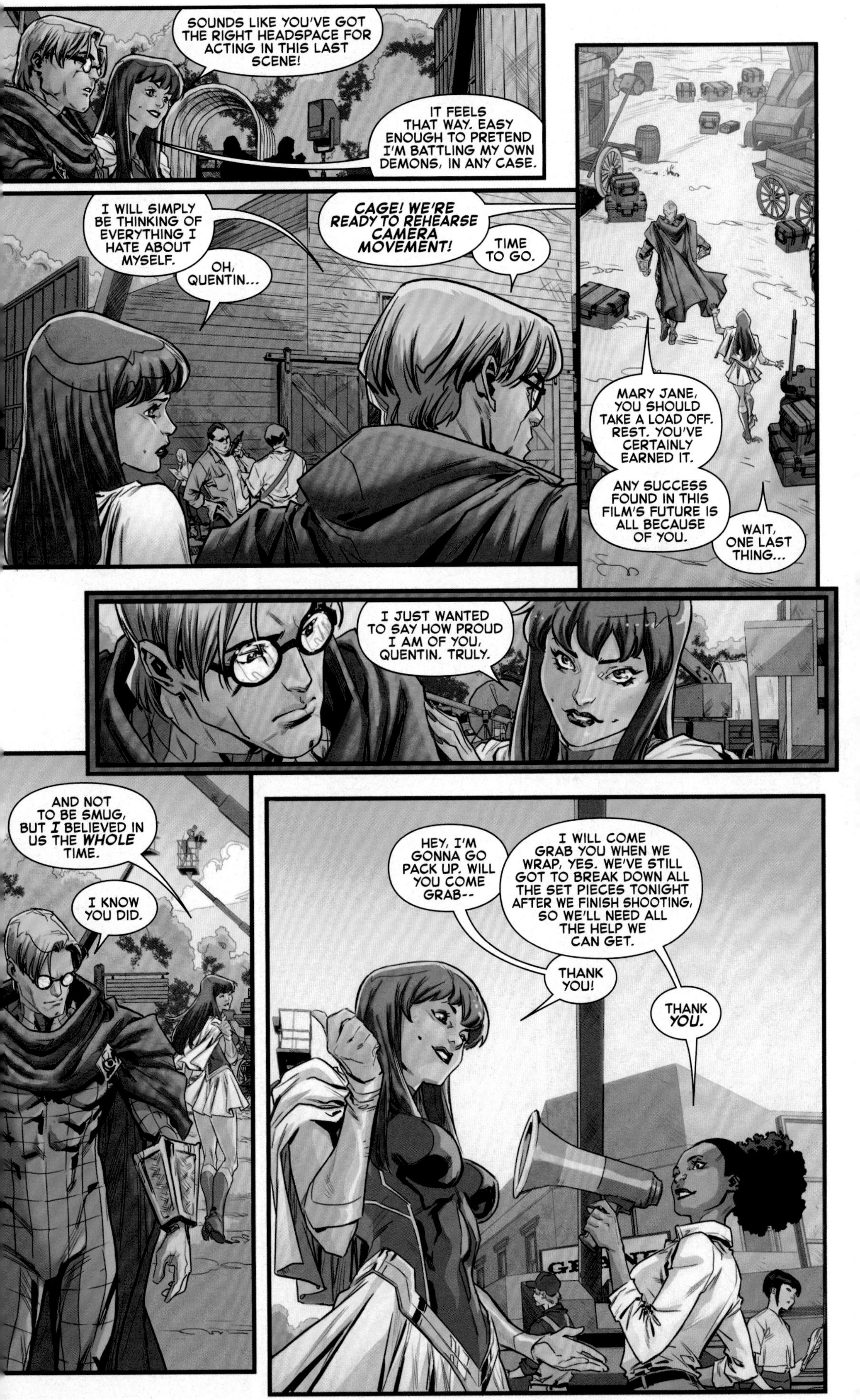
SOUNDS LIKE YOU'VE GOT THE RIGHT HEADSPACE FOR ACTING IN THIS LAST SCENE!
IT FEELS THAT WAY. EASY ENOUGH TO PRETEND I'M BATTLING MY OWN DEMONS, IN ANY CASE.
I WILL SIMPLY BE THINKING OF EVERYTHING I HATE ABOUT MYSELF.
OH, QUENTIN...
CAGE! WE'RE READY TO REHEARSE CAMERA MOVEMENT!
TIME TO GO.
MARY JANE, YOU SHOULD TAKE A LOAD OFF. REST. YOU'VE CERTAINLY EARNED IT.
ANY SUCCESS FOUND IN THIS FILM'S FUTURE IS ALL BECAUSE OF YOU.
WAIT, ONE LAST THING...
I JUST WANTED TO SAY HOW PROUD I AM OF YOU, QUENTIN. TRULY.
AND NOT TO BE SMUG, BUT I BELIEVED IN US THE WHOLE TIME.
I KNOW YOU DID.
HEY, I'M GONNA GO PACK UP. WILL YOU COME GRAB--
I WILL COME GRAB YOU WHEN WE WRAP, YES. WE'VE STILL GOT TO BREAK DOWN ALL THE SET PIECES TONIGHT AFTER WE FINISH SHOOTING, SO WE'LL NEED ALL THE HELP WE CAN GET.
THANK YOU!
THANK YOU.

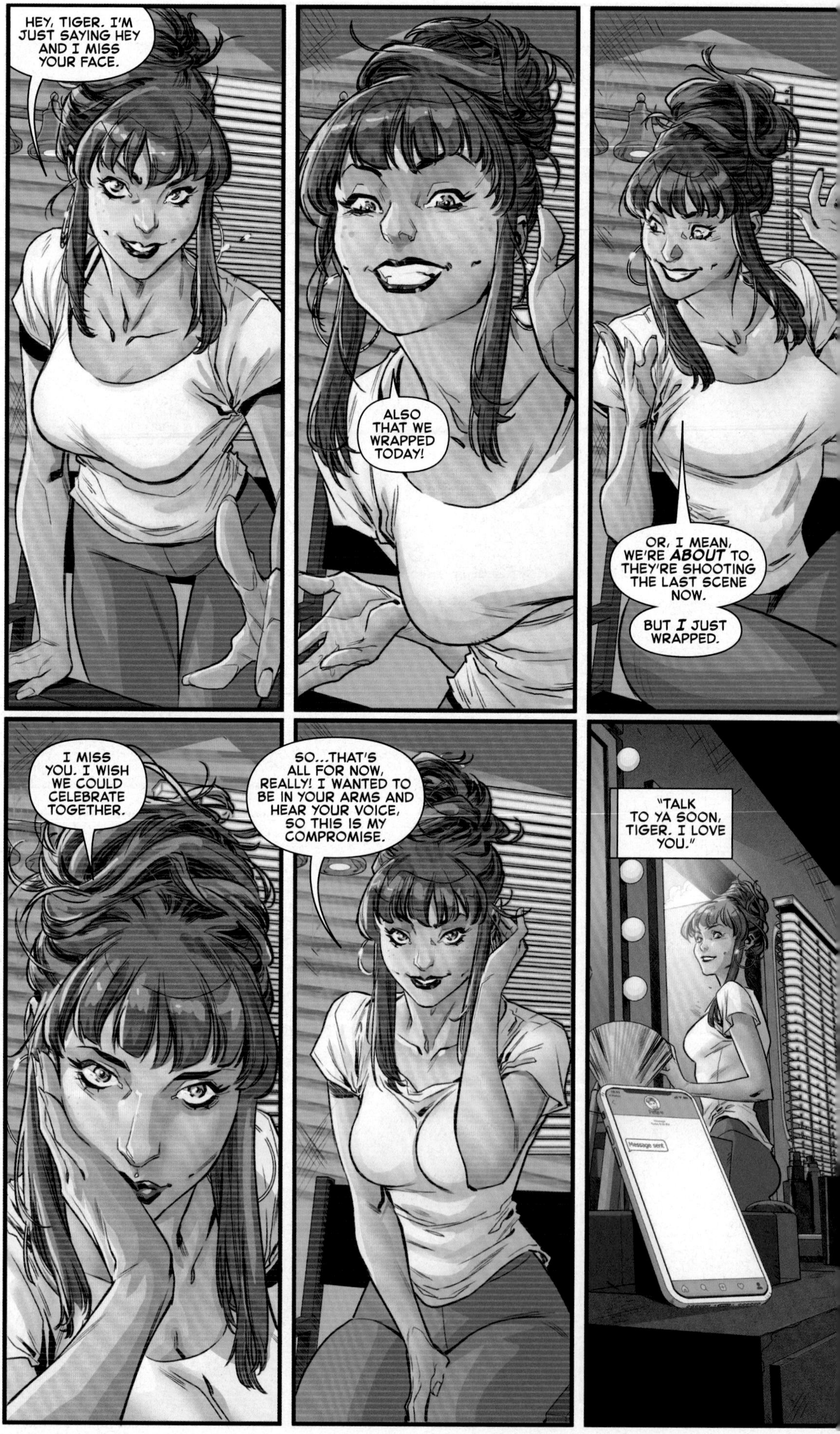
HEY, TIGER. I'M JUST SAYING HEY AND I MISS YOUR FACE.
ALSO THAT WE WRAPPED TODAY!
OR, I MEAN, WE'RE *ABOUT* TO. THEY'RE SHOOTING THE LAST SCENE NOW.
BUT *I* JUST WRAPPED.
I MISS YOU. I WISH WE COULD CELEBRATE TOGETHER.
SO...THAT'S ALL FOR NOW, REALLY! I WANTED TO BE IN YOUR ARMS AND HEAR YOUR VOICE, SO THIS IS MY COMPROMISE.
"TALK TO YA SOON, TIGER. I LOVE YOU."
Message sent

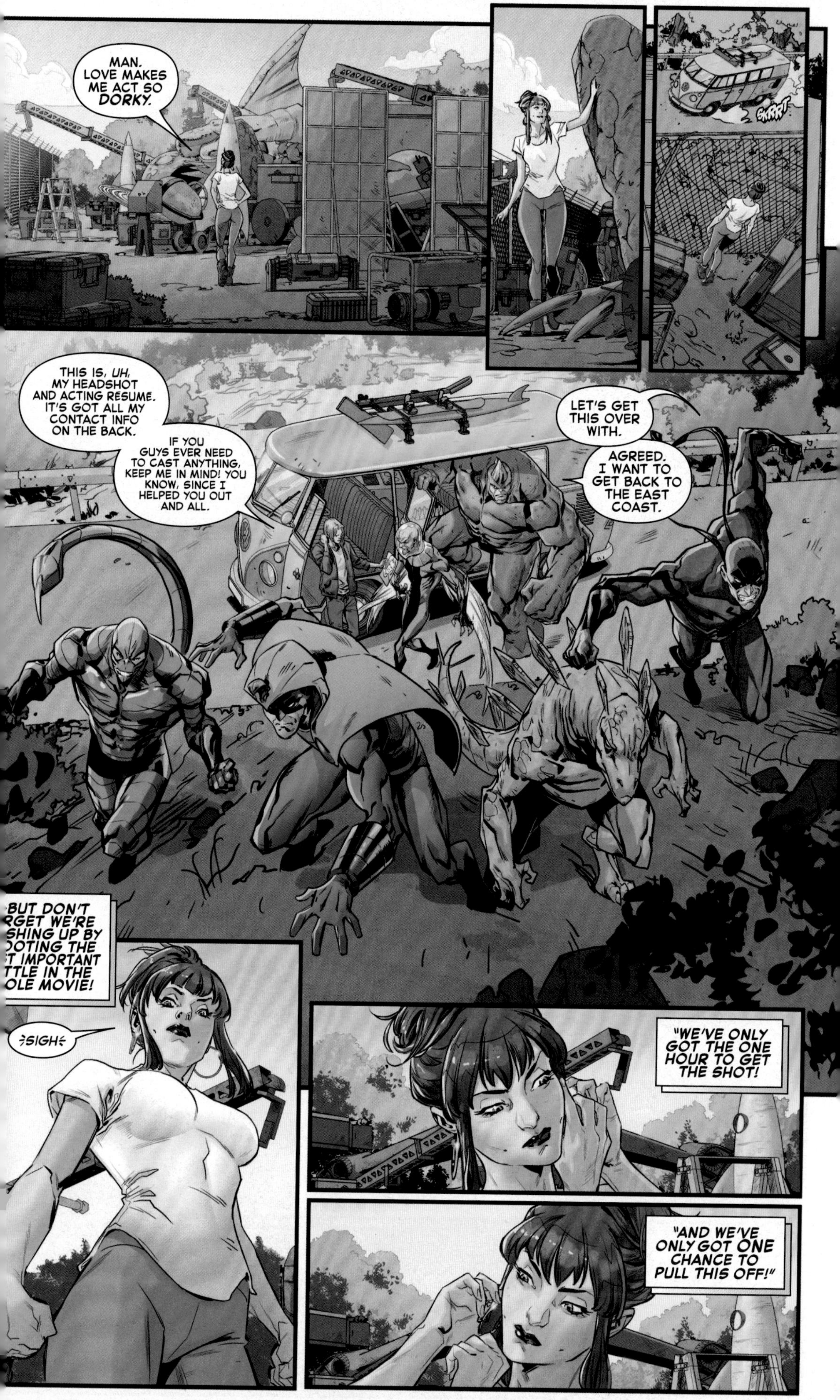

MAN. LOVE MAKES ME ACT SO *DORKY.*
SKRRT
THIS IS, *UH,* MY HEADSHOT AND ACTING RESUME. IT'S GOT ALL MY CONTACT INFO ON THE BACK.
IF YOU GUYS EVER NEED TO CAST ANYTHING, KEEP ME IN MIND! YOU KNOW, SINCE I HELPED YOU OUT AND ALL.
LET'S GET THIS OVER WITH.
AGREED. I WANT TO GET BACK TO THE EAST COAST.
BUT DON'T RGET WE'RE SHING UP BY OOTING THE T IMPORTANT TTLE IN THE OLE MOVIE!
SIGH
"WE'VE ONLY GOT THE ONE HOUR TO GET THE SHOT!
"AND WE'VE ONLY GOT ONE CHANCE TO PULL THIS OFF!"

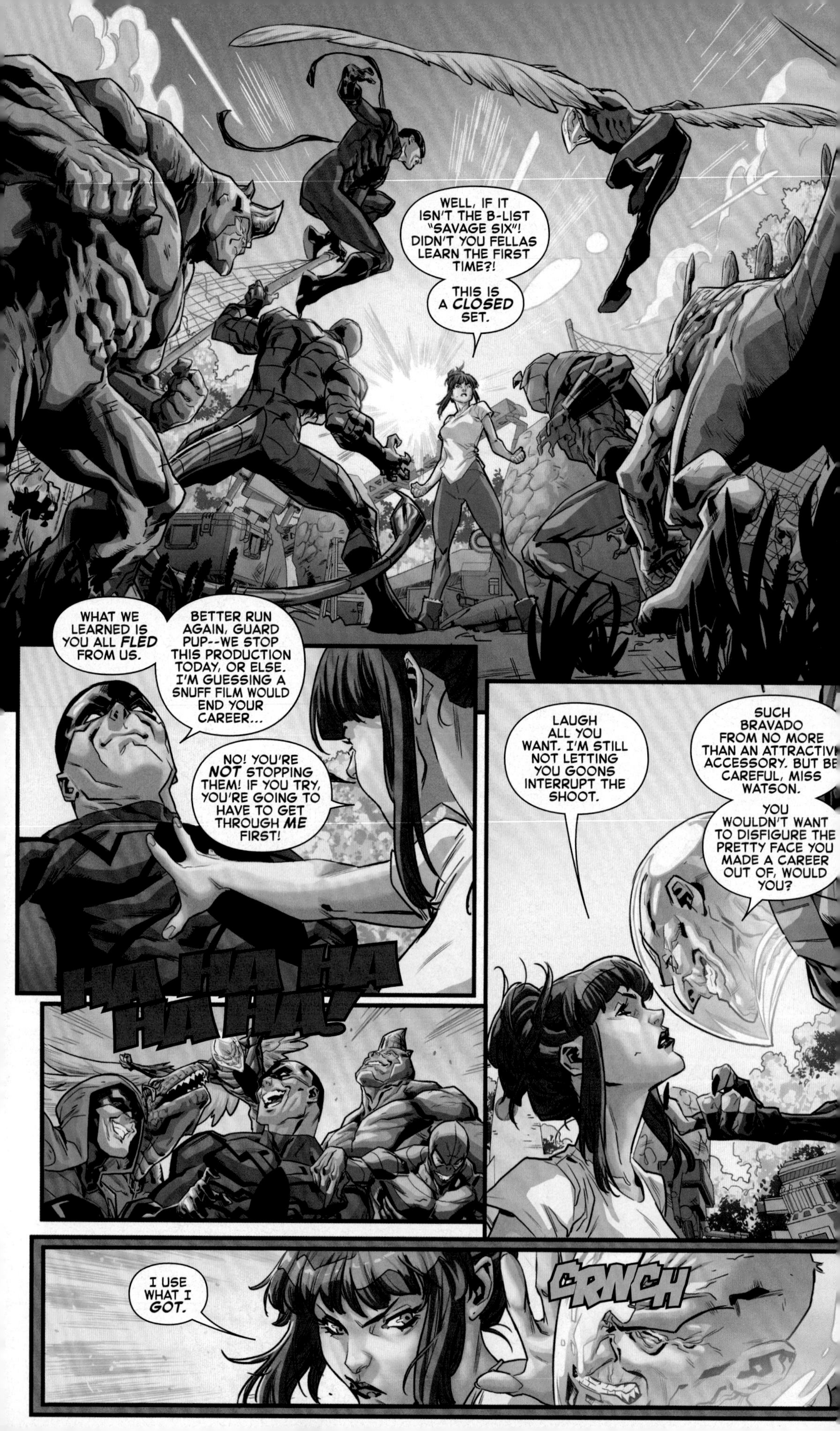
WELL, IF IT ISN'T THE B-LIST "SAVAGE SIX"! DIDN'T YOU FELLAS LEARN THE FIRST TIME?!
THIS IS A CLOSED SET.
WHAT WE LEARNED IS YOU ALL FLED FROM US.
BETTER RUN AGAIN, GUARD PUP--WE STOP THIS PRODUCTION TODAY, OR ELSE. I'M GUESSING A SNUFF FILM WOULD END YOUR CAREER...
NO! YOU'RE NOT STOPPING THEM! IF YOU TRY, YOU'RE GOING TO HAVE TO GET THROUGH ME FIRST!
HA HA HA HA HA HA!
LAUGH ALL YOU WANT. I'M STILL NOT LETTING YOU GOONS INTERRUPT THE SHOOT.
SUCH BRAVADO FROM NO MORE THAN AN ATTRACTIV ACCESSORY. BUT BE CAREFUL, MISS WATSON.
YOU WOULDN'T WANT TO DISFIGURE THE PRETTY FACE YOU MADE A CAREER OUT OF, WOULD YOU?
I USE WHAT I GOT.
CRNCH

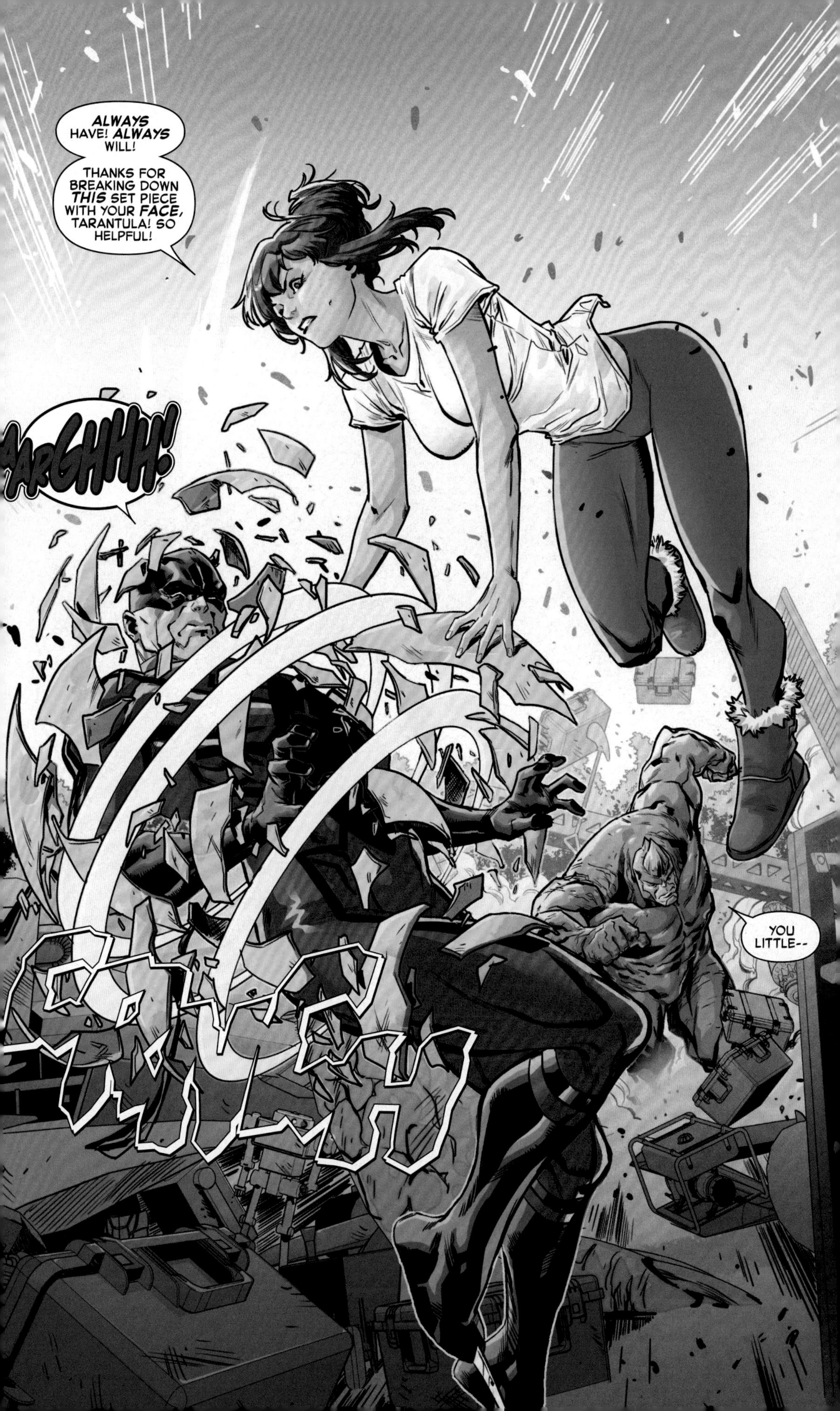
ALWAYS HAVE! ALWAYS WILL!
THANKS FOR BREAKING DOWN THIS SET PIECE WITH YOUR FACE, TARANTULA! SO HELPFUL!
AARGHHH!
YOU LITTLE--

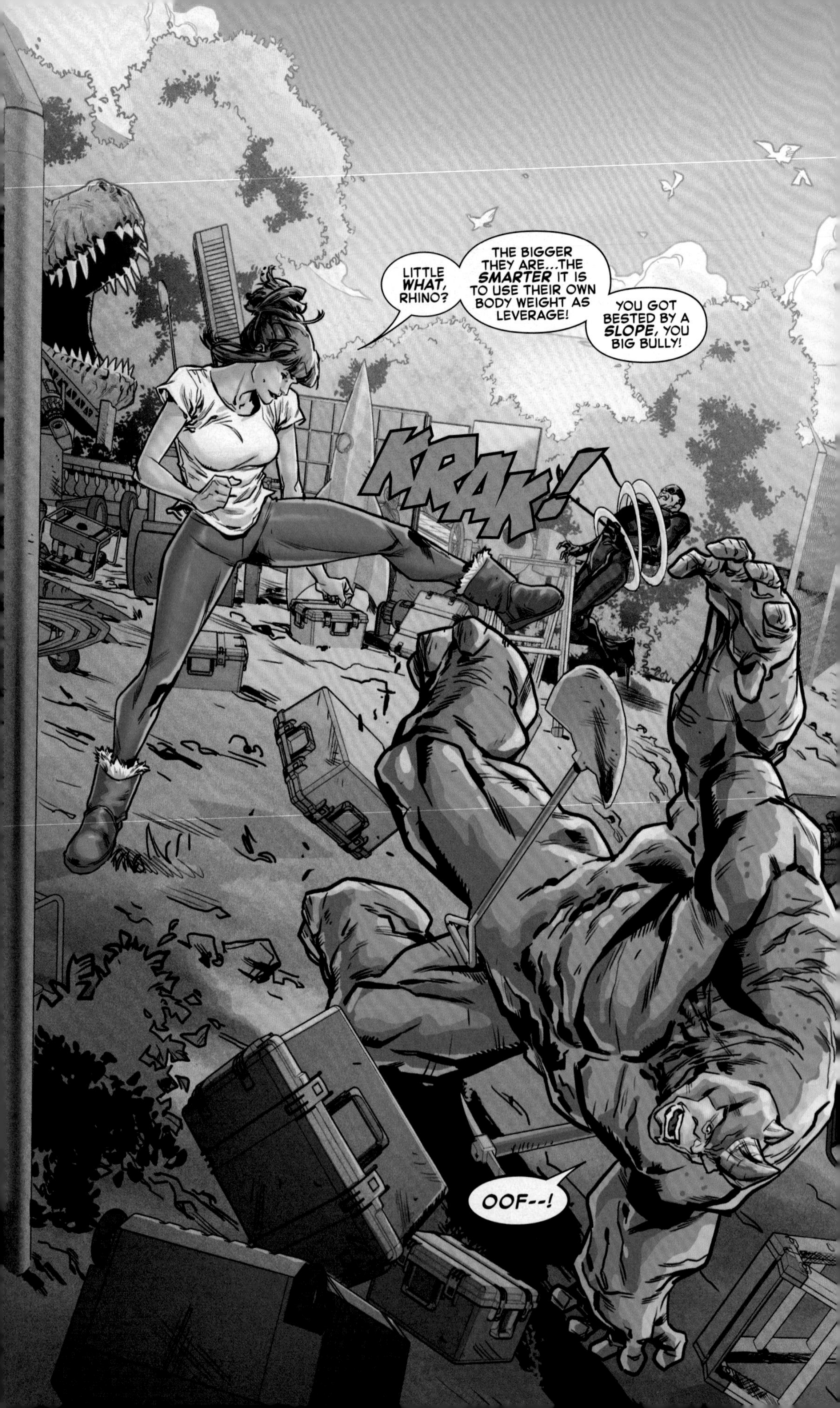
LITTLE WHAT, RHINO?
THE BIGGER THEY ARE...THE SMARTER IT IS TO USE THEIR OWN BODY WEIGHT AS LEVERAGE!
YOU GOT BESTED BY A SLOPE, YOU BIG BULLY!
KRAK!
OOF--!

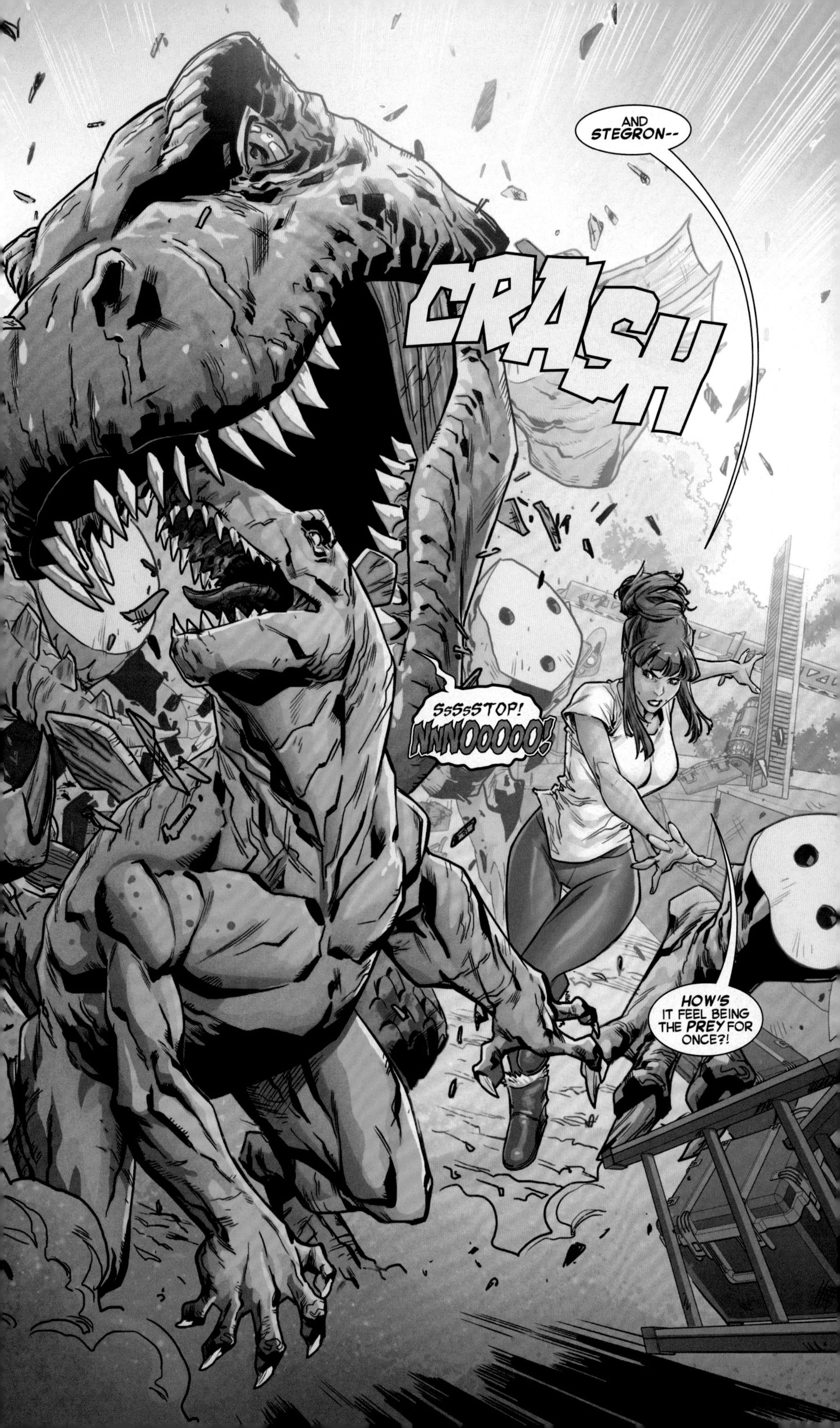

AND STEGRON--
CRASH
SsSsSTOP! NNNOOOOO!
HOW'S IT FEEL BEING THE PREY FOR ONCE?!

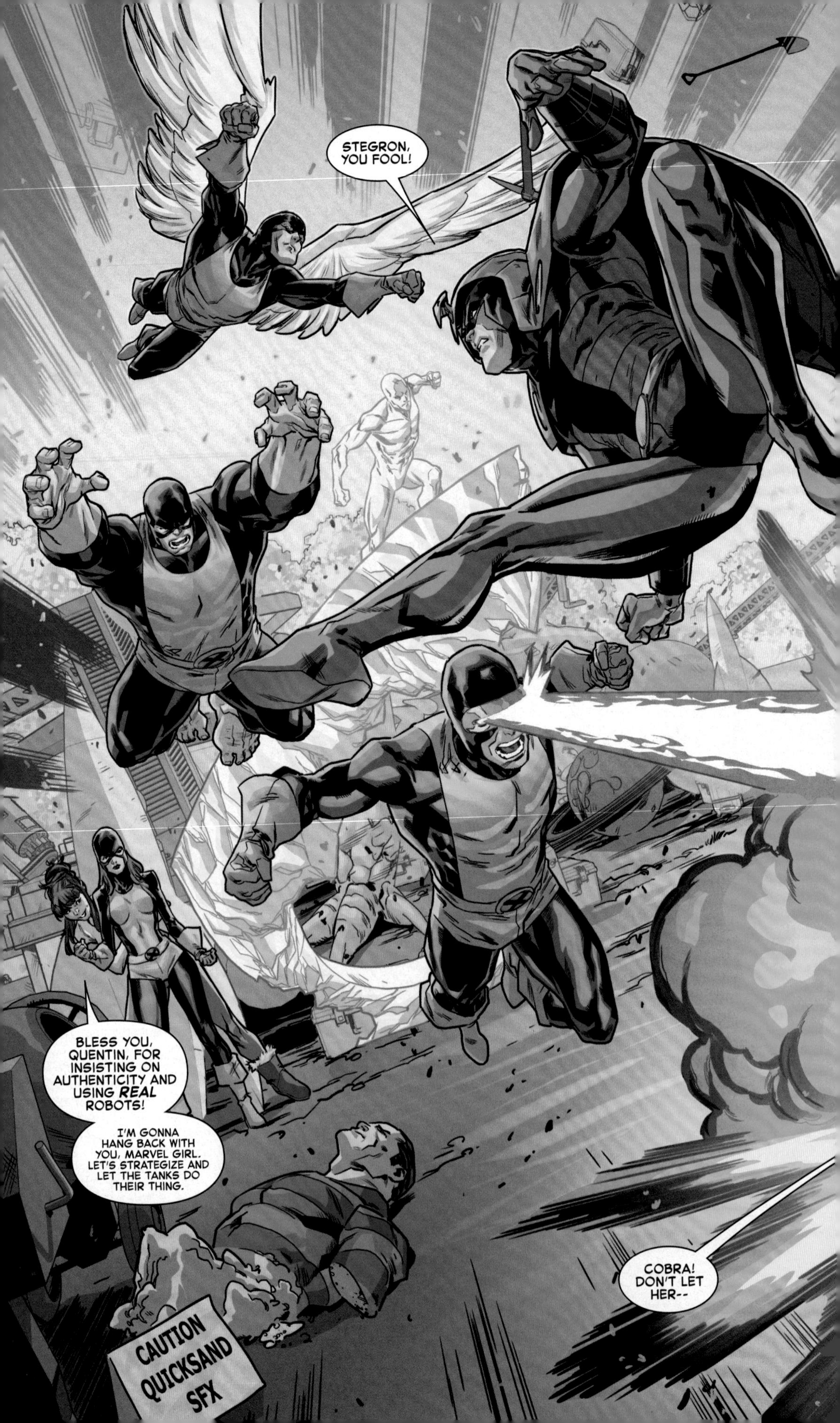
STEGRON, YOU FOOL!
BLESS YOU, QUENTIN, FOR INSISTING ON AUTHENTICITY AND USING *REAL* ROBOTS!
I'M GONNA HANG BACK WITH YOU, MARVEL GIRL. LET'S STRATEGIZE AND LET THE TANKS DO THEIR THING.
COBRA! DON'T LET HER--
CAUTION QUICKSAND SFX

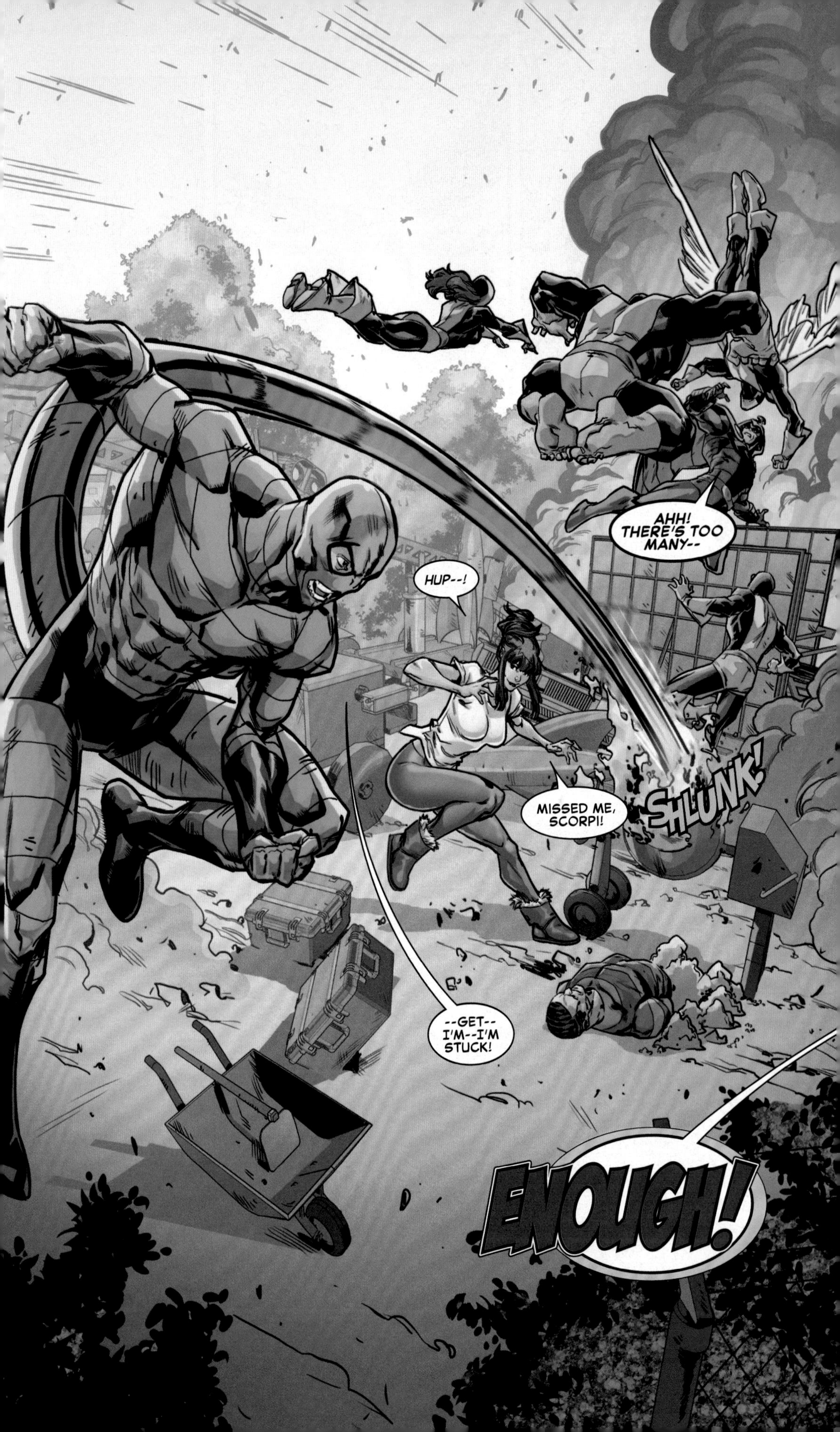
AHH! THERE'S TOO MANY--
HUP--!
MISSED ME, SCORPI!
SHLUNK!
--GET-- I'M--I'M STUCK!
ENOUGH!

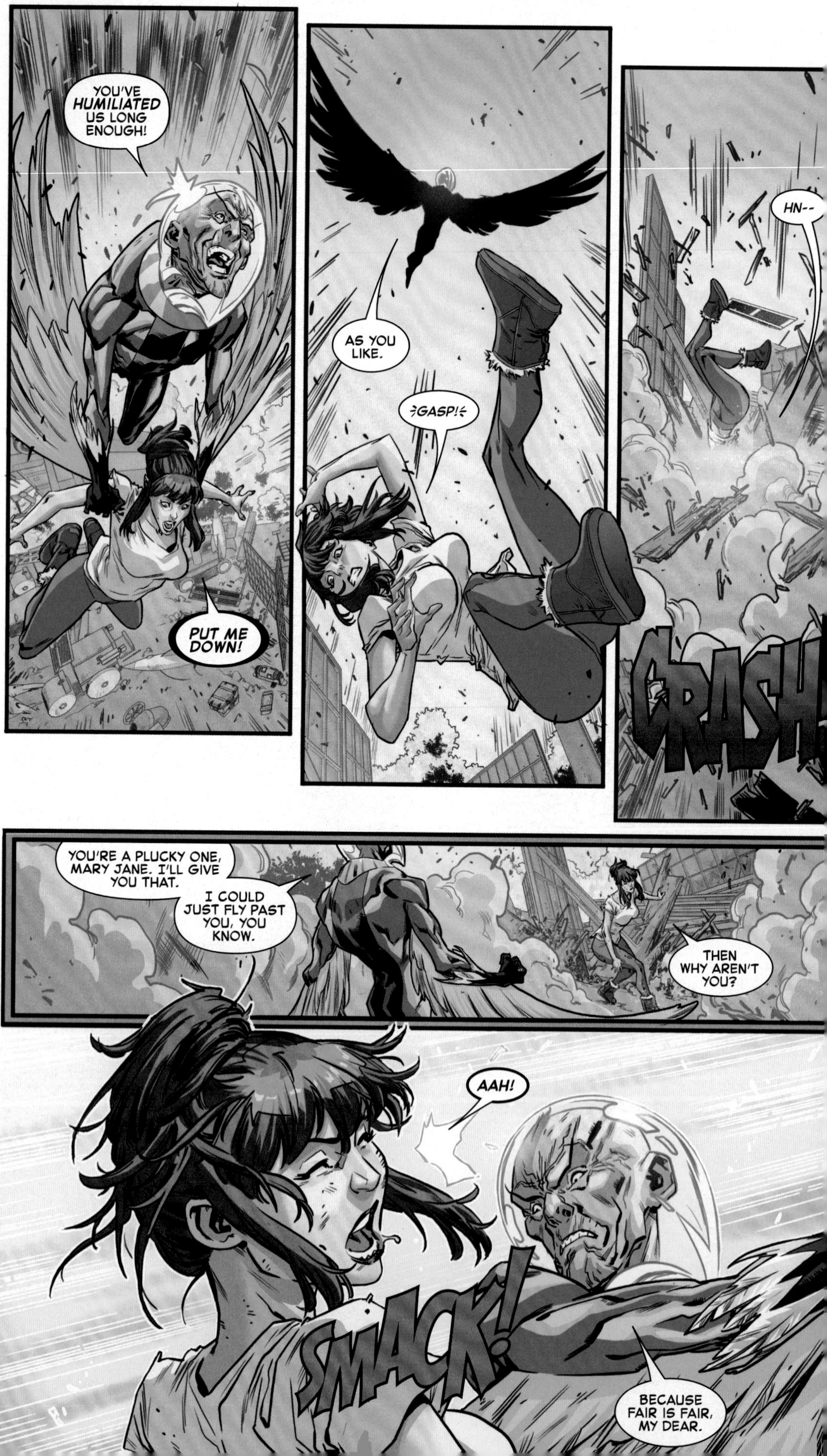

YOU'VE *HUMILIATED* US LONG ENOUGH!
PUT ME DOWN!
AS YOU LIKE.
GASP!
HN--
CRASH!
YOU'RE A PLUCKY ONE, MARY JANE. I'LL GIVE YOU THAT.
I COULD JUST FLY PAST YOU, YOU KNOW.
THEN WHY AREN'T YOU?
AAH!
SMACK!
BECAUSE FAIR IS FAIR, MY DEAR.

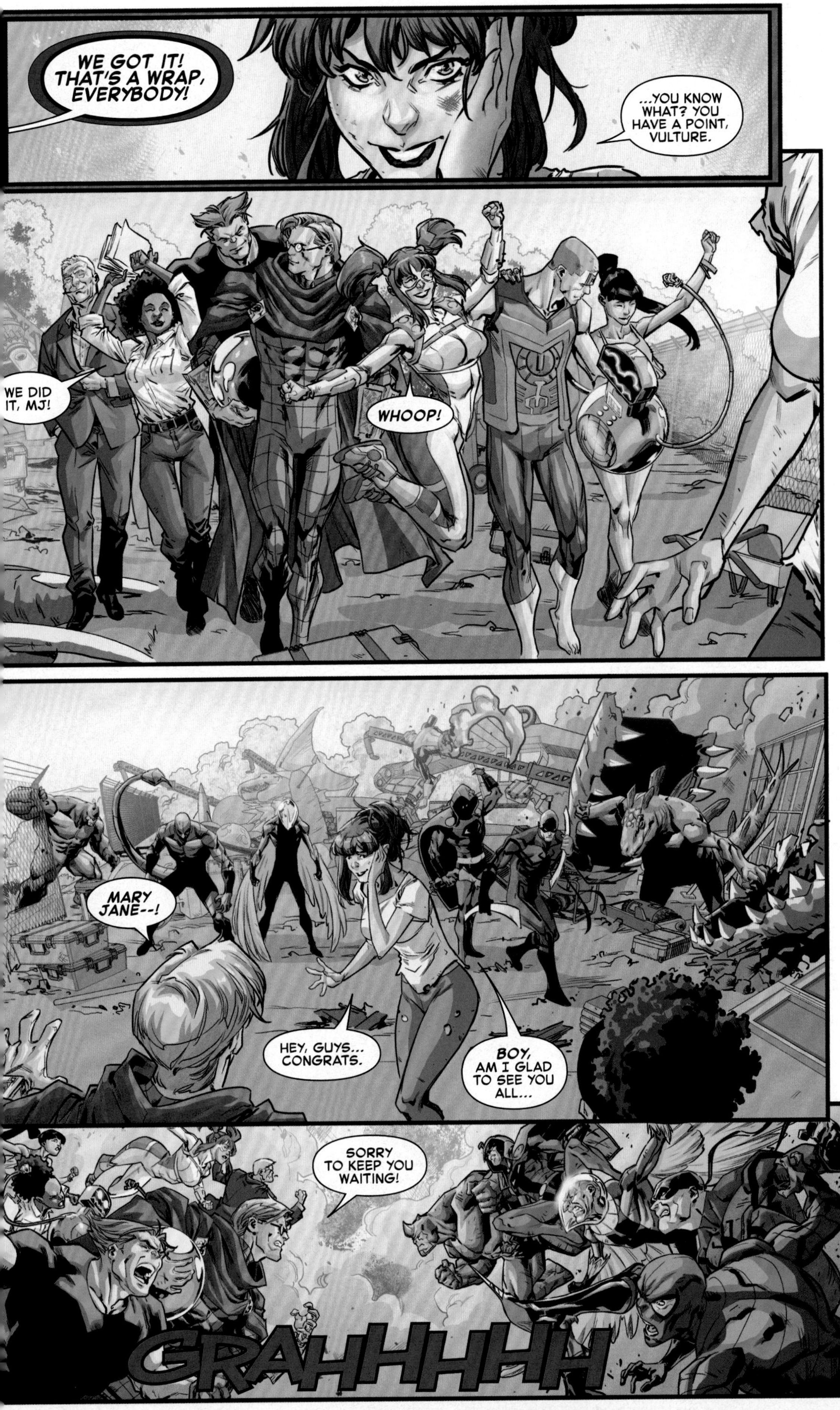

WE GOT IT! THAT'S A WRAP, EVERYBODY!
...YOU KNOW WHAT? YOU HAVE A POINT, VULTURE.
WE DID IT, MJ!
WHOOP!
MARY JANE--!
HEY, GUYS... CONGRATS.
BOY, AM I GLAD TO SEE YOU ALL...
SORRY TO KEEP YOU WAITING!
GRAHHHHH

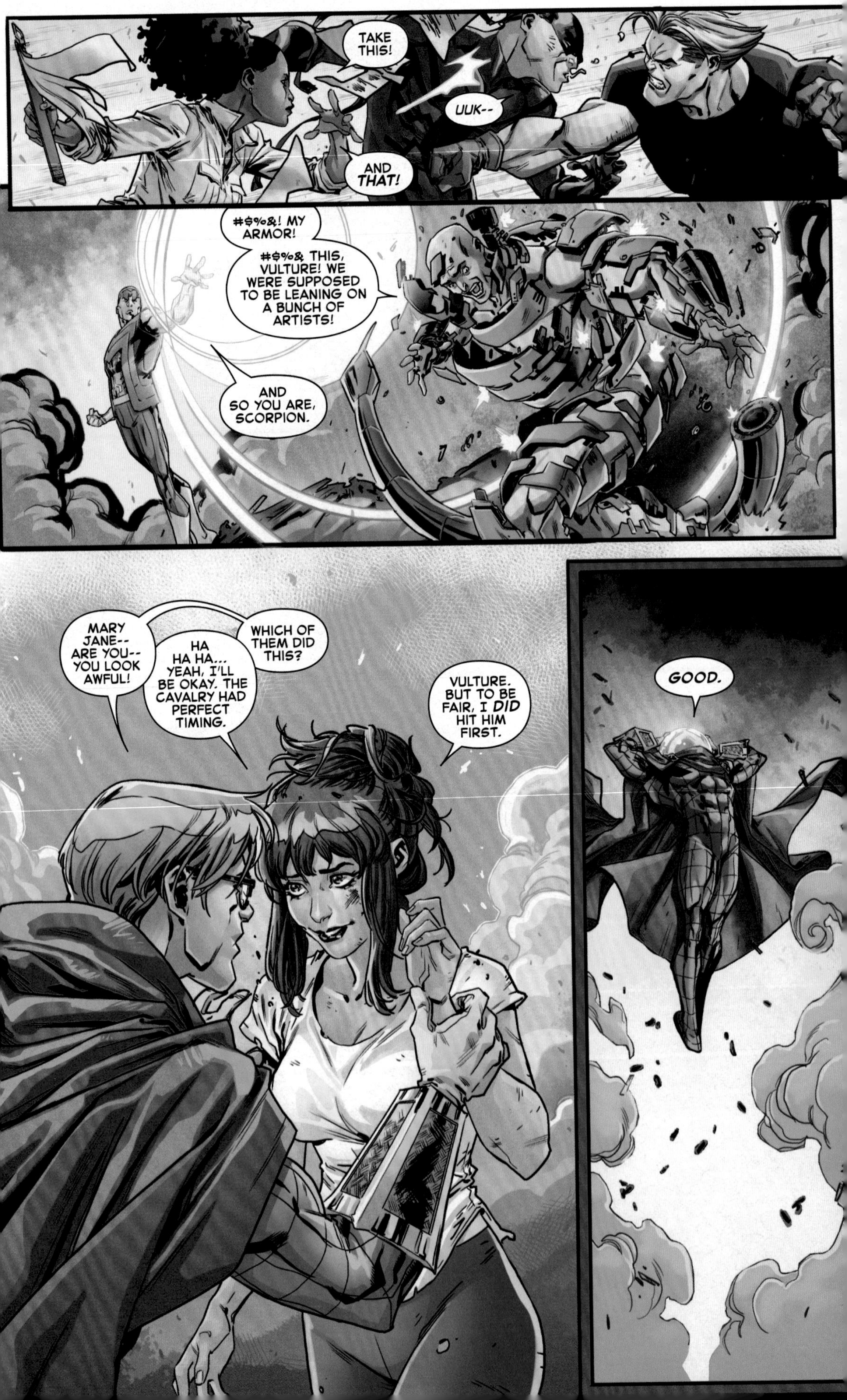
TAKE THIS!
UUK--
AND THAT!
#$%&! MY ARMOR!
#$%& THIS, VULTURE! WE WERE SUPPOSED TO BE LEANING ON A BUNCH OF ARTISTS!
AND SO YOU ARE, SCORPION.
MARY JANE-- ARE YOU-- YOU LOOK AWFUL!
HA HA HA... YEAH, I'LL BE OKAY. THE CAVALRY HAD PERFECT TIMING.
WHICH OF THEM DID THIS?
VULTURE. BUT TO BE FAIR, I DID HIT HIM FIRST.
GOOD.

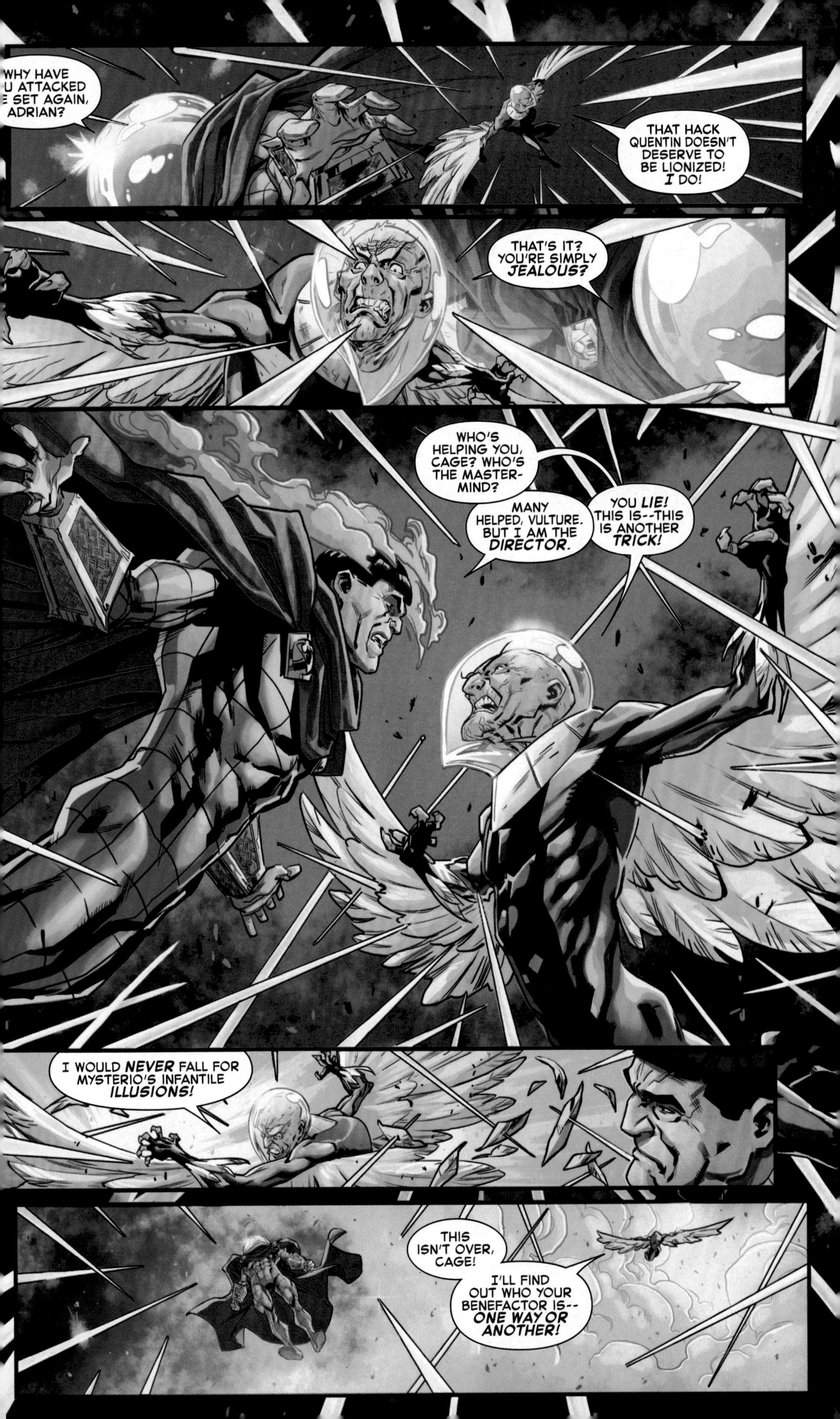
WHY HAVE
U ATTACKED
E SET AGAIN,
ADRIAN?
THAT HACK QUENTIN DOESN'T DESERVE TO BE LIONIZED! I DO!
THAT'S IT? YOU'RE SIMPLY JEALOUS?
WHO'S HELPING YOU, CAGE? WHO'S THE MASTER-MIND?
MANY HELPED, VULTURE. BUT I AM THE DIRECTOR.
YOU LIE! THIS IS--THIS IS ANOTHER TRICK!
I WOULD NEVER FALL FOR MYSTERIO'S INFANTILE ILLUSIONS!
THIS ISN'T OVER, CAGE!
I'LL FIND OUT WHO YOUR BENEFACTOR IS-- ONE WAY OR ANOTHER!

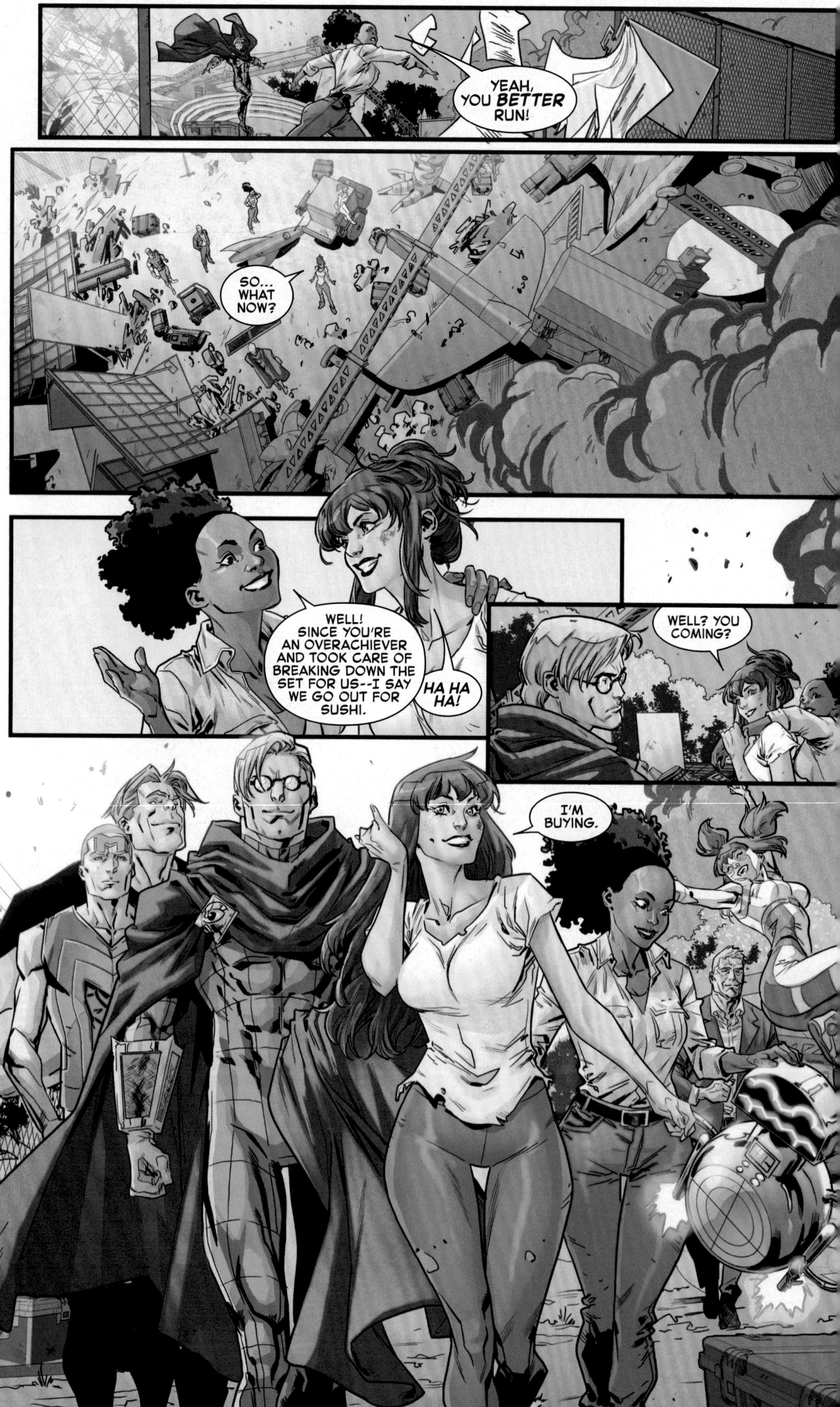
YEAH, YOU BETTER RUN!
SO... WHAT NOW?
WELL! SINCE YOU'RE AN OVERACHIEVER AND TOOK CARE OF BREAKING DOWN THE SET FOR US--I SAY WE GO OUT FOR SUSHI.
HA HA HA!
WELL? YOU COMING?
I'M BUYING.

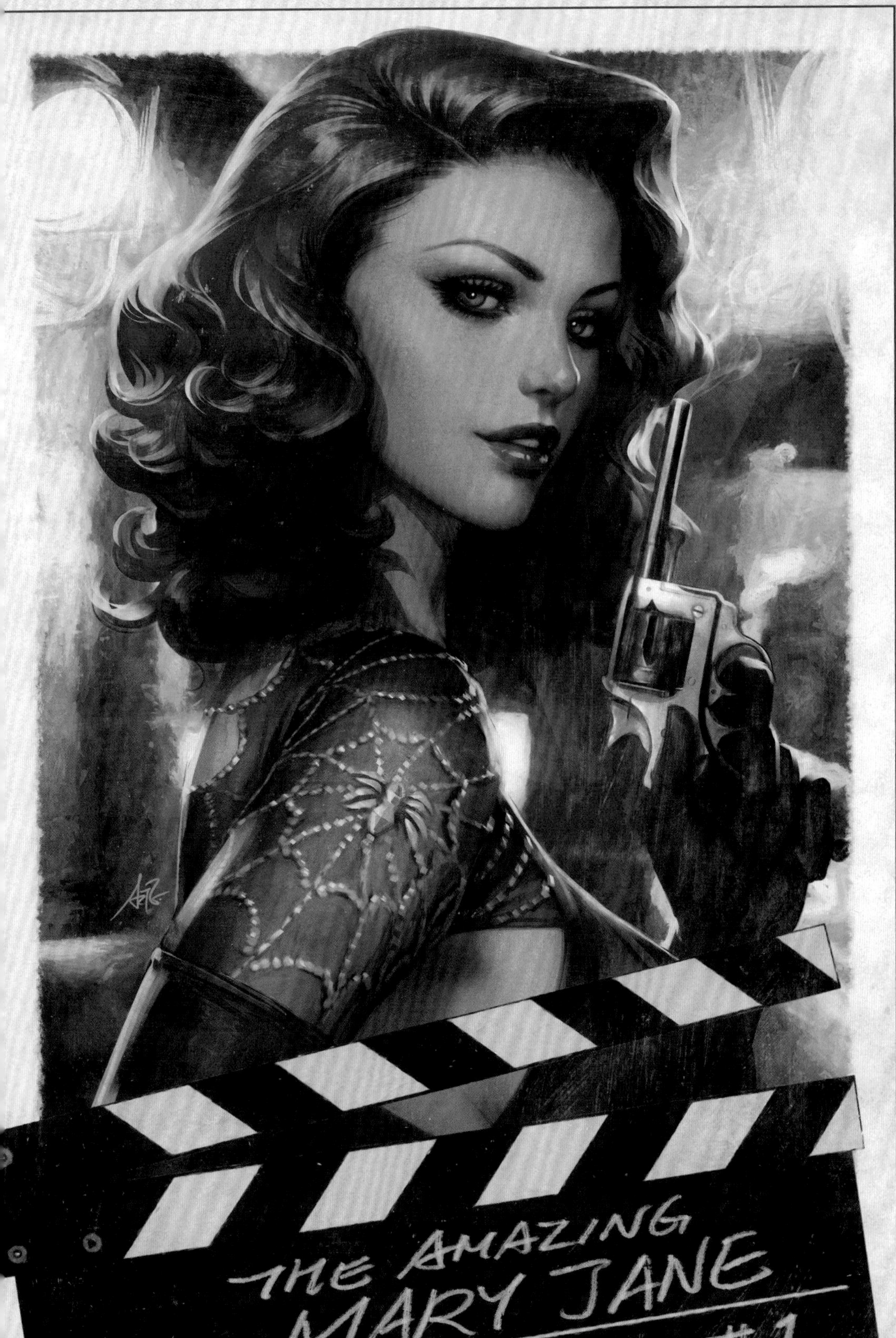
THE AMAZING
MARY JANE
#1
TITLE

1 VARIANT BY **STANLEY "ARTGERM" LAU**

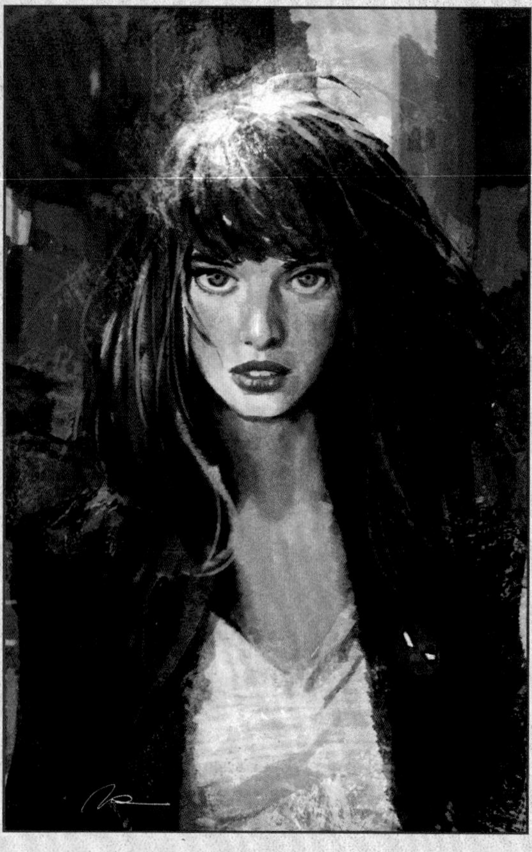

1 VARIANT BY
GERALD PAREL

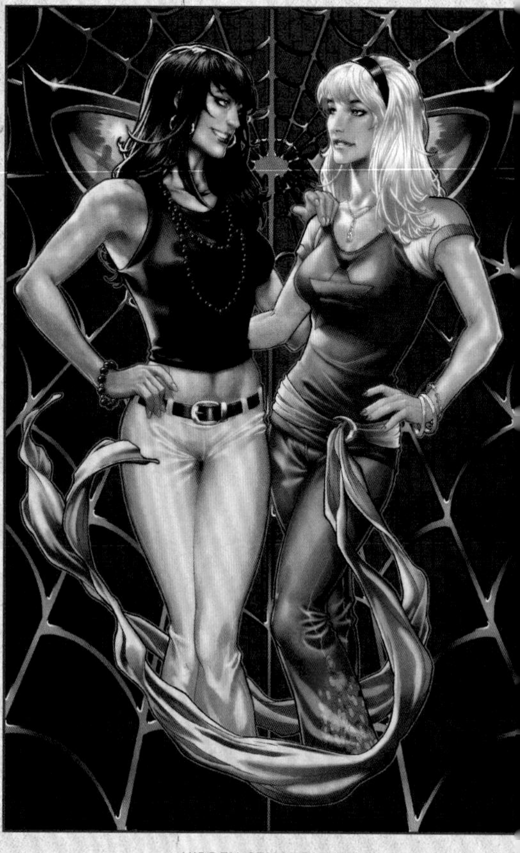

1 HIDDEN GEM VARIANT BY
MARK BROOKS

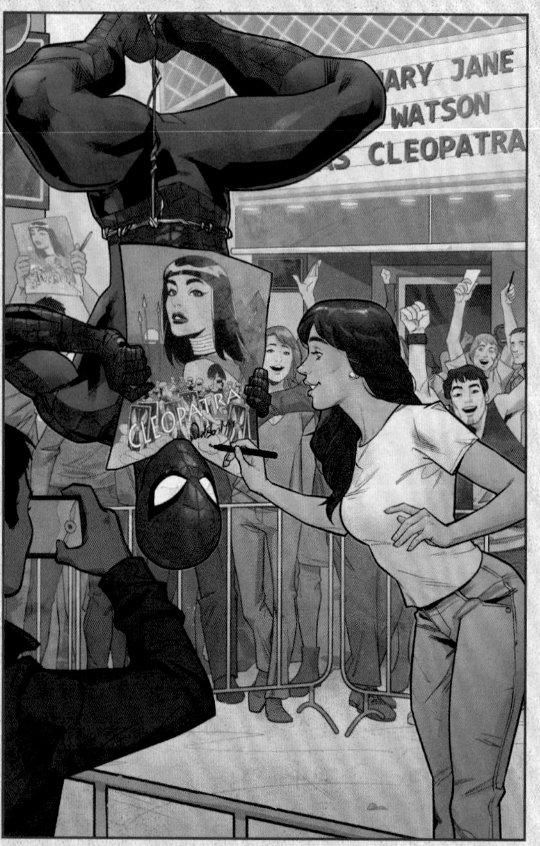
WATSON
CLEOPATRA
CLEOPATRA

1 VARIANT BY
ANNA RUD

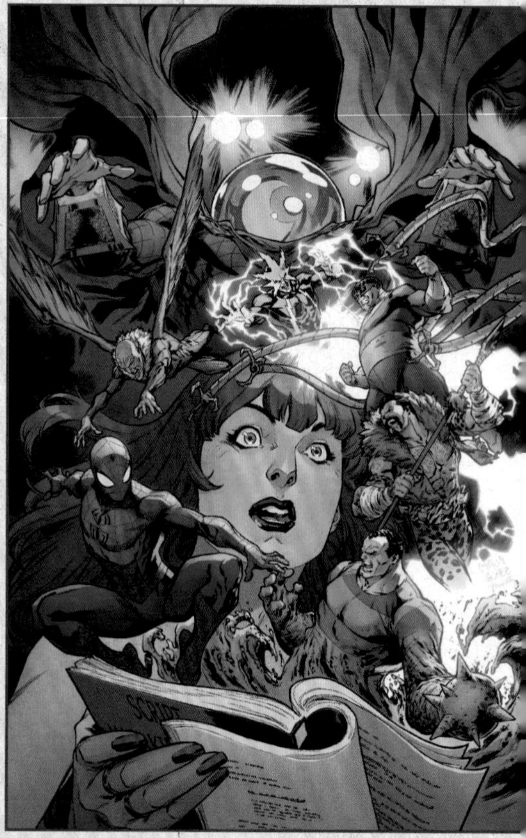

1 VARIANT BY
CARLOS GÓMEZ & TAMRA BONVILLAIN

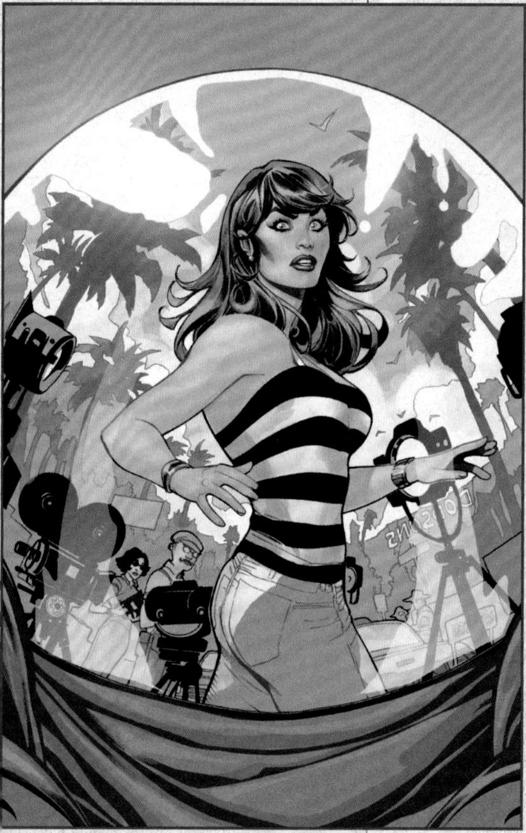

2 VARIANT BY
TERRY DODSON & RACHEL DODSON

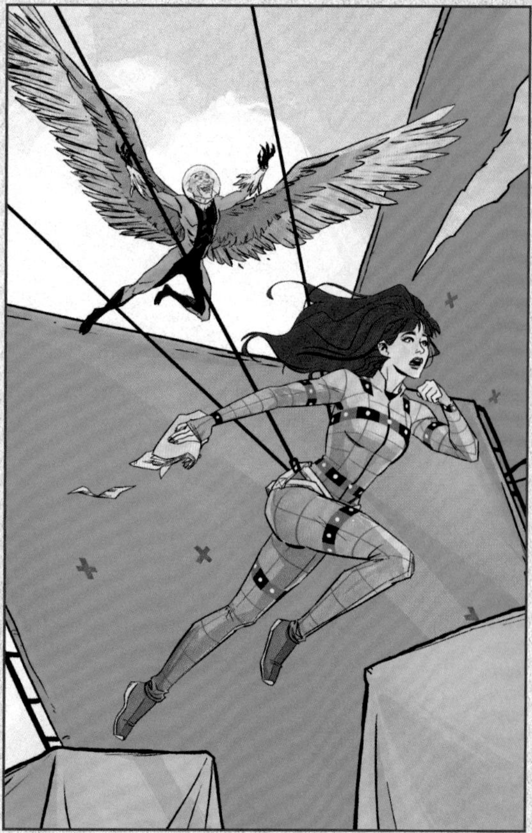

3 VARIANT BY
ANNIE WU

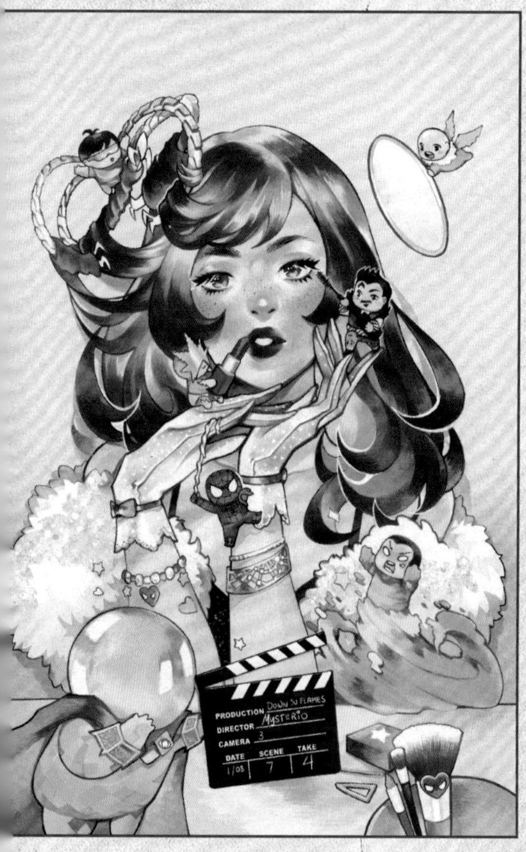
PRODUCTION
DIRECTOR
CAMERA
DATE
SCENE
TAKE

4 VARIANT BY
RIAN GONZALES

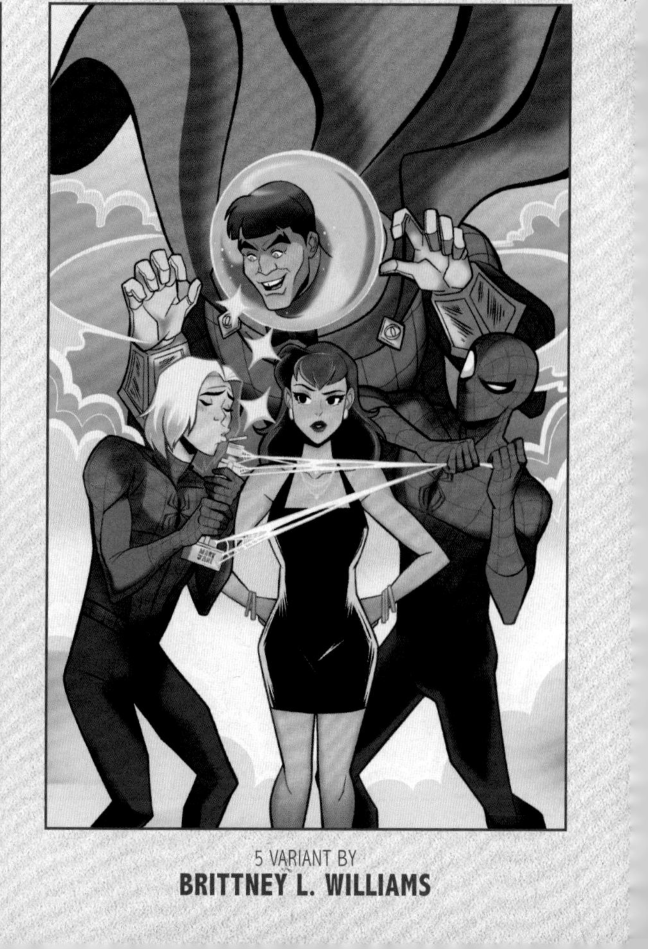

5 VARIANT BY
BRITTNEY L. WILLIAMS

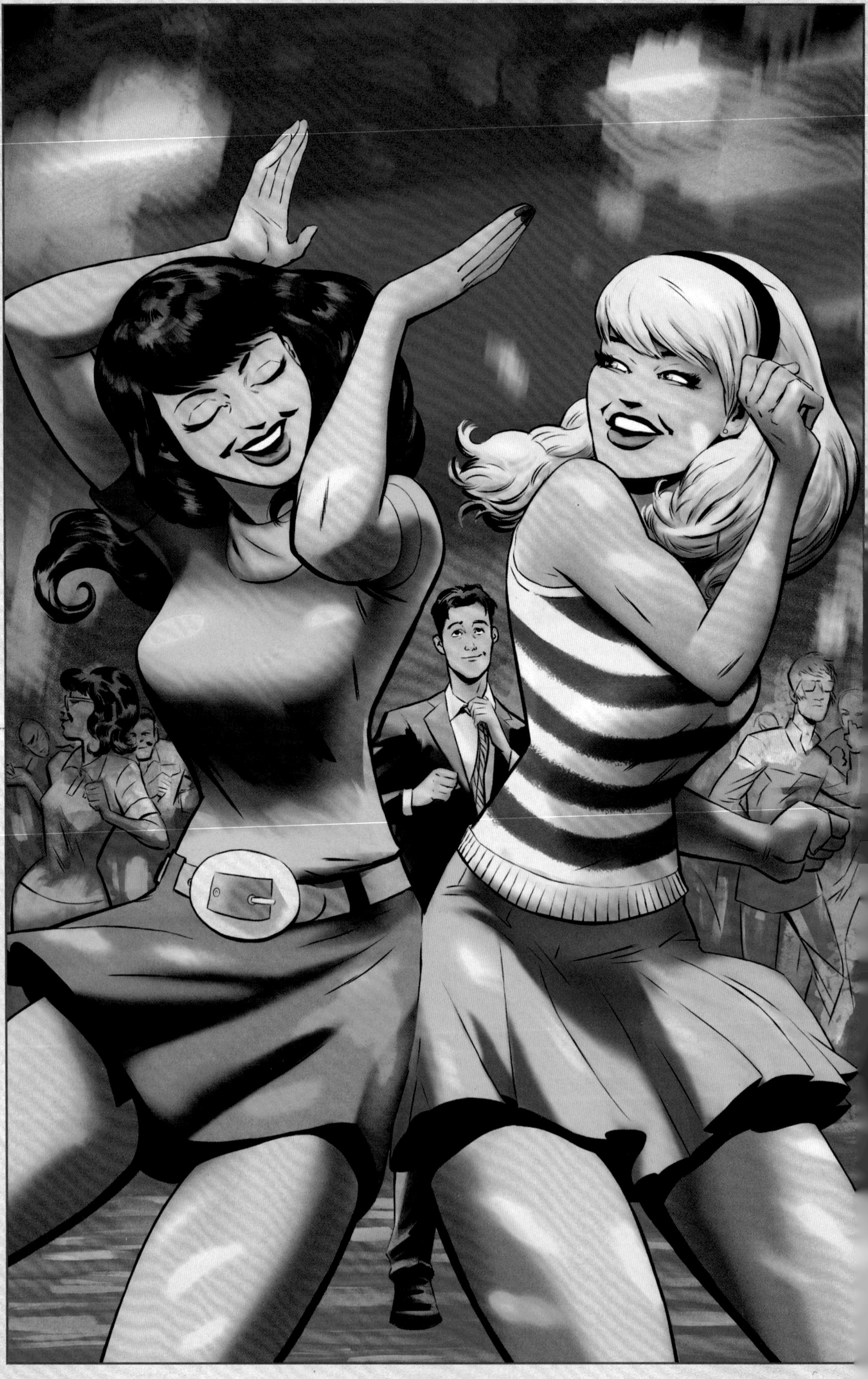

5 GWEN STACY VARIANT BY **JAVIER RODRÍGUEZ**